J. ARTHUR ___

- The Rise and Fall of His Film Empire -

GARETH OWEN

Published in the United States of America by:

BearManor Media
1317 Edgewater Dr #110
Orlando FL 32804
bearmanormedia.com

Printed in the United States.

All photos used with permission.

Typesetting and layout by DataSmith Solutions

Cover by DataSmith Solutions

ISBN — xxx-x-xxxxx-xxx-x

Contents

PART 4 – TODAY

Introduction

Up until his death in 1972 J Arthur Rank presided over a film concern, that became a film empire, that became Britain's largest ever integrated film combine with studios, laboratories, distribution and exhibition along with a stable of contract directors, producers and artistes.

Yet he was one of the most unlikely figures ever to become involved in the unstable and risky business of film finance and production. His involvement, he said, came through the guidance of God.

Many mocked him, many didn't understand him, but all – ultimately – were in awe of him.

Through the Rank Organisation's film production and distribution arm, some seven-hundred plus commercial films were made possible – and that doesn't take into account those produced for children (the Children's Film Movement), animation, religious films or documentary series (*This Modern Age* & *Look At Life*).

The output of the Rank Organisation's film division was formidable, and all were graced in their opening titles by a man hitting a large golden gong.

Through an extensive series of interviews the author conducted from 1999 onwards, this book charts Rank's initial involvement in film, through to the many experiments and initiatives he backed, the crises he carried the British film industry through, to the company's ultimate downfall and disposal – with all film divisions being sold in the late 1990s and early 2000s.

Finally, this book examines the ongoing business of the Rank Group (as it is now called), and the charitable foundations that bear the Rank name.

Part 1

Beginnings of an Empire

∝ 1 ∝

Joseph Rank

Before anyone can begin to explore the life and career of J Arthur Rank, and in particular his motives and his drive, you really have to first touch upon his father's background and the work ethic that he – Joseph Rank – instilled in his youngest son.

From the mid-sixteenth century the Rank family had been farmers in Yorkshire, and it was only when J Arthur Rank's great grandfather, John, rented a flour mill in Sproatley back in 1825 that the family entered the business that was to become their fortune and legacy.

Long before the electric light bulb had been invented, when horses were still the main mode of transportation and the telephone hadn't been thought of, Joseph Rank was born – on March 28, 1854 at his father's flour mill near Hull. It was the same month the Crimean War began.

Joseph was the second of four brothers, though the eldest died in infancy, making him the senior of the Rank children.

Having barely celebrated his fourth birthday, Joseph's mother died. It was said she never fully recovered from the birth of her youngest son the previous year.

His father, James, soon re-married and that marriage produced four more sons and a daughter though the arrival of a stepmother had a profound impact on Joseph's life – he did not like her, or her influence over his father. This was reflected in Joseph's total disinterest in all things academic, and pretty much everything else come to that – he excelled at nothing!

James Rank, somewhat unkindly, described his son as being 'lazy and dull'.

1.1 Joseph Rank

1.2 Emily Rank

James had fully expected his eldest son to inherit the family business but vocally expressed just how unimpressed he was with the boy's singular lack of achievement. He didn't believe Joseph deserved to be the heir – unless of course he drastically changed his ways. In order to help him do so, James took his then 14-year-old son out of school and started him to work at the family mill in the lowliest of all positions – carrying sacks and sweeping up. Joseph had to prove himself worthy of any future piece of the business by working his way up the ladder where 'ambition and a business aptitude' would also be installed.

However, Joseph wasn't quite so convinced and though he undertook all the tasks, he maintained what his father described as 'dubious company' outside working hours. So, James arranged to send his son far from home and all the bad influences that he felt were distracting him – to Scotland where a miller friend had offered to take Joseph on as a favour.

This new, strange, environment with its cold conditions and very long days did little to enthuse Joseph as his father had hoped, but then, in 1875, with Joseph having turned 21, his father died.

Joseph was still in Scotland when it happened and when he realized his father's view of him hadn't changed, as was reflected in the will. Although James Rank had amassed a fortune of £30,000 young Joseph was refused any part in the continuing family business or fortune.

The eldest Rank son was effectively frozen out, and disowned.

If ever Joseph needed any inspiration and motivation, this was certainly it. He became singularly determined to prove his father wrong and demonstrate he did indeed have what it took to run a business, so set up in competition with his own family.

By virtue of turning 21, Joseph was able to take hold of the £500 that his mother had left him in trust when she died. With it he moved across to the other side of Hull, the Yorkshire town where the family still lived and where his father's milling business operated, to set up a mill of his own. It was said from his mill in the Holderness Road you could see another 21 mills through to the banks of the River Humber.

Over the next five years he began building up his company, drawing inner strength from his deep religious beliefs in God's guiding hand and that he felt, along with hard toil, would help him make a success.

In 1880 Joseph Rank married his love Emily Voase, the daughter of a farmer from whom he bought grain. But when Joseph took stock of his business prior to his wedding he discovered his fortune had dipped to £300.

He knew he needed to produce more flour and so began looking for another mill with a greater capacity. Luckily, he found just the one, again in Hull, and bought a part share for cash. The young couple soon recovered Joseph's £500 nest egg, and more.

Joseph and Emily lived a modest lifestyle, dedicating themselves to work with only one day off a week – the Sabbath which they maintained should be kept sacred at all costs.

Three years into their marriage the couple attended an evangelistic mission run by Simpson Johnson at Waltham Street Methodist Chapel. By the end of that evening they had decided to follow Methodism – a religion founded by John Wesley in the 18th century.

The Methodist mission statement is quite simple: to respond to the gospel of God's love in Christ and to live out its discipleship in worship and mission. 'Get all you can, give all you can, save all you can' was John Wesley's motto. It is one Joseph Rank observed throughout the rest of his life; he read his bible daily and reportedly thought long and hard about devoting his life to the church by becoming a missionary. However, it was suggested that he could better help the cause of evangelism by making money to fund it – and that is exactly what he decided to do.

1.3 The terrace was known as Chestnut Villas, located at 171 Holderness Road in Hull, where Joseph and Emily eventually settled to raise their family, designed by architect William Alfred Gelder, who also designed many of Joseph's mills and lived at the opposite end of the terrace himself. (John Scotney)

With improving prospects and wealth, along with 'the guidance of God', the couple soon found that Joseph's original fortune had increased by almost 50 per-cent to £731, and steadily increased thereafter. Whatever his income, Joseph decreed they should live on half and put the rest back into the business. They were in fact able to live on a much smaller fraction as their fortunes improved.

Towards the end of the 19th century, the Methodist Church embraced the temperance movement to set a good example against widespread drinking problems in the society of the day. Ministers at one time had to take a pledge not to drink, which encouraged their congregations to do likewise. Joseph Rank took the pledge.

Joseph's prudence and forethought served him well. Gone were the day when he carried sacks to market on his back or on a handcart, as he now owned a pony and cart! The mill was running at full capacity, and demand for flour was ever-increasing. Further expansion of the empire was called for. Joseph introduced steel rollers into his mills, rather than traditional mill stones. He was the first in the country to do so, and further technological advances came when, frustrated at his measly output when the wind did not blow, Joseph saw the time – and pennies – slipping away, and so acquired a steam engine to drive the rollers. He also recognized the value of importing cheap wheat from overseas though many British farmers claimed ruination at his hands, but it was to be the key to his fortune heading into millions.

Recognising the ships importing cheaper wheat were the key to maximizing profit, Joseph decided to build mills at the docks – Victoria Docks in London, Barry Docks near Cardiff and, a little later, at Birkenhead. The grain came straight off the ships into his mills, and the flour sacks left via the same route. It was a massive efficiency improvement.

Along with a growing empire, Joseph and Emily were overseeing a growing family too. Between 1881 and 1888 the couple had three sons and four daughters.

In the early 1900s Joseph decided they should leave Hull for London, where the business was going great guns and where he believed their greater fortune lay. They relocated to Tooting Beck, and it was there he became a Methodist Sunday School Superintendent, taking classes in the afternoon and evening. It was a religious path his youngest son, Arthur, followed him on.

In wishing to spread the word, whilst also helping the neediest of the area, Joseph Rank funded the majority building of a Mission in Tooting in 1910 (costing £30,000). On November 10 that same year Tooting Central Hall was opened and Joseph described it as one of the greatest moments in his life. Seventeen hundred worshipers regularly gathered there on Sundays – mainly working-class people who would never have dreamed of darkening the door of many of the middle-class churches in the area.

With the outbreak of WWI in 1914, Joseph Rank's fortunes swelled as the demand for flour almost outstripped his capacity to produce it. Although

1.4 Joseph Rank's first mill in Hull

he had immediately offered his services to Prime Minister Lloyd-George and the government he was promptly turned down – what would they want with a 'simple Yorkshire miller', they asked?

Spurred by his annoyance, Joseph pursued his business interests with even greater vigor to the point it was reckoned that the 'simple Yorkshire miller' made over £2 million during the 1914–1918 conflict. He gave the majority away to various charities and with Methodism forming a hugely important part of Rank's philanthropy he funded Southfield's Central Hall to a cost of £40,000.

Though during the war period, in 1915, tragedy befell the family when Emily died. It was all very sudden and a day after she returned home from visiting her grandchildren; she complained of a terrible pain in her head but before the doctor arrived she had passed away.

Together she and Joseph had worked diligently to build the business and raise their family. Emily was industrious, economical, strong and – when required – could be very forcible. Though prudent she only ever bought the best food, best clothes, linen and furniture for the family – she never skimped when it came to the children. She was a most generous hostess and encouraged her children to bring friends home whenever possible, as she particularly enjoyed the company of young people.

It's easy to see how the family were all devoted to her.

Joseph was grief-stricken and turned his energy to working even longer hours, and often traveling between his mills in the north, Wales, Ireland and London. Next he began acquiring a number of competitors' mills – Riverside Milling, John Ure & Son of Glasgow, Buchanan's of Birkenhead – were bought up as were the mills of Henry Leetham & Sons jointly by both Rank and competitor Spillers Ltd.

Then came Cleveland Mills at Thornaby-on-Tees, Milnar's of Elland, Herdman & Sons of Edinburgh, Sutcliffe & Sons of Manchester, Kirby's of Selby, J Appleby & Sons in Liverpool, Hanley & Sons of Doncaster and Appletons Mill in Hull. All fell into the Rank fold, modernized, remodeled and/or merged with neighbouring mills controlled by Rank. The 'aggressive expansion' made him some enemies though his sons and son-in-law increasingly shouldered the majority of work as Joseph delegated much of the day to day running to them, allowing him to dedicate more time to his religious and charitable interests.

Joseph and Emily's sister, Annie, were united in a shared grief. They spent lots of time together and grew close. In 1917 they married, and left Tooting Beck for the leafy suburb of Reigate in Surrey where, for many years, Joseph continued in a daily routine of rising at 7am, exercising, and then taking a train to his London office.

Business continued to boom and by 1933, aged 79, Joseph Rank embarked on his biggest deal yet: a controlling interest in London Flour Millers, with an issued capital of £1,530,000.

He then formed Ranks Limited with share capital of £7,295,600. Joseph Rank was now suggested to be 'the richest man in England' by the press and his mills were grinding one seventh of all the flour eaten in Britain.

It is ironic to think as a boy he was deemed 'good for nowt' by his own father, but between 1920 and 1939 Joseph Rank used his wealth wisely and donated over £2.4 million to the Methodist Missionary Society, in addition to hundreds of thousands of pounds to other good causes.

He also set up various charitable trusts, which survive to this day, though now merged as the Joseph Rank Trust.

Tragically in 1940, Annie died of a stroke and three years later, on November 13, 1943, at the grand old age of eighty-nine, Joseph Rank – who only two weeks earlier presided over a company Board meeting – himself passed away.

He left £1 million to Methodist charities, and the press eagerly awaited news of the Revenue's claim in death duties – but were astounded when the estate of 'Britain's richest man' was announced to be just under £71,000.

Joseph Rank was prudent and astute in life, and he wasn't going to be any different in death! Thanks to his foresight in transferring the business to his sons, and other gifts and tax-exempt transfers, Joseph's heirs were millionaires.

Joseph Rank has been described as one of the greatest philanthropists of his time.

He once said 'I have found as much or more real joy in handing out as I have in raking in.'

2

J Arthur Rank

The youngest, and some say favourite, child of Joseph and Emily Rank was Joseph Arthur Rank, born on December 22, 1888, at 171 Holderness Road, Hull. The house was part of a terrace of four, known as Chestnut Villas, and after some years of near-dereliction was sympathetically restored in 2016. The architect of this terrace, William Alfred Gelder, also designed many flour mills for Joseph Rank, and lived at the opposite end of Chestnut Villas himself.

Despite not having much of an education himself, Joseph ensured his sons all received a private schooling, though Arthur – much like his father – was said to 'excel at nothing!'

Of the other Rank boys, James (the eldest) attended Hymers College in Hull whilst Rowland attended The Leys Public School, in Cambridge, as did Arthur – though unlike Rowland, Arthur was quite content to be bottom of the class.

None of the Rank children were offered the chance to go on to university, and instead all left school in their teens to go into the flour business. They, like Joseph had to, worked their way up from the lowliest sweeper-up and sack carrying jobs with long hours as Joseph certainly didn't believe in spoiling the children, moreover he believed hard work would instil a greater capacity for work and ambition in them – he called it character building. He was right, particularly in Arthur's case.

Arthur left school at 17 and joined the Mark Lane Corn Exchange in Hull and, from there, he was offered a year-long apprenticeship with a Luton-based miller, W Looker of Exchange Roller Mills – a friend of his father's.

1.5 A plaque marking the birthplace of J. Arthur Rank at Chestnut Villas (John Scotney)

Following his apprenticeship, young Arthur joined the family firm and started at one of the family's Hull mills, working 15-hour days. Then, aged 20, Arthur felt ready to spread his wings a little further, and moved to work at Premier Mills in London.

The following year, 1909 and aged 21, Arthur first met Ellen, daughter of Lord Marshall and later Lord Mayor of London who was a millionaire wholesale newspaper distributor with a passion for philanthropy, and Methodism. They actually met when Joseph Rank set up his Mission in Tooting and invited Lady Marshall to open the building … and in turn she was accompanied by her daughter, just as Joseph Rank was accompanied by his youngest son.

Romance soon blossomed and the young couple were married in 1917.

Meanwhile, during WWI, Arthur commenced his military service in The Royal Army Medical Corps, as part of an ambulance unit based out of Edgware Railway Station. Amongst the others who joined up at the same time was Roy Hake, later to become a partner in Arthur's Religious Film productions. Promotion soon followed, as did duty in France, where Arthur Rank had twenty ambulances under his charge. Upon demobilisation after the war, and having attained the rank of Captain, Arthur returned to the family flour business – and married life.

Joseph Rank had always believed the oldest son, James, would inherit and run his business whilst Arthur and Rowland were gifted a not insignificant number of shares in the company, Joseph Rank Ltd.

1.6 Joseph Arthur Rank

1.7 Joseph Rank with his three sons on his 80th birthday

Arthur's brothers were making names for themselves outside of the family business – James was the biggest racehorse owner in Britain, and just prior to WWII had some 70 racehorses in his stables; whilst Rowland bought Aldwick Place in Bognor Regis and bred racehorses – very successfully. Neither of the older brothers inherited their father's deep religious beliefs and both shunned the idea of becoming teetotal. Rowland Rank died in 1939, aged just 54 – he had been gassed during the first war and his health never fully recovered.

Arthur was mindful that there probably wouldn't be a full-time job when James took

1.8 Portrait of Joseph Rank aged 80

over, and so decided to acquire an existing business: Peterkin's Self-Raising Flour. It was not a success. Arthur sold out a few years later and returned to the family business, which was then still under his father's control. By the time Arthur celebrated his fortieth birthday he was on the Board of the company, and lived just a short distance away from his father in Reigate.

Arthur didn't seem to have any great ambitions outside the family firm, he was quite content in his modest life with wife Nell (Ellen). Like his father he was prudent, and invested the money he earned in property – namely Sutton Manor, a 12,000 acre estate in Sutton Scotney, Hampshire. He appointed former wartime friend Roy Hake his estate manager.

He also rediscovered his faith, which he had somewhat rebelled against when he moved to London and had avoided going to church. In fact, once ensconced in Sutton Scotney, he and Ellen became regular worshipers at the local Methodist church.

1.9 Endike Lane Methodist Church in Hull, built thanks to the generosity of J. Arthur Rank. He made it a condition any new churches he funded should all be designed with a projection room (see hatches above door)

That faith, they declared, helped them through the greatest tragedy of their lives, when their only son died at birth.

They had two other children, both girls, Ursula and Shelagh.

Arthur's private life was just that – private. He rarely talked about it outside the family, and in later life always shunned any type of personal publicity. Not a great deal was known about him, other than a general knowledge of his pastimes such as golf and shooting ... and his regular attendance of a local Sunday school. In fact, such was the passion he developed he became a regular speaker there, though admittedly was not a very animated or exciting speaker so Arthur wondered how he might liven up things and after discussions with Roy Hake, decided he might try showing a religious film.

Arthur entered into his 'real career' late in life. The hiring of his first religious film was to launch him to becoming the biggest force in British films – ever.

1.10 The same church, which along with the mandatory projection room, had space above the choir and pulpit area to also accommodate a screen

～ 3 ～

The British Film Industry

In the early 1930s the British film business was still coming to terms with the new exciting development of 'talkies'. In 1930 itself there were over one hundred films produced between studios at Elstree, Twickenham, Isleworth, Beaconsfield, Shepherd's Bush, Islington, Cricklewood, Welwyn, Teddington, Wembley and Walton-On-Thames.

Many were 'Quota Quickies'- films made in response to the 1927 Cinematograph Films Act introduced by the Government in a bid to try and stem the great influx of American films when, in 1927, the UK generated $165m in box office revenue and produced 44 films (4.8 per-cent of films shown), against 723 US film imports (81 per-cent). The UK provided 30 per cent of US film export earnings for the year. The American imports looked set to smother British cinema and film production.

The Act was introduced to 'enhance and increase British film

1.11 Sir Alexander Korda

production' by requiring a certain number of British films to be shown at cinemas (7½ per-cent, which rose to 20 per-cent over the next eight years). Far from instigating production of quality, commercial British films, the Act was viewed negatively and merely an obstacle to overcome for the American companies in order that their product could be exhibited; and resulted in a great deal of hastily produced quota-fillers, or 'quota quickies' as they were termed. Typically, they were of no more than 75 minutes in duration and generally cost around £6,250 each (£1 a foot). Often shot in two weeks, they were then edited and dubbed in another two weeks.

US studios set up production arms in the UK to 'churn out' inexpensive movies in order they could hit the minimum Government requirement and show the films that the British cinemagoers really, in fact, wanted to see – American movies!

There were two main cinema circuits at this time, Gaumont-British and ABC (Associated British). Monopoly, or duopoly, was certainly a prime concern.

Gaumont-British was run by five men: AC Bromhead, Isidore Ostrer, Charles Moss Woolf, Michael Balcon and Lord Beaverbrook.

Its rise to power is interesting. The Ostrer brothers (Isadore, Mark and Maurice) played an important part in the British film industry (and in Rank's story). They came into the industry in a relatively small way, their background being in merchant banking and finance, in acquiring control of the Gaumont production company and its studio in Shepherds Bush. They then bought into cinema and distribution companies and merged all their interests into Gaumont-British Pictures Corporation. For a decade, they were industry power brokers.

Of the other company directors it was perhaps CM Woolf who became the most legendary. He was a highly respected distributor. He entered the industry, having left the family fur business, in the 1920s as joint owner of a film renting company, W and F, with his partner Freedman. It was a modestly successful operation having acquired some of the American films cinema owner Sol Levy had imported for his chain (primarily in Birming-ham). W and F were able to book these into cinemas in other towns where Levy did not have a theatre.

When Levy's company secured the UK distribution rights for Harold Lloyd's films, the deal in turn made W and F a fortune!

Woolf developed his business and began re-investing in British productions. In 1922 one of the projects he helped make possible was *Woman to Woman*. It was produced by Michael Balcon. The other main investor was a Jewish scrap metal merchant from Birmingham, Oscar Deutsch. Among the notable cast and crew was a young art director named Alfred Hitchcock.

Balcon and his colleague Jack Cutts next formed a £100 company called Gainsborough. Together they went to see Colonel A C Bromhead and his brother Reginald, directors of the burgeoning Gaumont Company. Balcon and Cutts struck a deal with Gaumont to finance their next film, *The Passionate Adventure*. It was again to be distributed by CM Woolf's company.

After the 1927 Cinematograph Act came into being, the Ostrer brothers were keen to expand their Gaumont Company into distribution. They made an approach to CM Woolf. Although he said he would never give up his autonomy, Woolf was persuaded by Isidore Ostrer to sell and join the Board of the new Gaumont-British (G-B) company. During negotiations, Woolf had suggested that G-B make a more formal financing arrangement with Balcon's Gainsborough Pictures. Indeed a few months later, true to their word, the Ostrers floated Gainsborough Pictures (1928) to be 'associated with but not controlled by' G-B.

Under their banner of G-B, the Ostrers now had CM Woolf and Michael Balcon on their board. They had cinemas, distribution and production interests.

Along with the studios Balcon controlled in Shepherd's Bush, he took control of Islington Studios, where he had made a number of his earlier films. G-B was perhaps the UK's first film combine.

The Associated British Picture Company (ABPC), meanwhile, was run by ruthless Glaswegian John Maxwell, was the only real competitor of Gaumont-British. A trained solicitor, and failed Parliamentary candidate, Maxwell acquired an interest in a Scottish exhibition company in 1912. To supply his chain, he moved into distribution, acting as Scottish agent for a London based renter, Wardour Films (which he later bought control of). His little empire expanded slowly,

After the introduction of the 1927 Quota Act, he launched a mainstream production company called British International Pictures (BIP)

and formed his studio base in a new complex at Borehamwood – which he soon had to spend a fortune on to accommodate the arrival of sound. His first talkie was Britain's first talkie, Alfred Hitchcock's *Blackmail.* The studio became known as 'the porridge factory' for reasons more likely to do with the quantity of films that the company turned out, than their quality.

His most famous director, Hitchcock, made a huge number of films for BIP between 1927 and 1933, before he defected to Gaumont-British.

The Associated British Cinema chain (ABC), was a company formed by Maxwell to take care of his exhibition interests, and in 1933 Maxwell gathered together all of his companies: ABC cinemas, Pathé Pictures, Wardour Films, British International Pictures and British Instructional Films and re-branded them as the Associated British Picture Corporation.

Maxwell too controlled a studio, production company, distribution arm and cinema circuit.

Into this world of duopoly and established, experienced film-makers, distributors and exhibitors stepped flour magnate J Arthur Rank. He realised that far from making a profit, he was likely to lose money. He could afford to do so if it was in the pursuit of 'spreading the word'.

The Cinema of God

The Sunday school religious film screening idea became a reality and a big hit. Rank purchased a film projector for the Methodist church in Reigate, and soon afterwards many other Methodist churches throughout the country. In 1933 he formed the Religious Films Society (RFS) to supply projectors, and films, to Sunday Schools and churches.

In fact when Rank made grants towards construction of new Methodist chapels, one condition was that they should be designed with a projection room. Two such chapels were built in Hull for example: the original 1933 building (demolished 2007) at Derringham Bank Methodist Church and Endike Lane in 1934 – the latter chapel still has projection hatches above the door from the lobby, and the choir & pulpit area was visibly designed to accommodate a film screen.

It was a time of great excitement in the British Film Industry with Alexander Korda producing an unparalleled box-office hit with *The Private Life of Henry VIII*. Though J Arthur Rank admitted to having no interest or desire to be involved in commercial films he was, though, acutely aware of their influence on modern day life and society.

Korda and Rank were like chalk and cheese: Rank's prudence was countered by Korda's extravagance. Everything Korda boasted in abundance, Rank did not. They made an interesting pair of businessmen – one ambitious and ruthless, the other the most unassuming ever.

Together they were about to dominate and rule the British Film industry though curiously, they never quite ruled together – as one's company flourished, the other's always floundered.

It was really through Korda's success that Rank became drawn into the movie business when the Methodist Times, keen to point out in view of Korda's success with what should really have been called *The Sex Life Of Henry VIII*, claimed that good wholesome family stories, devoid of crime and sex, had all but vanished from screens since the arrival of talkies. Of course, there was also Hollywood and its more liberal stories to contend with too, and their total disregard for religious morals.

Just as the Methodists were growing suspicious – maybe even envious – of cinema, Rank was growing disheartened with many of the films he hired in for his Sunday shows; both in quality and subject matter. He decided to make a film that would reflect the values the Methodists held so dear.

In 1934 Rank proposed *The Mastery of Christ* (based on material written by him and W H Lax, a preacher from London's East End) as a film he would like to finance for the RFS.

He proposed to apply his everyday business principles to film, which amused many in the business. A flour miller making films!

Rank enlisted a former journalist Aveling Ginever, who had enjoyed success with a religious film called *In Our Time* to write and direct his project. *Mastership*, as it was re-titled, was completed in one week at Merton Park Studios in 1934, ran for 20 minutes and cost £2,700. Ginever employed over 100 actors. The story followed a quarreling family making their separate way to one of Lax's meetings and leaving united after hearing him speak.

As Rank's intention was to 'spread the word', the next step was to take his film around churches to interest them in screening it. Though never shown commercially, *Mastership* was a success and was even taken to foreign fields by missionaries.

Rank later admitted – with hindsight – that it was a 'lousy film' but went on to add that on its first showing in a Yorkshire coalfield 'nineteen people were brought to Christ'.

Rank and Ginever discussed a full-length film to follow-up and even buying Wembley Studios to undertake an ambitious film programme. Plans fell through, and the couple parted after an argument about theology.

Claiming that Ginever was not prudent enough in his budgeting, and not particularly caring for his modern-day approach and personal beliefs, Rank decided to find a new partner for future films. When word of the wealthy miller seeking someone to make films and spend his money went out, potential partners were banging on his door.

Enter John Corfield, a law graduate and producer of a low budget quota film. Corfield's meeting with Rank came about after a friend and colleague of Corfield's, Graham Glegg, had set up a meeting with Rank to talk about making a religious film. Unfortunately, the day before the meeting, Glegg's son was involved in an aeroplane crash and broke both his legs. Glegg asked Corfield if he would mind keeping the appointment with Rank in his place.

Rank ran *Mastership* for Corfield and asked how much he would charge to produce the film. Corfield replied £2,000 (a pound per foot, as per the Quota films). Impressed that it was £700 less than he had paid for the actual production, he immediately asked the producer to sign a contract to produce religious films at £2,000 each. Corfield – cannily – added that it was a bare cost, and they should add another 10 percent … or 'how about two films for £4,500'. It was agreed.

Rank commissioned him to produce two more shorts in 1934: *Inasmuch* which was the story of St Francis of Assisi, with Greer Garson in her first role and Donald Wolfit as St Francis; and *Let There Be Love*. Combined they cost £4,500.

J Arthur Rank found promoting his films an uphill slog within the Methodist Church, with many believing that a man of such traditional religious beliefs should not behave in such a 'revolutionary manner'. One must remember that many Methodist Ministers still claimed film was the work of Satan at this time, and religious films were a form of blasphemy. His own father was even dubious as to his involvement in the medium too.

Rank continued nevertheless, in his crusade to furnish Methodist churches with projectors, and one day visited Wardour Street, the heart of the film industry.

There he made enquiries at powerhouse Gaumont-British (G-B) about buying a number of projectors, and ever the businessman demanded a discount for quantity.

Rank struck up a friendship with managing director Ian Cremieu-Javal, and persuaded him that the company might make three films for the Religious Film Society. He saw them as an efficient and proven production company. Rank and the Religious Film Society fast became one of G-B's best customers. Production of the films moved from Merton Park to the superior Rock Studios (later British National) at Elstree.

The religious films were taken all round the country, into prisons and youth clubs, schools and Women's Institute gatherings, and even to the Prime Minister's country estate, Chequers. Rank footed the bill for all of this personally.

Whilst generously writing out cheques, the ever-prudent Rank began thinking of ways to economize in his expanding venture. In examining the costs involved he realized that his main costs were the writer, production company (G-B), and then a facility for studio space. The greatest of these costs was studio space. Surely rather than rent space, it would make more sense to use facilities that he owned?

An old cinema in Gypsy Hill, in the London suburbs of Norwood, was taken over by Rank for that very purpose. In the summer of 1937, Mrs Rank officially opened the building. The first film to move in was a 45-minute biography of William Tyndale, the great Christian scholar.

Obviously, there were drawbacks with the facility – limited space, poor sound proofing being two – but it proved adequate for a number of religious films including *Fishers of Men* and *Who Then Can Be Saved?*

The relative success of these films saw J Arthur Rank becoming increasingly more interested in the commercial sector of film production, and the greater audiences therein which he might reach.

Rank's actual move into commercial films came after the challenge from the *Evening News* to the *Methodist Times* who had (again) attacked the low

1.12 Lady Yule's yacht 'Nahlin'. The first inclining of a British constitutional crisis was reported when King Edward VIII chartered Nahlin for he and Mrs Simpson

moral standard of modern films – namely *The Private Life of Henry VIII* – that was all very well, maintained the *Evening News*, but why didn't the Methodists produce 'family' films of their own in response?

Rank decided to take up the challenge.

British National

Lady Annie Henrietta Yule, millionairess widow of jute baron Sir David Yule, became active in the film industry in the early 1930s. She had inherited an estimated £15 million upon her husband's death in 1928.

With her daughter Gladys, Lady Yule travelled the world to fuel her passion for big game hunting. Her St Albans home was full of stuffed animal heads and a huge bear which she shot in the Rocky Mountains.

Despite her tendency to shoot big game, she was an animal lover. She funded a home in the South of France for mistreated animals, instructed jockeys on her horses to never use a whip, and kept a veritable menagerie in her garden – wallabies, penguins, seals along with dogs and horses.

Arabian horses were certainly her main interest in life; and she expended every luxury on them at her Hertfordshire stud farm.

Though perhaps she might have been viewed as somewhat eccentric, she moved in impressive circles. Her financial advisor was Lord Catto, later the Governor of the Bank of England.

Catto no doubt steered her towards a number of conservative investment opportunities, but all lacked the excitement she craved. She described herself as being acutely bored. The idea of becoming involved in films was one that intrigued her, and one she thought might be fun! She would have very little interest in whether a film made a profit or not; in fact, she had little interest in any financial matters relating to production. She simply enjoyed the glamour associated with it.

Like Arthur Rank, she was a teetotaller. Wealth and a dislike of alcohol were two things the unlikely movie moguls had in common.

Among Lady Yule's possessions was an enormous yacht, *Nahlin*, boasting a crew of fifty-one, which played host to King Edward VII and Mrs Simpson – leading up to the abdication.

John Corfield had met Lady Yule after making a Quota Film for low budget production company Butchers. He was on holiday in Bermuda at the same time as Lady Yule was there on *Nahlin*. There he invited her to a cinema show – the film being his own of course. The film was bad, very bad, and Lady Yule wasted no time in telling Corfield so.

'What do you expect for £8,000?' he asked (considerably more than the usual quota cost of £2,700). To which Lady Yule reportedly said that he should not let money stand in the way of quality and agreed to back the producer in a new project.

Corfield began telling his friend Rank of his proposed venture with Lady Yule and made mention of an idea to film *The Pilgrim's Progress*. Although it never materialised, it was enough to secure Rank's firm interest in making a feature, with good family values. A meeting was organised between Rank and Lady Yule; and together they agreed a joint venture. British National Films Ltd was formed in 1934 with Rank, Yule and Corfield becoming company directors.

One of Rank's first concerns was that he should continue making religious films, but now through British National. He asked his fellow directors to consider making them for him 'at cost' without the company taking a

1.13 A, B , C, D Cast and crew from Turn Of The Tide

1.13 A, B , C, D Cast and crew from Turn Of The Tide

1.13 A, B , C, D Cast and crew from Turn Of The Tide

1.13 A, B , C, D Cast and crew from Turn Of The Tide

production fee, typically 5 per-cent. Corfield readily agreed however Lady Yule retorted: 'You believe in Christianity with 5 per-cent don't you Mr Rank?'

Fiercely annoyed, Rank held his tongue.

Turn of the Tide

In 1935 British National produced their first film, *Turn of the Tide* at British & Dominion Studios in Borehamwood.

The story was based on Leo Walmsley's 1932 novel *Three Fevers*, which was inspired by the author's life in Robin Hood's Bay on the North Yorkshire coast. It was reported that Rank knew Robin Hood's Bay from childhood visits and, having read *Three Fevers*, saw the opportunity to provide a true reflection of everyday life in Britain as opposed to the Hollywood-style stories coming from Alexander Korda at Denham; which Rank believed bore little relation to British life and values. The story is a simple one based on the rivalry between two fishing families, the Lunns and Fosdycks, after the Lunns acquire an engine for their boat. This prompts the Fosdyck family to start sabotaging lobster pots and to keep their daughter away from John Lunn, with whom she is romantically involved.

The film was superbly photographed by Franz Planer and boasted a fine cast which included Wilfrid Lawson, Moore Marriott, and Geraldine Fitzgerald. It was edited by Ian Dalrymple and an uncredited David Lean. It was warmly received by the critics, and even won a prize at the Venice Film Festival.

A distribution agreement had been sealed with Gaumont-British, guaranteeing a London premiere followed by a national run with British National netting 25 per-cent of the box office. A not unreasonable deal.

However, in practice, the national run was not all Rank had been led to believe it would be. It was actually run as a second feature – and the box office mechanics meant the bulk of profit share was made to the main programme, not the supporting one.

Rank was furious. John Corfield went to meet the Ostrer brothers at G-B, saying he was representing J Arthur Rank.

'I've never heard of him,' replied Mark Ostrer. The Ostrers had indeed heard of Rank. He and Lady Yule were the talk of Wardour Street. But it

1.14 Turn of the Tide trade show of film

would seem that the Ostrers were disappointed having been approached by the burgeoning movie moguls, that the only offering for their distribution circuit was a modest moralistic Yorkshire fisherman story. They decided to treat the project just as they would any other with which they held mild distain.

Rank deemed the release highly unsatisfactory, particularly when production costs of £30,000 had not been recouped.

A valuable lesson had been learned: producing films was all well and good, but one had to have control of distribution and exhibition in order

1.15 Charles Boot purchased a country estate with a plan to build a film studio

to make a profit. The film actually recouped just £18,000 on its release through G-B. Rank was deeply unhappy and angry with the way he and his film had been treated.

The Ostrers had cheated the wrong man!

As well as thinking about distribution, Rank also applied his milling background to film production. During the making of *Turn of the Tide* he witnessed many inefficiencies of filming on just one of the three-stages of the B&D complex. Whenever a new set was called for, everything stopped for the new sets to be brought in and lit.

Distribution, exhibition, and production facilities – Rank realised these were areas he would be wise to investigate further.

Pinewood Studios

In the early 1930s the wealthy Sheffield building tycoon Charles Boot (of Henry Boot Ltd) was drawn into the world of film with a view to establishing and building a British studio to rival those of Hollywood. Writing in the October 1, 1936, edition of trade paper *Kinematograph Weekly*, he said: 'Sir Auckland Geddes had been touring the United States and had closely studied Hollywood, its studios and its film production activities, and he came back enthusiastic regarding the growing possibilities of a similar Film Industry in Great Britain. He and another far-seeing man [Sir John Henry] discussed in a definite and detailed manner the organisation which would be necessary to ensure success.'

Initially, plans were made to build a complex at Elstree, but the project fell through due to Boot's then considerable business interests in, and frequent travel to and from, Greece. His interest in a film studio, however, did

1.16/1.17 Heatherden Hall in Iver Heath, Buckinghamshire.

not diminish. In 1934, Heatherden Hall, a lavish mansion in Iver Heath, Buckinghamshire, came up for auction on the death of its Canadian owner, Lt Col Grant Morden. Formerly the MP for Chiswick and Brentford, and a multi-millionaire in his own right, Morden had been declared bankrupt and left only £10 in his will.

Morden had spent thousands of pounds on the Hall, adding a magnificent 76 ft ballroom, 30 ft high with a sprung polished floor and a ceiling heavily moulded in the Grindling Gibbons style; a swimming pool 44 ft long and 24 ft wide with dressing rooms, shower baths and a spectators' gallery (thought to be the first in a privately owned house in Britain); a

1.16/1.17 Heatherden Hall in Iver Heath, Buckinghamshire.

Turkish bath; billiard room; glass-covered squash courts; tennis courts and ornamental garden.

He had 10,000 roses planted and funded expeditions to the Himalayas to bring back rare rhododendrons. He also brought trees, shrubs and plants from Japan, Canada, India, Australia, and other exotic climes, many of which are still in the gardens at the studio: a Judas Tree, Wellingtonias, Tulip Tree and a magnificent Lebanon Cedar. Morden also owned borzoi dogs and deerhounds, and regularly held grouse and pheasant shoots in the grounds for his guests. Unsurprisingly, the Hall became a popular retreat for politicians and diplomats and was valued at £300,000.

1.18 The one-hundred acre estate included an ornamental bridge and pond

On November 3, 1921, when the Irish Free-State treaty was signed at the Hall (in the room which is now the studio's main bar) by the Rt Hon Earl of Birkenhead; the Rt Hon Viscount Long of Wraxhall; the Rt Hon Viscount Younger of Leckie, Chairman of the Conservative and Unionist Party; Sir Malcolm Fraser, Principal Agent, the Conservatives and Unionist Party; and Lt Col Grant Morden.

After Morden's death, the auction of Heatherden Hall was held on September 25, 1934, by Goddard & Smith of London. The auction brochure described the property thus: 'Luxuriously appointed imposing Georgian Mansion (upon which vast sums have been spent from time to time) with its valuable furniture and contents … It contains: Porte Cochère entrance, Outer, Inner, Lounge and Staircase Halls, 4 Reception Rooms, Billiard Room, Magnificent Dance Room (76 ft by 30 ft), 39 Principal, Secondary and Staff Bedrooms, 2 Marble Bath Rooms, 9 other Bath Rooms, Exceptionally Fine Swimming Bath, Turkish Bath Room and adequate Offices.'

Boot bought the house and grounds for what must have seemed a bargain – about £35,000.

1.19 The Porte Cochre entrance

Boot's idea was simple: build a studio to rival the best that California had to offer. So, with his general manager James Sloan he set to work designing his new studio complex.

J Arthur Rank had made no secret of his annoyance at the inefficiency of small studios. He wanted better to produce films more efficiently and effectively, and Charles Boot was able to offer them.

Unsurprisingly, Rank and Lady Yule soon joined forces with Boot and became major shareholders in Pinewood Studios Ltd. The name Pinewood was chosen, according to Boot, because 'of the number of these trees which grow there, and because it seemed to suggest something of the American film centre in its second syllable.'

GCFC

In 1936 a film-finance company called 'The General Cinema Finance Corporation' (GCFC) was set up to help change the fortunes of British film production; after the Quota Act did little to break Hollywood's grip on British film, and the British box office. Lord (Wyndham) Portal, the paper

1.20 Stately front elevation

magnate, was commissioned by the Board Of Trade to 'do something to turn things around' and, as Chairman of the company, he pulled in directors Lord Luke (Bovril), Paul Lindenburg (Japhet's Bank), L W Farrow (accountant) and rising noise in the film industry J Arthur Rank. The GCFC had an extremely sound and prestigious backing with its distinguished directors. The company also, rather ironically, bought a 25 per-cent share in American film company Universal Pictures, which had recently run into financial problems. The GCFC had the potential to become a powerhouse. Yet, bizarrely to the outsider, it was guided by two men whose main business interests lay in paper and flour.

With a finance and production company in place Rank next turned his thoughts to distribution. He had no idea where to start? It was suggested that he should contact C M Woolf.

Charles Moss Woolf, the former managing director of G-B (who had left a few months ahead of the release of *Turn Of The Tide* to pursue his own interests), was considered a leading name in distribution and when Rank asked who the best film salesman was, without hesitation, his was the name that came back. Since leaving G-B, Woolf had set up a small company called General Film Distributors (GFD). His parting from G-B was not a particularly happy one and was in fact the result of a growing number of disagreements between Woolf and the Ostrers.

GFD grew fast. In two years since forming the company, by the end of 1936 Woolf had handled some twenty-four films including several from Alfred Hitchcock.

In the 1930s, distributors had a stranglehold on British film production. They reserved the right to vet any script and make casting decisions. The producer was often the puppet to which they controlled the strings. They demanded cuts, re-shoots, and re-edits as they saw fit. Creativity on the part of the filmmakers was suppressed. Basically, if you controlled distribution, you pretty much controlled production too.

Rank met with Woolf and whilst the latter had no interest in becoming involved in moralistic or religious films, he did offer to help Rank learn the ropes of distribution and guide him along Wardour Street, said to be 'shadowy on both sides'.

Rank and Lord Portal had together bought some shares in GFD in 1935, and in exchange for his 'distribution education' Rank signed cheques to help fund Woolf's activities.

The General Cinema Finance Corporation, if it were to have any impact on bettering British Film's fortunes, obviously needed a foothold in distribution. Given Rank and Portal's existing involvement with GFD, it made logical sense for the GCFC to follow suit. Thus, in March 1936, GFD was taken over completely by the General Cinema Finance Corporation.

One may wonder why a seasoned sales veteran such as Woolf would so keenly agree for his company to be absorbed into the GCFC and lose his independence much as he had done previously with Gaumont-British. The answer was simple. The GCFC was cash rich, allowing Woolf to back any projects he wanted, and it owned a 25 per-cent share in Universal. The American market was always the one British companies yearned, yet failed, to crack. Woolf would now have a significant foothold in the US for his films; and he also absorbed Universal's British interests into GFD, thus guaranteeing himself a flow of quality American films for British screens in the process. Plus, in this case, Woolf was not selling out to a film combine, as with the Ostrers, but a finance company who had no real experience of

1.21 The first privately owned indoor swimming pool

filmmaking. They valued him and his knowledge and were quite happy to give him a free reign.

Woolf was very conservative in his choice of British films he would back. He turned down epics in favour of a staple diet of comedies, thrillers, and musicals. He turned away maverick filmmakers such as Powell & Pressburger, Alexander Korda and Gabriel Pascal. He preferred to let the American companies take such risks, allowing him to buy up their successes for his company; and leave well alone their failures.

GFD's logo – thought up by C M Woolf's secretary – was the now legendary 'man with the gong'; Carl Dane was the first to assume a role, followed by Bombardier Billy Wells, Phil Nieman, Ken Richmond and (an unused) Martin Grace. Curiously, Dane struck the gong three times whilst his successors only struck it twice. The golden gong was to grace all of Rank's future films, through to the company's last in 1997.

Lady Yule, not overly keen to get involved in distribution matters, declined the opportunity to partner British National with GFD – marking the beginning of her split with Rank. In 1937 Rank withdrew from British

1.22 Charles Boot's sister, Mary Reis (nee Boot), laid the foundation stone for Pinewood in 1935 (Matt Boot)

National to concentrate on activities through GFD, and Lady Yule withdrew from Pinewood Studios. She sold her shares in Pinewood to Rank, and he sold his shares in British National to her. John Corfield remained with Lady Yule and continued to produce films for the company through until 1948, including the popular *Old Mother Riley* comedies, the superior *Gaslight* and later *One of Our Aircraft Is Missing* with Powell & Pressburger at the helm. British National Films financed and produced 71 films from its inception through to 1948 when, with ailing health, Lady Yule withdrew from all film interests. She died in 1950. Three years later, having not produced any other films, John Corfield died aged 60.

Pinewood

'I am one of the very few', recalled Sir Anthony Havelock-Allan in an interview with the author in 1999, 'and perhaps the only surviving person, to remember staying at Heatherden Hall when it was a country club, some 20 years or more before anyone thought of buying it for a film studio. It was a delightful venue with marvellous facilities, particularly the dining room, and it was a wonderful place to stay. I recall vividly news of the signing of the Anglo-Irish agreement in what was then the smoking room of the Hall.'

W G King, a gardener at the Hall, remembered with fondness the early days on the estate. 'Heatherden Hall was functioning as a country club under the management of a Major Rawlings. The garden staff was increased to 18 (from six) under the supervision of Ian Morrison, the son of the head gardener of Mr Boot's estate in Derbyshire. The gardens were transformed from the wilderness they had become to their former glory. Where Car Park One (opposite the canteen) was later situated, a vast area of glass houses stood along with a vineyard, peach house and so on. This was surrounded by a two-acre walled kitchen garden full of fruit trees of every variety. The Heath Farm was once a fully operational farm; also, in that area was the generating plant attended by the estate electrician, engineer Fred Clifford. The water came from the tank on the lot and supplied the ornamental lake in the garden, with the little waterfall which tumbles over the rock, behind the bridge which crosses the lake. The Deer Park was the grassed area outside the front door of the old Hall which, in those days, came within 12 yards of the porch with its stately pillars. Eventually, the progress of the British film industry changed the landscape of Heatherden Hall, and we were privileged to see the start of Pinewood Studios. Soon, everything north of the Hall had gone.'

The first brick of Pinewood Studios was laid in December 1935 by Boot's sister Mrs Mary Reis, and a new stage was completed every three weeks. The cost of building the studio ran to over £1 million.

Some Construction and Equipment Facts and Figures

Men employed during construction	: 1,500
Steelwork erected	: 2,300 tons
Concrete	: 20,000 cubic yards
Patent glazing	: 25,000 sq ft
Asphalting	: 15,000 sq yards
Thatchboard	: 24,000 sq yards
Soundproofing	: 300,000 sq ft
Floor area of buildings	: 7.5 acres
Bricks used	: 6,000,000
Ventilating trunking	: 3,300 ft
Capacity of air inlet fans	: 8,100,000 cubic ft / min
Feet run of heating pipework	: 50,000
Number of radiators	: 700
Heating surface of radiators	: 25,000 sq ft
Electrical wire	: 60 miles
Bare aluminium conductors	: 2.5 miles

(Kinematograph Weekly, 1936)

J Arthur Rank was appointed Chairman; Ronald Crammond, Vice Chairman; Richard Norton, Managing Director; and C M Woolf as a director.

With a background in banking, Captain Richard Norton (later Lord Grantley) had been in charge of production at United Artists in the early 1930s prior to joining British & Dominion. In 1936 he was appointed the first managing director of Pinewood. The monocle-wearing aristocrat and his assistant, Anthony Havelock-Allan (himself later knighted), were charged with keeping the studio busy.

Havelock-Allan had begun his career in the entertainment business as a cabaret manager and subsequently as a casting director, giving him an extensive knowledge of actors, both established and up-and-coming. Richard Norton persuaded him to join B&D and now, through a twist of fate, Havelock-Allan found himself back at Heatherden Hall, although this time it was to be his home for two years.

1.23/1.24 The studio under construction. It took Boot twelve months in total

1.23/1.24 The studio under construction. It took Boot twelve months in total

'We moved to Pinewood in the early part of 1936,' he remembered, 'when there was only one stage and the dressing rooms completed. Captain Richard Norton and I took suites on the top floor of the old house and Pinewood became our home until the end of 1938. It was absolutely ideal for me, as I could get out of bed and be at work almost immediately. I can honestly say that as well as being a lovely studio, I was tremendously happy there and, indeed, met my first wife Valerie Hobson there. It was the happiest period I have ever had in the film business. The ease and comfort of being there was wonderful.'

Having transferred with Wilcox's B&D outfit, assistant editor Richard Best (who went on to cut such notable films as *Ice Cold in Alex, The Dambusters* and *Woman in a Dressing Gown*) recalled the first day in 1936. 'Pinewood had an air of relaxed efficiency – the same as it has today, only less bustling. The first impression on entering was of its elegance and good planning, emanating not only from the original house and grounds but in the choice of pale-whitish brick work and off-white stages. The car park was finished in light gravel to match and was surrounded by a low chain rail.'

Production at Pinewood began after a mishap at another studio. A fire at Elstree early in 1936 persuaded the director Herbert Wilcox to transfer his British & Dominion (B&D) productions to Pinewood, after brief stints at 'Sound City' (Shepperton) and Warner Bros Studios in Teddington. It was said that with the whole of his studio gutted – bar the vaults and cutting rooms – Wilcox now had more money than ever, thanks to his insurance claim. The studio's first equipment was purchased from B&D and transferred from Elstree. It cost £75,545 which included the sum of £61,999 for sound equipment supplied by the Western Electric Company Ltd.

The news was announced in the Kinematograph Weekly on May 28, 1936: 'Shareholders of the British and Dominions Film Corporation at an extra-ordinary general meeting held on Tuesday approved unanimously the scheme under which B&D will become part-owners of the Pinewood Studios by virtue of an investment of 50 per cent in the capital of the studio owning company … The present share capital is £150,000 which is to be increased to £300,000, of which B&D is to take £150,000 … It is proposed that the directors of B&D join the board of the Pinewood company and that Captain R Norton be appointed managing director. Captain Norton has agreed to apply part of the remuneration payable to him by Pinewood towards reducing the remuneration payable to him by B&D. Certain of the equipment and stores at Elstree which were not affected by the fire will be taken over by the Pinewood Studios, and B&D will also manage Pinewood Studios for a term of 10 years.'

On September 30, 1936, a special opening ceremony was performed by the Parliamentary Secretary of Trade, Dr Leslie Burgin. According to a report in the Daily Film Renter, 'Guests are being taken down to Iver from Paddington by special train and motored thence to the studios. A strong muster of trade and production celebrities is expected.' Over 1,200 guests assembled for the event and a special lunch was served on D Stage. A guided tour of the stages, dressing rooms, powerhouse, workshops, administration buildings, and the club house and gardens followed. Herbert Wilcox was shooting *London Melody*, which was already partly completed before transferring to Pinewood, and the guests were allowed a peek at the first film ever shot at the new studio. (Released by GFD in 1937, *London Melody* was dubbed by Variety an 'excellent compilation of bromidial mush, beautifully produced and directed.') The day's events ended at 4.00pm when 'vehicles [were] available to convey guests to Iver Station.'

Pinewood fast made its mark as a remarkably modern production centre. Yet the refined elegance of the once stately home was not lost as the art gallery, drawing rooms, guest rooms and gardens were beautifully maintained. It was, however, a difficult time for filmmakers and, as they suffered, so too did the rental spaces that so desperately relied upon their activity. Denham struggled under Korda, who found himself £1 million in the red owing to poor box-office on the likes of *The Four Feathers* and *Elephant Boy*. Twickenham Studios found it impossible to stay in business. It was a bad time to be in film ... unless your name was Mr Rank.

In 1937, Rank decided to consolidate his not insignificant film industry interests in one company, The Rank Organisation. It was to become the greatest of all the British film combines.

❧ 4 ❧

Rank and Korda

As Rank was celebrating his success, the Ostrer brothers were beginning to experience what was to become a spectacular fall from grace. Financial difficulties in the Gaumont-British empire (which included 60 subsidiary companies) had seen them run up an overdraft of £1 million.

Mark Ostrer famously once said he had 'never heard' of J Arthur Rank. In the months and years that followed, he heard a great deal about Rank!

Alexander Korda's production programme meanwhile had generated more flops than successes, and his ambitious Denham studios and its 2,000 employees was haemorrhaging money.

Quota Quickies

Korda had begun his British film-making career in Quota Quickies at Borehamwood, after a successful period of making films in his native Hungary, Hollywood, and Paris. Korda was described as charm personified.

'They paid one pound per foot of film, and wouldn't pay any more if you went over one hour fifteen, as that was 6,250 feet!' recalled Sir Anthony Havelock-Allan, who was responsible for all of B&D's quota films. 'Quotas were not really regarded with much affection, apart, of course, from those who got their start in them. Vivien Leigh made two, although she always denied it; Rex Harrison first appeared in one, as did Wendy Hiller and Margaret Rutherford. George Sanders got his first starring role in one too.

Young writers also got a break: Terry Rattigan and Robert Morley wrote scripts for me before they became famous.'

Simplicity was the key to these productions. There was no heavy camera coverage, post-synchronisation, or sound effects recordings. Library tracks were used for both music and effects. They were usually well cast, with reasonable scripts, and proved a springboard for many famous names of the future. Actors in the Pinewood films included Patrick Barr, Greta Gynt, Jimmy Hanley, Wendy Hiller, and Edward Rigby.

Conversely, just as they were a starting ground for many aspiring filmmakers, they also marked the end of the line for some of the great silent movie directors, George Pearson being one. Film director and Oscar-winning lighting cameraman Freddie Francis worked on many of the 'quota' films, two of them with George Pearson, at the beginning of his Pinewood career. 'He was a strange chap,' said Francis, 'as he always used to wear his overcoat and trilby hat on set. He never really came to terms with sound either, as he would quite often talk in the middle of a scene or shout out directions.'

But what of the other filmmakers? 'There were many people around the studio at that time,' continued Francis, 'who really knew very little about making films and I have to admit I learnt a lot from their mistakes! They just found themselves in the situation of having to make these films and muddled their way through as best they could. Of course, the in-joke with the quota films was that nobody other than the cleaners at the Plaza would ever see them, as the films were often run in the mornings to fulfil the requirements of the quota act – but they were a good training ground.'

The ten-year life span of the 'quota quickies' came to an end in 1937.

Denham Studios

Korda had expanded his London Film Production's company programme rapidly and rented studio space at Worton Hall in Isleworth, and the nearby Shepperton Studios, making films such as *The Private Life of Don Juan* and *The Scarlett Pimpernel*. In the mid 1930s however, he became determined to have his own permanent home, and settled upon a 193-acre estate called The Fisheries in Denham, Buckinghamshire. In 1935 building commenced.

In May 1936, Britain's largest film studio, with seven stages, opened. It boasted the best of everything and even had a film processing laboratory on site.

With a great fanfare *Wings of the Morning* was the first production to move in. It was the first Technicolor film shot in the UK and starred Henry Fonda, Anabella Power, and Leslie Banks.

Big budget productions followed such as *The Four Feathers, Elephant Boy, The Divorce of Lady X* and *I, Claudius* but non shared the commercial success of *Henry VIII*.

Korda's big-budget pictures – which Woolf resolutely refused to try and emulate or invest in – could not deliver the box-office returns so desperately needed to ensure a continuing programme. Ever-increasing debts stretched beyond £1 million and the patience of Korda's 'patron', the Prudential Building Society, wore thin. In 1938 the Prudential sought to recoup some of the vast investment they had made.

Rank saw his opportunity to move in. Working with Prudential, he bought out Korda's interests in Denham in 1939 and combined the studio with Pinewood. The Hungarian mogul may have lost his home, but he saw it as an opportunity to again become an independent. His and Rank's paths would cross again, with fortunes reversed, as we will see.

Rank formed Denham & Pinewood Studios Ltd and incorporated the activities of both studios under the D&P banner. It was a further six years before Rank bought out all of Prudential's interests in the studio.

The company had been registered as a private concern with a nominal capital of £750,000 in £1 shares. The objectives of the company were listed as being to 'acquire London Film Productions (Korda's production company) and Pinewood Studios, and it will adopt agreements with (1) London Films and Prudential Assurance Company, and (2) Pinewood Studios and Equity and Law Life Assurance Society.' The eight appointed directors were E Ronald Crammond, E H George, Sir Connop Guthrie, E H Lever, Captain R Norton, J Arthur Rank, Spencer M Reis, and P C Stapleton.

It should be added that in 1939 Rank added another studio to his stable when he purchased the newly built Amalgamated Studios in Borehamwood. Aware that ABPC's John Maxwell was close to tying up a deal, Rank wrote a personal cheque for the full asking price and pipped Maxwell to the post. In a canny business move, Rank then leased the studio to the Government for records storage. After the war, the studio did re-open, after Rank sold it to MGM for their British base.

Pinebrook

As Rank's meteoric rise was playing out, in 1938 a new Films Act had been introduced to rid the screen of the quota quickies.

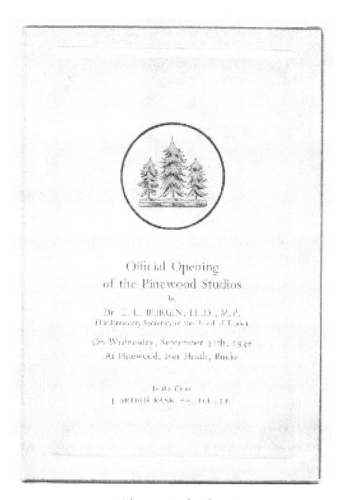

1.25 The opening lunch party

1.26/1.27 The famous sign which graced Pinewood from the moment J. Arthur Rank formed The Rank Organisation

In its place a 'treble quota' system was brought in, the idea being that producers would opt for more expensive or better films, but certainly fewer than under the previous Act.

It provoked a massive crisis: investors were wary that bigger budget 'quota fillers' would be treated with equal disdain as their cheaper predecessors by distributors, exhibitors and the public.

It caused a massive down-turn in production.

Pinewood meanwhile had a staff to pay, and with empty stages a crisis was not far off.

Managing director Richard Norton developed an idea to keep the studio busy and technicians employed. He formed Pinebrook Films to make

1.26/1.27 The famous sign which graced Pinewood from the moment J. Arthur Rank formed The Rank Organisation

low-budget films when there were gaps in studio bookings. He did not have to pay for stage space, and rather than pay a crew to sit around doing nothing, he could now at least gain something.

Along came such pictures as *Lightning Conductor* with Gordon Harker and *Spot of Bother*, starring Roberston Hare and Alfred Drayton. One of the most successful productions was *The Lambeth Walk* with Lupino Lane and Sally Gray, directed by Albert de Courville. Thought to be one of the many 'lost' films of the period, the discovery and remastering of a French-subtitled copy was greeted with jubilation in the mid 1990s. The stage revival of *Me and My Girl*, source of *The Lambeth Walk*, still plays to packed houses on both sides of the Atlantic. Better was to follow with *This Man is News*. Shot for £14,000, it made almost £150,000 at the box-office. But the Pinebrook venture proved to be a double-edged sword. Studio staff wages still had to be paid and Norton found it a struggle. He then persuaded his cast and crew to take a lower salary and invest the remainder in the film. If the film made a profit, then salary deferment would earn a sizeable amount. *This Man is News* was the first film ever to offer profit participation, rather than just a straight fee. It is interesting to note that Pinebrook never lost money.

1.28 J. Arthur Rank and Alexander Korda deep in discussion over lunch at Denham Studios

Meanwhile, playwright George Bernard Shaw was being cajoled into allowing one of his plays to be made into a film. He had turned down many previous requests, but a 40-year-old Hungarian called Gabriel Pascal persuaded him otherwise. He was a very canny producer. From studying farming at the Hungarian National Economy college and serving as a lieutenant in the Hungarian Hussar Regiment during the Great War, he progressed to producing silent films in Italy and decamped to Britain in the mid-1930s. He won Shaw over against all the odds, and when C M Woolf rejected the opportunity to distribute the film and hence guarantee the finance, Pascal manoeuvred himself in the direction of Richard Norton (who was no great friend of Woolf) and arranged a meeting with

1.29 Zoltan Korda, Gabriel Pascal and Alex Korda

J Arthur Rank himself. Ignorant of Woolf's decision, Rank agreed to back the film.

The splendid *Pygmalion* starred Wendy Hiller, and Leslie Howard, who co-directed with Anthony Asquith. The film was nominated for four Academy Awards – Best Picture, Script, Actor and Actress. It also caused some controversy when Wendy Hiller delivered what was then considered an outrageous line: 'Not bloody likely!' It was the first of Pascal's collaborations with Rank and was box-office dynamite. Rank had evidently made a wise decision.

On Christmas Eve 1938, Pinewood Studios closed its doors. Lack of productions and mounting operating costs had rendered it non-viable. Rank moved all production over to the busier Denham Studios. Rank's interests in other areas of film, meanwhile, were growing further. When Oscar Deutsch, of the Odeon chain of cinemas, needed further investment to fund his 'invasion' of North America, the vital missing link in Rank's empire was finally put in place.

⤳ 5 ⤳

Oscar Deutsch

Oscar Deutsch had entered the film industry in the 1920s with school friends Michael Balcon and Victor Saville. He part funded some of their films. He was more interested in exhibition than production and in 1930, the son of a Hungarian scrap metal merchant, built a cinema in Perry Barr, Birmingham. It was the very first Odeon.

A few years later, Odeon cinemas were popping up all over the country. The cinemas were luxurious, well designed and well constructed. The exteriors were extravagant in every aspect – set to lure people in. Cannily, Deutsch designed each interior to be virtually identical. The idea being, just as it was said you could walk into any Woolworths shop and find the same layout, people on holiday in different parts of the country would willingly visit the local Odeon as it would remind them of their home-town Odeon. As each cinema opened, Deutsch would engage the Dagenham Girl Pipers to be on stage, ahead of Deutsch leading local dignitaries on.

Initially Deutsch met with great opposition. The established networks did not want competition, and they certainly flexed their muscles with their suppliers. So much so, Deutsch found it difficult to secure films from distributors. He then made a deal with United Artists (UA), who were in turn finding it difficult finding British cinemas to exhibit their films.

It looked, for a while at least, as though Odeon would become linked with Alexander Korda. The producer had a deal with United Artists, and it seemed an obvious move for UA to rent the films they financed for Korda, to Odeon. Korda was poised to take a stranglehold on British film

1.30 The J. Arthur Rank Boardroom at Pinewood Studios

production. But then came Korda's financial problems at Denham when his backers, the Prudential, stop signing cheques.

By 1933, Deutsch had 26 cinemas. Odeon, incidentally, was alleged to be an acronym for 'Oscar Deutsch Entertains Our Nation'. By 1937 there were 250 in the chain including the flagship, the Leicester Square cinema.

Odeon not only brought audiences the latest British and Hollywood movies, but also a standard of contemporary design. With their cloud-piercing towers and sweeping lines, Odeons were a promise of the shape of things to come. For less than a shilling (five pence), coal miners, railway workers, teachers, nurses, servicemen, typists, and clerks could disappear into a shining world of futuristic dreams, a whole dimension away from the grim economic and political reality.

In 1938, with his company enjoying great success at home Deutsch set his sights on establishing his cinema chain in other countries; notably, North America. In order to fund an American expansion, Deutsch obviously needed finance. Enter J Arthur Rank.

Rank, through the GFFC, had a few theatres under his control, but knew all too well that if his distribution arm was to have any great success, then he needed a far more sizeable exhibition chain behind him. Rank bought

1.31 General Film Distributors (GFD) produced melodramas and comedies, such as this with Will Hay.

7,000 preference shares and 4,000 ordinary shares in Odeon – and took his place on the board.

Tragically, in 1941, at the age of just 48, Deutsch died of cancer. Driven by a great enthusiasm Deutsch had worked around the clock to build his empire, but despite huge success he never lost touch with his working-class roots. Deutsch had travelled the country almost continuously and made frequent trips to London with a team of secretaries and assistants on the train with him. Telegrams would be typed as soon as the train left the station; and as the express slowed for Coventry, bundles of telegrams, letters and other instructions would be thrown from the train, to be picked up and dealt with by station staff.

It was often said that should a member of his staff find themselves in financial difficulties, he would offer them an interest free loan.

Upon his death, Deutsch's widow sold their remaining and controlling interests in the company to Rank.

1.32 Oscar Deutsch – founder of Odeon Cinemas

However, there was an unforeseen and potential complication. In 1937 when Odeon became a public company, with a capital of some £6 million, and in the wake of some of Korda's recently reported flops, Deutsch guaranteed to his shareholders that Odeon would never become involved in the risky business of film production. Shareholders now feared that Odeon, by virtue of it becoming part of Rank's empire, would find itself involved (albeit indirectly) in film financing, with the property value of its sites alone offering substantial collateral against which Rank could theoretically raise production finance.

War

When war arrived in 1939, Pinewood Studios were requisitioned by the Army. Denham was still open thanks to Pascal and his over-running production of *Major Barbara*.

As well as the Army using Pinewood for storage purposes, the Royal Mint moved onto one of the stages and Lloyd's of London were installed in the main house and admin building. Lloyd's, in fact, moved into the studio the weekend before war was declared. Some 500 staff, mostly women, were involved in the move and every one of them was offered a local billet. Five thousand such billets were secured through house-to-house canvassing in anticipation of the whole city market evacuating; wherever Lloyd's went, it was assumed, the Marine Insurance companies and brokers in other sections of the market would surely follow. On September 4, 1939, Lloyd's opened for 'business as usual' at its new base.

The decor of Pinewood was transformed dramatically. Gone were the off-white colours and in their place was camouflage paint. Several members of the Lloyd's staff had received ARP training in London before war was declared, and these men and women formed the nucleus of a Lloyd's Pinewood Fire Guard which developed into an enviable team covering fire, first-aid and wardens' duties. There were no air-raid shelters at the studio at the time, so the staff were given rather vague instructions to 'disperse into the surrounding woods on warning being sounded.'

In 1941, the Crown Film Unit, Army Film and Photography Unit (AFPU), Royal Air Force (RAF) Film Unit and the Polish Air Force Film Unit made their base at Pinewood and had use of the studio and general production area. A wire fence was erected diagonally across the car park and the road alongside the administration building in order to separate the house and gardens from the main studio area.

Gaumont-British

In 1941 Rank declared that the film industry had got into the hands of the wrong people'. And so, in what was to become his inimitable style within the industry, he set out to buy Gaumont-British Picture Corporation (G-B): the largest producer-renter-exhibitor in Britain and the dominant force in the industry.

He had never really forgiven the Ostrers for their treatment of him with *Turn of the Tide*.

The company had two production arms: Gaumont-British, based at Shepherd's Bush, produced 'quality' pictures; while Gainsborough's studios at Islington were dedicated to 'lower-budget' productions, mainly comedies and melodramas for the home market.

A complicated financial structure saw control of the company invested in a small trust, the Metropolis and Bradford, with the Ostrers owning 51vper-cent of the voting shares and 49vper-cent owned by American company Fox – to whom the British-born Ostrers had sold a significant chunk of the business in order to fund their theatre's conversion to sound in the late 1920s and early 1930s.

John Maxwell, the head of ABC, was also extremely keen to take over G-B. In fact, in 1936 he purchased £600,000 of shares, but mistakenly assumed he was buying 'A class' voting shares. He did not. He had bought non-voting 'B class' shares. Fox meanwhile also realised their holding was not quite what they had expected. They were not allowed representation on the G-B board, as company law stated non-British shareholders could not have voting rights. However, no one could buy the company without their consent – and that was really the sole power they could exercise over it.

Maxwell needed Fox's agreement to buy any voting shares. The Ostrers offered him 5,100 for a sum just under £1 million, and Maxwell duly entered into discussions with Fox, but they ended abruptly. It is unclear as to why. Some say it was due to Maxwell haggling excessively over minor financial matters, whereas others maintain it was due to MGM stepping in. MGM's Nick Schenck was the brother of Fox's Joe Schenck, and it is said he felt that if Maxwell combined his ABC circuit with G-B then he'd have a vast chain that would mean, theoretically, he'd be in a position to dictate terms to Hollywood.

Whatever the reason, Maxwell was denied his chance to assume any control of G-B.

He, unsuccessfully, brought a lawsuit against the Ostrers and had no choice but to then sit back, consoled only in the knowledge that the Ostrers could not sell control to any other party as he had a five year exclusive option on the said voting shares.

Though in ailing health, Maxwell expanded his circuit by buying up the Union Cinema chain – he now owned some 431 theatres compared to 345 belonging to G-B and it was thought he may mount another challenge.

Sadly, he never did. Maxwell's ill health which worsened considerably over the Ostrer affair, took its toll. John Maxwell died in 1940.

Along with him ABPC's interest in taking over G-B died and G-B, perhaps feeling certain Maxwell would come back and increase his offers, found itself floundering. Its overdraft was spiralling out of control with no visible means of further investment. The company owned two studios, 345 cinemas and Baird Television. It was a very tempting purchase for any would-be film mogul.

Ironically, the Ostrer brothers had been quick to mock Rank's foray into film. He was now about to pounce and take them over!

C M Woolf met with Isidore Ostrer, and as their former Managing Director Woolf was now about to offer them a lifeline with the financial backing of Rank. A deal was struck whereby Rank / GFD would finance 50 percent of G-B films and distribute them through General Film Distributors. Gaumont's Islington studio would continue producing a few films each year, whereas the Shepherd's Bush studio would be slowly wound down in favour of moving all production to the re-opened Pinewood by the late 1940s.

The Ostrers never quite lifted themselves out of their financial difficulties until, somewhat surprisingly, The General Film Finance Corporation announced, in October 1941 that it had paid £750,000 to buy a controlling interest in the Bradford and Metropolis Trust. This was thought to be precipitated by Isidore Ostrer wanting to spend more time with his seriously ill wife and relieve himself of the stress of handling G-B's affairs. But whatever the reasons, Rank, as Chairman of the GFFC, owned 25 per-cent of the G-B share. Other 'ordinary' shareholders were furious that he seemed to come in and swoop to buy a controlling share without them being consulted. The industry reported it as Rank 'taking control' of G-B, which was not strictly correct, but 6 months later Isidore Ostrer did decide to sell control of the company to him.

Rank managed to re-negotiate Fox's veto right, by offering to change the company's articles and thus give them representation on the Board.

C M Woolf was appointed joint managing director with Mark Ostrer, but soon after – in 1942 – C M Woolf died and Rank's other chief partners, Lord Portal and Lord Luke, gradually began to withdraw from the business, leaving J Arthur Rank centre stage.

Within nine years, the millionaire miller had advanced from renting simple projectors at church Sunday schools to becoming Britain's most powerful and influential film mogul. His film empire consisted of studios at Pinewood, Denham, Islington, and Shepherds Bush; he had cinemas (totalling 600) and distribution.

Indeed, the government became worried about his and ABC's growing monopoly of studios and cinemas they commissioned the Palache Report in 1944. It found that, although Rank had growing interests, he by no means had a monopoly – less than half the operational British studios were controlled by Rank and he owned only 15 per cent of cinema screens. It was agreed that ABC and Rank should have to ask permission from the Board of Trade before opening further cinemas.

Meanwhile, Rank met again with G-B's Ian Cremieu-Javal, whom he had met many years earlier when searching for film projectors for his Sunday schools.

'Now I'll find out how much those projectors you sold me really cost!' he exclaimed.

Independent Producers

At Denham, Rank had funded a group of independent filmmakers in a film production programme. Independent Producers Ltd comprised Ian Dalrymple and Marcel Hellman, Anthony Havelock-Allan and Ronald Neame, Leslie Howard, Frank Launder and Sidney Gilliatt, Michael Powell and Emeric Pressburger, David Lean and Alfred Watkins. The idea was to bring together distinguished filmmakers of the day, promote co-operation between them and enable them to make the best use of facilities and manpower. Rank also offered them a cut of the profits. They were very much independent, Rank funding their operations with the minimum of interference. Finance, creative freedom, stories, casting and 'final cut' were all part of the deal. All the more amazing: no party in the company was under any form of contract.

'Independent Producers was the brainchild of an agent called Christopher Mann – quite an extraordinary chap,' remembered Cineguild's production manager, Norman Spencer. 'He suggested that the leading filmmaking talent of the day should form a conglomerate where each would take a place on the board and, although they would make their own films, they would assist each other. Tom White was the general production manager, and his assistant was Peggy Hennessey. I remember that each of the production managers from the various companies such as Archers, Cineguild, Wessex etc would meet every Monday in the Pinewood boardroom to discuss matters and how projects were running and so forth. It was a marvellous company with a tremendous, unified spirit.'

Independent Producers Ltd operated from 1944 to 1947. James B Sloan had come over from Pinewood to act as chief production manager and the group's managing director was George Archibald. Their functions were administrative rather than creative and they took seats on the board with J Arthur Rank as chairman. Of the filmmakers, Leslie Howard died soon after the company's formation when a plane he was travelling in was shot down by the Luftwaffe over the Bay of Biscay. Marcel Hellman then left after making two indifferent pictures with the group, *They Met in the Dark* and *Secret Mission*. Alfred Watkins, meanwhile, did little but offer his production services and expertise. Even so, many notable productions came from the Independent Producers stable, not least *Black Narcissus, A Canterbury Tale, A Matter of Life and Death* (which was inspired by a government request to improve Anglo-American relations and became the first Royal Film Performance), *Great Expectations* and *Oliver Twist*.

GHW

Whilst Rank concentrated much of his attention into developing his film combine, he never lost sight of the reason he had entered the film business in the first place.

The Religious Films Society was doing well in the mid 1930s, but its films were never really shown outside of church circles. Rank was keen to make commercial religious films that would play at cinemas.

He discussed this with Norman Walker, the director of *Turn of the Tide*, and suggested he would like to form a new company for this purpose. He also sought to involve former Methodist Times editor, Dr Gregory and his wartime friend and estate manager, Roy Hake, as company directors.

GHW Productions (the initials taken from the names of its three directors) was formed to produce films with a religious message. Rank also stated he would supply new 16mm projectors to churches in order these films could be shown.

The films would boast high production values, and in 1936 Rank threw open the doors of his newly christened Pinewood to his colleagues.

Norman Walker, having worked at much smaller studios, was delighted with the state-of-the-art complex and commenced work on *The Way of Salvation* before moving on to *The First Easter*. Just months prior to the outbreak of the Second World War, Walker completed location filming in Norway for *Beyond Our Horizon*.

In the build up to war, there was a great demand for cinemas – the only source of newsreels for the public – to open. Sunday was of course sacred to Rank. The idea of opening his cinemas on the Sabbath was not one that he felt comfortable with. However, he realised that he had a duty to satisfy public demand and set about thinking how he might use Sunday screenings to help spread the word.

He decided, after discussing matters with the Religious Films Society, to include a three-minute short film at the start of each programme. *A Thought for the Day* was conceived. It would involve Dr Goodfellow leaning over his garden gate and talking to the audience. An ex-silent film star named Stewart Rome was awarded the role, and filming took place at Norwood Studios, and the tiny Gate Studios in Borehamwood, which Rank had now also taken control of. Norman Walker directed most of them and they were scripted by Peter Rogers, who later went on to produce the *Carry On* films.

GHW's first film was *The Man at The Gate* (1940) starring Wilfrid Lawson and Mary Jerrold. It was based on a poem by Louise Haskin, involving a mother who lost two sons at sea and fears for her third and her husband at the front. In listening to the King's Christmas broadcast, she rediscovered her faith. It was said to be Rank's favourite religious film.

Part 2

The Rise of the Empire

~ 1 ~

Post War – Pinewood Open for Business (1946–1950)

J Arthur Rank maintained that his film activities still stemmed from duty and obligation. He wanted to give the Americans a run for their money and was passionate about ensuring his films received good distribution throughout the world. In the summer of 1945, he had visited Hollywood and was given an almost royal reception by the assembled moguls. The mild-mannered Sunday school teacher was an enigma to the American press: he controlled everything and yet appeared so unassuming, quite unlike his American counterparts. One of these – David O Selznick, the producer of *Gone with the Wind* – was so keen to work with Rank he formed a new company in England just to make one (unrealised) film.

Rank was shown around Universal Studios, of which he was a share-holder, and was so impressed with American production efficiency that he later sent over his own technicians, producers, and directors to study Hollywood methods. Pinewood was to benefit greatly from the expertise they brought back with them.

During this time John Davis, an accountant from Oscar Deutsch's reign at Odeon, was fast becoming a powerful figure within the Rank Organisation. He was a hard worker, with an unstinting loyalty to J Arthur Rank, and was considered to be the voice of prudence. Every penny should turn a profit, as far as Davis was concerned.

In 1946, Pinewood re-opened for business.

2.1 J. Arthur Rank on the set of Black Narcissus with Michael Powell

The first film onto the stages was the Launder-Gilliatt production of comedy-thriller *Green for Danger*, starring Alistair Sim, Trevor Howard, Rosamund John and Sally Gray. A couple of the Independent Producers' films also made use of Pinewood, most notably David Lean's *Great Expectations* and Powell and Pressburger's *Black Narcissus* – the second film to shoot in Technicolor at the studio and winner of Academy Awards in 1948 for art direction and cinematography. The production recreated the Himalayas in the back lot and gardens, as production manager Norman Spencer recalled.

'My office was on the first floor of the old house overlooking the gardens and one could really have been forgiven for thinking we were in the Himalayas, especially with the light at certain times of day. Hundreds of rhododendrons were brought in, as they are found in that area of the world in abundance, and the gardens looked fantastic; albeit with nuns everywhere!'

Anthony Havelock-Allan returned to produce Ronald Neame's *Take My Life*, a thriller in the Hitchcock mould with excellent performances from Hugh Williams, Greta Gynt and Marius Goring. 'The post-war atmosphere was much more professional,' he claimed. 'There had been a "gifted amateur" feel to the place with the grand house and gardens before, which, although never inhibiting the making of films, was perhaps a little too pleasant on the whole. You got away from the fact that what you were doing was making an industrial product and probably the riskiest one there is. You're putting a great deal of money into a piece of celluloid and nobody knows what might happen. But that industrial feel was present on our return, perhaps through the influence on Rank of John Davis.'

2.2 Michael Powell was one half of The Archers, with Emeric Pressburger (left)

The first post-war year for Pinewood was a good one. But better was to come in 1947, for one of the greatest stories ever told was created on C Stage: *The Red Shoes*.

Powell and Pressburger, who had initially met at Denham, chose the story having completed *The End of the River*, which had been a strange departure for the filmmakers and a critical and commercial disaster. *The Red Shoes* was a very simple tale of a great ballet dancer and how she is torn between love (with Marius Goring) and her career (with Anton Walbrook) and then driven to suicide when she has to choose between them. Nothing like it had been seen before; the subtle use of colours, the special effects and the wonderful characters and performances all combined to form a beautifully textured film. The Red Shoes received three Academy Award nominations for Best Picture, Best Story and Music; Brian Easdale won in the latter category. Powell and Pressburger were back on form. And of the many new techniques and effects employed in the film, the 'gunshot' travelling matte must rate as the best: Moira Shearer danced with a newspaper.

2.3 The Red Shoes on Pinewood's C-Stage

Editor Noreen Ackland collaborated on all of the Powell and Pressburger films at Pinewood and remembered *The Red Shoes* with particular affection. 'Micky and Emeric were wonderful. Exciting. Everything was new and they made you a part of the whole company making it. I was only second assistant in those days but was made to feel just as important as the stars. Pinewood was a fantastic place to work – a truly magical film made at a truly magical studio. It will always be my favourite film and holds so many precious memories for me, and whenever anyone mentions Pinewood to me, *The Red Shoes* always springs to mind.'

Following the highly successful and critically acclaimed *Great Expectations*, Cineguild decided to film another Dickens classic, *Oliver Twist*. David Lean again took the director's chair.

'*Oliver Twist* was shot in its entirety at Pinewood,' remembered the film's production manager Norman Spencer. 'The fantastic, silent opening scene was all done on a stage and it was planned with military precision as each shot had to convey the mood of that scene – the girl's pain with the thorns,

2.4 David Lean's Oliver Twist shooting on D-Stage

the cold night with the clouds and so on. John Bryan designed the set. David [Lean] said that he wished he could start every film with a silent sequence as he felt it was a real tension-builder. He used the analogy of a man sitting in the cinema just about to light a cigarette, but he can't because he's so grabbed with what's happening on the screen. The baby we used in the workhouse scene was in fact the daughter of a local doctor. I had to find

2.5 ... and on the Pinewood backlot

a new-born baby, and the only thing I could think of was to phone a local doctor and enquire if any patients were soon to "produce". A lady doctor in Gerrards Cross, Dr Shipman, said that my luck was in as in two weeks she was due to give birth! The day after the child was born, we took the unit to her house and filmed the scene you see in the film. Incidentally, the baby was named Olivia, after the film's title.'

2.6 *Warning to Wantons was one of the first features made at Pinewood using 'Independent Frame'*

Independent Frame

Independent Frame (IF) was a technical project that Rank invested in heavily. Plans were hatched for the project as far back as 1944. David Rawnsley was the leading force behind IF, which was expected to revolutionise

2.7/2.8 David Hand's animation division included adventures with Ginger Nutt

filmmaking by shortening film schedules and saving money on set construction and location shooting. The idea appealed to Rank, especially in light of the ever-increasing excesses of some producers, because it offered an inexpensive production process and, moreover, a welcome means of supplying his distribution and cinema companies.

Rawnsley's idea stemmed from working on *49th Parallel* where he had shot a multitude of background plates (the location shots that would be projected onto screens in the studio, in front of or behind artistes, to give the impression of the artistes actually 'being there'). He thought that by taking the process a little further, it would be possible to combine projection, matte effects, and split screens into one great project: Independent Frame.

Painted backdrops would be wheeled in and out of the stages on Vickers rostra, and with the use of specially modified cameras all would combine to quicken the filmmaking process. Gone would be the lengthy construction times and changing of sets and stages and in would come a factory 'conveyor belt' system, as Charles Staffell, one of Pinewood's top special effects men, described it.

The sets were wheeled in, the artistes followed, rehearsed, and then shot the scene. Then they'd move to another stage while the sets on the first were being wheeled out and replaced, to shoot further scenes and so the process continued. There would, of course, be a massive library of backgrounds for use in multiple productions.

Bernard Hanson, who was assistant stage controller on the IF films, explained the technicalities of shooting. 'The whole stage was divided up into squares and each had a number. I then had to mark up the squares, once I received details from the art director on where the cameras had to be placed – otherwise the shot wouldn't fill the screen properly. I was just a youngster in those days and had to tell very distinguished cameramen where they would have to place their cameras!'

Alan Hume, who later went on to photograph many of the *Carry On* and James Bond films, was then a camera operator. 'Yes, the floor was marked up in yard-squares which were all numbered. We used to go on the floor and say, "We're shooting scene 28." The reply would come back "That's square 34 shooting towards square 19 and you'll be on the screen in such and such a position."'

The first IF film made at Pinewood was the comedy-drama *Warning to Wantons* (1949). Movement was severely restricted on the sets and the projection techniques were never totally satisfactory. It was a frustrating process synching the projector shutter frequency with that of the camera filming the action, and actors often had a give-away 'glow' around them in these scenes. The process was later modified and perfected by Charles Staffell, who won an Academy Award for his work in the projection process; the first and only Oscar awarded for technical work of this kind.

'Independent Frame was an ill-thought out project,' believed Norman Spencer, 'but Rawnsley was egged on by the likes of John Davis who wanted to save money on productions. Davis was never interested in films but paid them lip service and always tried to cut expenditure. The only useful thing to come out of it were the rostra!' Director Guy Hamilton agreed. 'The only useful remains of that ridiculous experiment were those excellent Vickers rostra – they're still in use today!'

Bernard Hanson added: 'I do remember that a hexagonal rostrum was made too – it had a revolving centre. The idea being that the hex would sit in the middle of the stage and other rostra could square onto the edges. I don't recall that one ever being used though.'

'The rostra are marvellous, but you must also remember that some bloody good projection equipment was developed as well,' says Alan Hume, 'which became invaluable in many of my later pictures. Independent Frame wasn't the success they thought it would be, but a few good things did come out of it.'

Warning to Wantons cost £100,000 and took 35 days to make – almost double what was anticipated on both counts. Naturally, these excesses were put down to teething troubles. But Rank had spent over £600,000 developing the technology – principally at Pinewood – and the resulting films were often poor quality box-office disasters. The great white hope in film production was soon dead in the water.

Animation

Around this time, the first creations from the Gaumont-British animation division came to life. In 1944, Rank head-hunted David Hand, a highly regarded American animator who had recently served as supervising director on Walt Disney's *Snow White and the Seven Dwarfs* and *Bambi*, among others. His brief was to mould the division, based at Moor Hall in Cookham, into one that could rival the Americans and produce cartoons for British audiences, incorporating British humour.

2.7/2.8 David Hand's animation division included adventures with Ginger Nutt

This was to be a particularly difficult task. At one point thoughts of turning newspaper cartoon strips into animated films were considered but quickly dismissed. Competition was fierce: *Popeye, Tom & Jerry* and the like were massively popular.

2.9 Chester Cat

Under Hands' leadership, a crew of some 200 personnel were assembled, and production began on two series of short, animated films: nine Animaland cartoons and ten more Musical Paintbox shorts. Hand divided his team to work on two concurrent film series, one headed by Burt Felstead (Animaland), and the other marshalled by Henry Stringer (Musical Paintbox).

Of the two, the Animaland cartoons are best known and featured a host of colourful critters at play – four starred a squirrel called Ginger Nutt and his pals Loopy the Hare, Corny the Crow and Dusty Mole, as well as Ginger's sweetheart Hazel. The studio was positioning young Ginger for animated stardom, and several licensing deals were struck in his name.

The other five cartoons in the series adopted a 'mockumentary' approach, observing animal antics from a distance with the aid of a narrator. But these sat rather awkwardly next to the Ginger Nutt films – Ginger's antics all took place in a woodland with talking characters, whereas most of the fauna in this second selection were non-speaking. Both sets of critters were united in one celebratory film Ginger Nutt's Christmas Circus.

Although technically faultless, lushly painted with fun characters the underdeveloped storylines and characterization made them seem like a pale imitation of the American shorts, rather than something distinctly British.

Their voices were awkward too. Ginger Nutt had a particularly weedy intonation.

The Musical Paintbox films meanwhile took audiences on a witty musical tour of Britain, introducing them to some eccentric characters, local folk tales, odd superstitions and customs. Beginning with a look at life on the River Thames. The ten films visited Wales, Yorkshire, Scotland, Somerset, Ireland, Cornwall, Canterbury and Devon, before concluding with a look at life in London.

Featuring a mixture of artwork, and limited animation, accompanying the narration and music, these were more adventurous tales, with abstract design, great backgrounds, and more playful characters.

The result of Hand's efforts were described as being stilted and unoriginal hodgepodge with very little of the madcap fun the American cartoons could offer. The animated films cost around £10,000 each and lasted no more than 10 minutes. In 1950 the division was closed down with losses of around half a million pounds.

This Modern Age

Another ill-fated project was *This Modern Age*, on which some of Hand's animators were kept busy. This was Rank's attempt to better the American newsreel magazine *The March of Time*. Production started in 1946 with *Homes For All*, a documentary about homelessness and poor housing. The series tackled some 41 topical subjects in its four-year lifespan and Rank gave the editorial team complete freedom, as he had done with his

Independent Producers, even though some topics and viewpoints were not to his taste. Initially popular, the series visited many countries and prided itself on its location shooting. One 21-minute film was produced per month and each featured music by Muir Mathieson. Every episode ended with the legend, 'The challenge must be met in This Modern Age.'

Bob Verrell, who edited many entries in the series, said, 'They were excellent little films with relevant subjects and, in my opinion, every bit as good as – if not better than – *The March of Time*. Their eventual downfall came because they were not supported by the distribution and exhibition circuits, as they ought to have been and as Rank hoped they would be. I know for a fact that J Arthur Rank was particularly saddened at the demise of the series, more so than anything else he had worked on setting up, because he was tremendously proud of the films and felt they said a lot about Britain.'

This Modern Age was eventually relegated to supporting programme time-filler status and, along with the cartoon initiative, was reluctantly discontinued.

Charming

Another idea of Rank's was the formation of the 'Company of Youth', which became known as the Rank Charm School. Rank had a strong contract artist division, and the Charm School was basically a finishing school for many of them: they would learn poise, screen techniques and all-round airs and graces. An academy was founded in a large house in Highbury, North London. Enrolment wasn't necessarily dependent upon acting ability, but rather looks, figure and potential. The most successful Charm School graduates included Joan Collins, Diana Dors, Jill Ireland, Christopher Lee, Roger Moore, and Anthony Steel.

'When I left the Army, I had no interest in acting at all,' observed Anthony Steel, 'although I did enjoy going to the theatre and films. But it was when I met up with two friends of mine, Guy Middleton, and Taffy [Hugh] Williams, in Berlin that the seeds were sown. We were having a drink and they mentioned that Olive Dodds and the Rank Organisation were wanting to create some stars for the future. Unbeknown to me, they

2.10 Corny Crow

had already spoken with Olive Dodds and said that I was someone she should meet.

'I eventually met with Olive and she asked if I'd ever thought about being an actor, and – in all honesty – I said "No"! She said that she'd let me know and that was that. However, a month or so later I received a letter saying that they'd like to offer me a two year contract. The money they offered was considerably better than what my old Army chums were making, and although they all said I was mad, it seemed like a good opportunity.

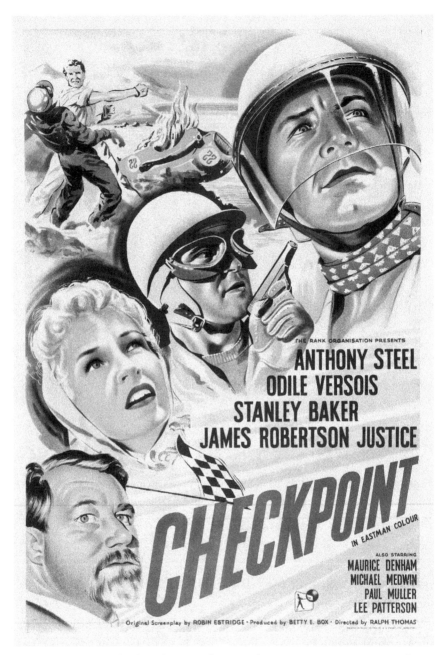

2.11 Rank Charm School graduate Anthony Steel went on to star in many Rank productions including Checkpoint with Stanley Baker

'I then went into the Charm School. It was quite an eclectic crowd – all ages from 17 onwards – and I went to Highbury Studios. Molly Terraine, who was in charge with Olive, had been a very successful actress and took me under her wing. After six weeks I said that it didn't really interest me. What I wanted was some practical experience. After a couple of little bit parts which gave me that experience, I landed The Wooden Horse – as they were looking for an unknown to co-star – and it was a great success. I then re-negotiated a new contract with Rank and stayed with them for quite some time.'

Charm School artistes were paid £20 a week whether they worked or not. The contracts were renewable annually (on the company's side) and when the artistes were hired out, or 'sub-let', to other producers Rank had it written into the contract that his organisation was entitled to 50 per cent of any profits. With most of Rank's top stars being in high demand for public appearances, charity functions and the like, quite often one of the Charm School artistes would be sent in their place. It didn't seem to matter that they were not of equal status to, say, Dirk Bogarde or Jean Simmons: they were stars simply because of their association with J Arthur Rank and were besieged accordingly.

Publicist Euan Lloyd explained how he also used Rank's stars to help achieve better relations with other sectors of the industry. 'My job was to bring a closer understanding between Wardour Street and Pinewood's producers as Mr Rank could sense a gulf which was becoming harmful. Salesmen and movie-makers rarely see eye to eye. John Davis approved my plan to invite salesmen and certain key exhibitors to the studio to see how the supply lines worked. An extension of that plan culminated in my escorting Mr Rank to GFD's countrywide branches. Actors became involved too, led mainly by Trevor Howard, Jack Hawkins, Stewart Granger, as well as new faces like Donald Houston. Personal appearances by the stars became a regular event, often lifting the box-office results. Glamour prevailed.'

Although the Charm School was kept busy, its graduates were not; there was no obligation for any of Rank's producers to engage them, which rather defeated the object of setting up the academy. Those who were engaged were often only used in small parts or walk-ons and many left the business as a result.

Highbury

After the abolition of 'quota quickies' the 'B' picture industry had suffered in Britain. In 1947 Rank decided to revive the curtain raisers as he believed, in tune with the Palache report of 1944, that Britain needed a flow of inexpensive films to act as a training ground for up-and-coming filmmakers. He purchased the two-stage Highbury Studios for this very purpose and every five weeks, at a cost of £20,000, a movie was made by talented newcomers, with seasoned heads of department overseeing production and providing the experience and know-how. Former Ealing Studios filmmaker John Croydon was brought in to run Highbury, where he was extremely innovative and turned its many constraints to his advantage. Preparation was everything with Croydon. He emphasised that time spent on planning and preparing sequences was invaluable once you moved on to the stage.

Highbury produced some admirable films, many transcending the material on which they were based, and provided a valuable training ground for actors, directors, and technicians alike.

Some of the films produced in 1947/48 included:

A Song for Tomorrow, directed by Terence Fisher;
Trouble in the Air, starring comics Freddie Frinton & Jimmy Edwards, plus Jon Pertwee and Bill Owen;
Penny and the Pownall Case starring Diana Dors & Christopher Lee;
Colonel Bogey, directed by Terence Fisher;
To the Public Danger, directed by Terence Fisher, starring Dermot Walsh & Susan Shaw;
Love in Waiting starring David Tomlinson; and,
A Piece of Cake, starring Cyril Fletcher & Jon Pertwee.

However, like the cartoon and documentary divisions, the B pictures did not make money for The Rank Organisation – second features earned only a small fraction of the box office – and the division was wound up, less than two years after it was formed.

Children's Films

Prior to 1944 the programme at children's Saturday matinees was composed entirely of films made for general distribution. At first Rank specifically imported films from America – comedies, adventures and westerns – but mindful of content and possible negative effects on children, the films were vetted and sometimes re-edited.

This led J Arthur Rank wanting to produce his own wholesome children's entertainment films, and his first attempt was a highly successful short film called *Tom's Ride* made by Gaumont British Instructional Films in 1944.

The success of *Tom's Ride* gave Rank the confidence to set up a unique division which would produce films especially for children. Thus, in 1944, the Children's Entertainment Film (CEF) division of the Rank Organisation was born.

Rank appointed an extraordinary woman, Mary Field, as director of this new division. Field, a former teacher, had made her name as producer of a ground-breaking series called *Secrets of Nature* and during the war had made official documentary films for the Ministry of Information before being recruited by Rank. She was an ideal director and in effect acted as a deputy for Rank as she shared his desire to mould and educate children's tastes by ensuring that CEF films would not only be entertaining but would also set a high moral tone and encourage good behaviour.

Field controlled a team of ten and used approximately 20 production companies all working on a freelance basis. Their productions were vetted by Field and the Youth Advisory Council which often left the film makers somewhat resentful as artistic and editorial control was removed from their grasp. Field and the Youth Advisory Council, which included representatives from the BBC, the Church, the Home Office and the Ministry of Education, were bent on providing children not with what they wanted but with what was believed to be good for them.

The film programme was only one part of the morning activities as also on offer for 'the betterment of youngsters' were singing lessons, general instructional classes in safety, hygiene, good citizenship etc. There was even a weekly song:

We come along on Saturday morning
Greeting everybody with a smile.
We come along on Saturday morning
Knowing it is well worth while.
As members of the GB club
We all intend to be
Good citizens when we grow up
and champions of the free.
We come along on Saturday morning
Greeting everybody with a smile, smile, smile.
Greeting everybody with a smile.

Every Children's Cinema Club member received a birthday card and free admittance voucher for the following week. Although moral messages were contained in the clubs' activities and films, Rank was careful not to preach: first and foremost, he wanted to entertain. Although the division lost money, Rank believed the social benefits outweighed financial gain. Under Mary Field, the division produced some good quality and entertaining children's films but, like many of Rank's initiatives of the 1940s, it ultimately failed to survive. The films stayed in circulation but took some 15 years to show any profits. Ironically, within a year of its closure, the government set up the Children's Film Foundation and appointed J Arthur Rank as chairman, with Mary Field as executive officer.

Crisis

In 1947, Britain was plunged into financial crisis as a consequence of an international 'dollar drain' and the government announced drastic measures to reduce imports and increase exports. Hollywood films were a major 'import' and substantial profits were flowing from British cinemas right back to the American producers. The ad valorem tax was rushed through Parliament, imposing a duty of 75 per cent on earnings of American films in Britain. Needless to say, the film industries on both sides of the Atlantic were furious. Rubbing salt into the wound, the Chancellor of the Exchequer stated that the tax would not be on actual earnings but predicted earnings, meaning that it would have to be paid in advance.

Hollywood reacted swiftly. The very next day an embargo was introduced preventing any new American films entering Britain. Rank was in America at the time, courting potential distribution partners, and American producers looked to him, the voice of reason, as the man who could turn around this ridiculous taxation scheme. He was unable to, and almost overnight his work in setting up distribution deals in America was brought into question. Added to that, his cinema circuits were starved of highly profitable and much-needed American product.

The government assumed that without American dominance of the British circuits, British filmmakers would be in a much stronger position; they would have to satisfy the demand by increasing production and would have nothing to fear from Hollywood. But did the post-war British film industry have the capacity to achieve this?

Pinewood was put into overdrive: six-day weeks and night-shifts were the norm as the production boom got into gear. It would be fair to say that although the 'quota quickie' legislation had been abolished almost ten years earlier, Rank was entering into that arena again with his new programme. Like the 'quota' films, it was destined primarily to feed the circuits and fill the gaps left by the American films.

In November, Rank announced plans for 47 feature films to be produced at Pinewood with investment of almost £10 million. But Rank's coffers were not as rich as he would have liked, and the investment programme could only be met by capitalising upon his other companies within the Organisation. J Arthur Rank announced plans that were effectively to involve Odeon shareholders in his production programme, which went totally against what Oscar Deutsch had stated when floating the company in 1937: 'This company will not engage in film production, either by itself or [through] any subsidiary company.'

Rank suffered at the hands of the financial press. They were particularly critical of his plans to absorb his General Cinema Finance Corporation into Odeon Cinemas, while merging that chain with Gaumont. And because Rank's programme could not be fully operational for several months – the projects needed to be developed before moving into production, and post-production to exhibition could take a further six months – the ill-thought-out scheme proved an unmitigated disaster.

By March 1948, Harold Wilson – in his capacity as President of the Board of Trade – reached a new agreement with the Motion Picture Association of America. When the Hollywood embargo was lifted – just as the first of Rank's films was released – there was a massive influx of previously unreleased American pictures. Filmgoers opted for the lavish Hollywood productions in preference to Rank's offerings and the Rank Organisation plummeted towards financial disaster. The company's overdraft at the end of the 1947/48 financial year was over £16 million. Rank's hopes and plans for a thriving British film industry, on which he had worked so tirelessly, were in tatters. He was slipping more and more into the red with ever-mounting debts. It would seem that his Midas touch was wearing off. Had it not been for the good will of the National Provincial, film production would have been abandoned altogether.

Eleven films were produced at Pinewood in 1948, including two Independent Frame films: the aforementioned *Warning to Wantons* and *Floodtide*, directed by Frederick Wilson and starring Gordon Jackson, Rona Anderson, John Laurie and Elizabeth Sellars in a drama about a young Clydeside ship designer. Other productions included *The Passionate Friends* and *The Blue Lagoon* from Cineguild and Individual, respectively.

The Passionate Friends actually led to the demise of Cineguild. Ronald Neame was to have originally directed Eric Ambler's adaptation of the H G Wells novel. David Lean didn't feel that Neame had what it took to be a good director, despite his having directed *Take My Life*, and ordered the script rewritten. Start dates were set, however, and Neame commenced filming with half the new script in place, only to be supplanted by Lean a few days later. The whole débâcle spelt an unfortunate end to one of Britain's most successful and talented production companies. Other members of the Independent Producers team were also showing signs of frustration and division. Powell and Pressburger were lured away to join Korda's revitalised enterprise, this time at Shepperton Studios; Launder and Gilliat felt that they were losing their independence as the free reins they had so enjoyed were being drawn in; and Ian Dalrymple's Wessex Films made their last film at Pinewood with *Dear Mr Prohack*. David Lean made one more film at Pinewood in 1949 – the disastrous *Madeleine* – before he too

2.12 The Passionate Friends was David Lean's 1949 romantic drama

left to join Korda. Anthony Havelock-Allan set up his own company, Constellation Films – it, too, ultimately controlled by Korda.

It was ironic that as Rank rose to great heights while Korda floundered during the war, the scales had now tipped the other way. Rank was struggling to keep his company afloat and his most prized and successful filmmakers were leaving to join Korda, who had sought and secured government funding.

⤝ 2 ⤞

THE JOHN DAVIS ERA –
PART 1 – (1950-1956)

In 1949, there were only seven British studios open and even they employed 2,000 fewer people than in the previous year. Rank lost more than £3 million in production expenditure, not recouped at the box-office. Just as the early 1940s had seen Rank's empire rise to astronomical heights,

2.13 John Davis at his desk in South Street, Mayfair

the end of the decade witnessed it plunging to new depths. Highbury Studios and the Charm School were closed, the children's film division was wound-up, and the Organisation was on the verge of collapse.

However, there was a man – or hatchet man – of the hour. John Davis, the young accountant who had joined Odeon in the 1930s, had worked his way up to the position of managing director of the Rank Organisation and, more importantly, had the total trust of J Arthur Rank.

2.14 Pinewood's Earl St. John (left) talking here to contract director Roy Baker. St. John was initially John Davis' assistant before being promoted to oversee all production at Pinewood

Earl St John

Now charged with turning the Organisation around, Davis stepped in with ruthless efficiency. The closure of Gainsborough's Islington and Lime Grove Studios (the latter sold to the BBC before being demolished in the early 1990s for a housing development) soon followed; Independent Producers was formally disbanded and George Archibald left; Denham Studios was wound down and all of the Organisation's production interests were transferred to Pinewood under the control of Earl St John. 200 jobs were sacrificed in the process.

Earl St John was born in Louisiana, USA, in 1892. His first taste of the film industry came when he peddled films across Mexico for his uncle. After the Great War, he came to Britain working as an independent exhibitor in Manchester before Paramount appointed him 'head of exploitation' in London. St John began to expand their cinema circuit and when Odeon bought out Paramount cinemas, the company took over St John's contract. Just prior to World War II, he became personal assistant to John Davis. 'JD', as Davis was known, subsequently installed him as executive producer at Pinewood where he would eventually oversee some 131 films.

'My lingering memory of Earl St John,' said director Ken Annakin, 'was that he was a slow reader, and often if you needed a verdict on some scene or synopsis, you'd find he'd retire into the toilet to concentrate on the matter – a joke amongst us, but it seemed to work!' J Lee Thompson's verdict was that 'Earl was always full of fun and confidence and he always gave you the feeling that whatever you were making would be a huge success. He was truly delightful and became a very dear friend.'

Davis's 'cut and cut' mentality towards films made him a figure of hatred among production personnel, even, to some degree, Earl St John himself. 'JD was rude, arrogant and harsh,' confirmed director Lewis Gilbert. 'That's a fact. His poor secretaries were often in tears as he treated them terribly at times. Most senior figures lived in fear of the man, even Earl St John. I remember going into a meeting with JD and Earl one morning and JD barked at Earl to get me a chair. I was relatively young at the time and Earl must have been in his sixties, so it was very embarrassing to see him dive off into a corner and rush a chair to me.

'But I always found that JD was the complete gentleman to non-contract filmmakers, such as me – I was never under contract – and when he agreed a deal it was a deal. It wouldn't change and there needn't be anything in writing: a deal was a deal. I started *Carve Her Name With Pride* without anything in writing, because I knew I had JD's handshake. He didn't know much about films and never pretended otherwise, but he knew what could work in terms of a deal and a story for his circuit. Never did he criticise a director or producer if the finished film didn't perform well at the box-office. He took responsibility for the good as well as the not so good, and that I admired in him.'

Ken Annakin agreed that Davis did have some redeeming features. 'I had many meetings with JD at Pinewood. He was the first of the hard-faced businessmen who have since come to run this industry and, basically, he wasn't a bad guy. He did try to understand the quality of film stories and encouraged those who made a good – and profitable – movie. If you managed to get into his good books, you were invited up to his suite

for lunches to impress jour-
nalists and top trade people.
If you got into his bad books,
then you just tried to cling
on – usually through Earl
St John. He may have made
mistakes, but there have been
many people in charge of studios, past and present, who
have no interest in stories or
the content of movies. I don't
think he did well with the
acting talent though, as British stars seemed to get out
of their contracts as quickly
as possible! He was lucky
to have Dinah Sheridan as
his wife for many years; she

2.15 Director Ralph Thomas

certainly tried to fill the creative gaps in his make-up. He did many silly
things but gave us all good breaks and the chance to make a really good
movie now and then.'

'I always got on famously well with John Davis,' recalled Rank contract
director Ralph Thomas. 'He could organise a picture within ten minutes if
he liked the idea, it was a good script and had a sensible budget – and it
would be done on a handshake. If he didn't like the idea or package, then
you'd never sway him! At least he was honest and up-front with you in that
respect and wouldn't mess you around. He always came into the studio
for one day a week and would see anyone with a problem or who wanted
something done – he'd always happily meet with you.'

In the space of a year, the company overdraft was reduced by almost
£4 million, thanks to Davis's measures coupled with the extreme patience
of Rank's bankers. Davis slashed all budgets and imposed a maximum ceiling of £150,000 per film. He amalgamated Pinewood Films, Two Cities
Films and Gainsborough under the banner of J Arthur Rank Productions
Ltd at Pinewood, and was keen only to produce commercial films, avoid-
ing the experimental initiatives that had cost Rank so dearly in the past.

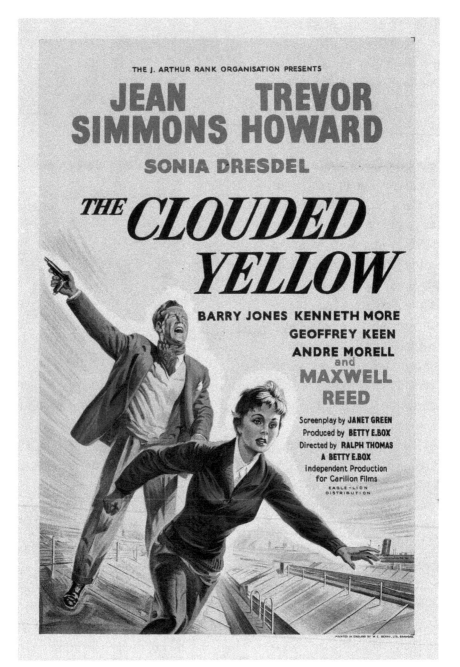

2.16 *The Clouded Yellow, for which Betty Box mortgaged her house to keep the production afloat*

All Rank employees who survived the axe faced a 10 per-cent pay cut, but even then, were not guaranteed job security. 'You'd know whether or not you were long for the company at the annual Christmas dinner,' said Sir Donald Sinden. 'Long tables radiated from where JD sat, and one's seating at the tables suggested one's position in the "Rankery" for the following year. If within touching distance of JD, then your star shone brightly, but if you were at the far end, you didn't have long to go!'

Dinah Sheridan, who was married to Davis for 15 years, had few fond memories. 'I'll give you the fact that he did honour the deals he shook on, but that's all I'll give you. I divorced him for cruelty [in the end] and it took 15 minutes.'

Through all this upheaval, Pinewood remained busy. Captain Richard Norton, now Lord Grantley, returned to the studio as Chairman of Javelin Films – Anthony Asquith's company – to make *The Woman in Question*, following it with a celebrated adaptation of Terence Rattigan's play *The Browning Version*. Elspeth March visited the studios with her husband Stewart Granger around this time and remembers seeing some graffiti in one of the corridors. 'Someone had written "Richard Norton is a ..." – well, it was rather a rude word! He'd obviously seen it as he'd scrubbed across "Richard Norton" and written "Lord Grantley", leaving the expletive intact. It really was terribly funny!'

Ken Annakin and Harold French brought three of Somerset Maugham's stories to the screen in a compendium film called *Trio*. Whilst *The Clouded Yellow* came from the Sydney and Betty Box stable: a Hitchcock-style thriller, it incorporated a chase across the Lake District. Ralph Thomas directed, and thus started a collaboration with Betty Box that would span a further 20 years. 'Betty mortgaged her house to keep *The Clouded Yellow* afloat,' he explained. 'You see, we had a contract with a company who were supposed to be financing films on behalf of the government and they withdrew after we'd started shooting. I was on a very complicated location in the Lake District when they pulled out and I needed money to keep going. It was three or four thousand pounds, which nowadays is nothing, but back then it was a lot of money and it was very brave of Betty and Peter [Rogers] to put their home on the line. She didn't tell me until the picture had finished, but then she made it all back plus some more. I'm rather proud of that film – Jean Simmons was lovely in it, and so was Trevor Howard. Sonia

Dresdel was very good value for money too. They don't make them like her anymore. It's my favourite picture.'

Television

In what was generally considered a positive move, the government introduced the British Film Production Fund in 1950, which became known as the 'Eady Levy' after its architect, Sir Wilfred Eady. The fund, derived from a percentage of ticket sales, would make available £3 million a year for the film industry, half of which would go directly to producers making films in Britain. Ironically, it was to be the more successful producers who stood to benefit most from the scheme.

Although the Eady Fund was welcomed with open arms, a new crisis was on the way. In December 1949, the first provincial TV station began transmission in the Midlands and viewers were set to increase in millions over the next few years as TV spread across the whole of the country. There was, of course, an instant distrust of the new medium from filmmakers who feared not only shrinking cinema attendances, but also that – if their films were sold to TV – they would lose much of their quality when broadcast. This was a view shared by John Davis, who felt that a massive depreciation of the Rank Organisation's films would ensue should TV start broadcasting them.

The BBC had been short of programming in the late 1940s and was struggling to maximise its capacity. Rank was aware of the impending competition and moved to see if a mutually beneficial compromise might be reached. His plans were for 'Cinema-Television', whereby live broadcasts were made to his cinemas offering more up-to-the-minute programming and news than film could provide. He saw this as the perfect compliment to cinema and as a public service. In exchange certain films from the library would be made available to the BBC.

Cyril Hayden was employed to bring together all of the Rank film negatives at Pinewood. 'They had the idea that all the films would be wanted for television, and there was a man called Alf Wilson who was employed just to examine all the negs, catalogue them, wrap them up in tissue paper and re-label them. A fantastic amount of work went into gathering negatives from all around the country – I remember some had even been stored in a barn somewhere.'

Both the government and the BBC were wary of the idea. They worried that if the scheme went ahead, Rank would eventually become more interested in broadcasting his own programmes instead of buying in from the Corporation. So Rank was continually refused a broadcast licence. Ironically, however, Rank had bought Bush Radio in 1949 which began producing and selling TV sets in addition to radios and proved to be one of his most successful interests.

Eventually, Rank was granted a short-period licence on the condition that he sold some of his films to the BBC. For several years' broadcasts were relayed from Pinewood to the Crystal Palace transmitter and in turn to five of Rank's West End cinemas. Sadly, there were never large enough audiences to test the broadcasts on and Rank's attempts to compete with domestic television proved, in the long run, fruitless. It did, however, make Rank and Davis realise that TV was now a force to be reckoned with, rather than one they could work with. As a result, none of Rank's contract artistes were allowed to work on television, though Rank himself later invested in Southern Television, one of the first independent companies in the ITV network.

Rank's output in the 1950s was, rather unfairly, considered lacklustre and boring. While it is true that a great many films of the period were characterised by blandness, John Davis reported that Rank's pictures were performing better at the foreign box-office than ever. Dwindling domestic attendances made cinema closures unavoidable, however, but in those cinemas that survived – and many underwent modernisation programmes – a new market was booming: ancillary sales such as ice cream and sweets were, in some cases, making more profit than the films. In fact, it was reported that the Rank Organisation made a profit of £1 million on sales of ice cream in 1951.

Ten films were produced at Pinewood that year. The most notable of these was Anthony Asquith's delightful production of Oscar Wilde's *The Importance of Being Earnest*, with the definitive portrayal of Lady Bracknell by Dame Edith Evans. Among the other films were Terence Young's *Valley of Eagles* and the David Niven vehicle *Appointment With Venus*, produced by Betty Box and directed by Ralph Thomas.

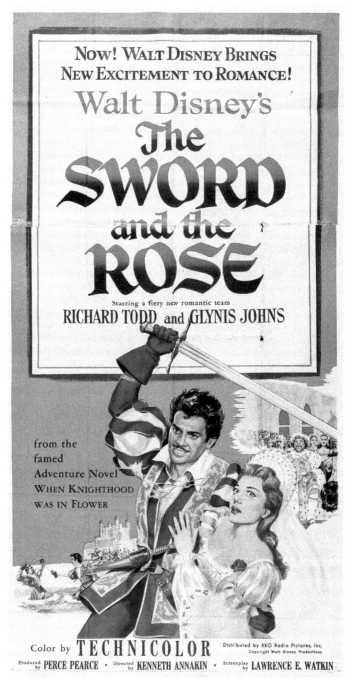

2.17 The Sword and the Rose was Disney's first film at Pinewood and ushered in the 'renters'

Rent

1952 proved to be a significant year, with the studio's first major 'renter' (a non-Rank associated company) arriving in the shape of Walt Disney. Under the guidance of associate producer Hugh Attwooll, Disney decided to capitalise upon the success of a couple of British films he'd produced by setting up a production programme at Pinewood. There was something special about Disney and his films that was summed up very succinctly by the late and much-missed Attwooll at the time of the studio's 50th birthday in 1986. 'Nothing went out of the studio that didn't have Walt's own personal stamp. I don't think he ever forgot what was contained in the script – he knew it mentally and visually. When he died, the films became the product of many people. They lost their magic touch.'

Ken Annakin concurred. 'Walt not only had his stamp on every picture, he was always an active creator. He had to okay all your storyboards and if you deviated, he wanted to know why! A Walt Disney movie was always Walt's concept and you did your best to flesh it out and interpret it. That doesn't mean to say you were a slave director unless you chose to be, but you were making his movie and glad to have all the facilities he provided. Walt was a genius and I loved working for him.'

Disney's first Pinewood production was *The Sword and the Rose*, with Annakin directing Richard Todd, Glynis Johns, James Robertson Justice and Michael Gough in the story of young Mary Tudor. 'Disney had made *Robin Hood* in and around Denham Studios,' Annakin pointed out, 'but they closed after that production. *The Sword and the Rose* therefore came to Pinewood where facilities were pretty much comparable – one or two stages in Denham were bigger, but we had the same art director in Carmen Dillon, so the look of the pictures was the same except, perhaps, a little more lavish and with wonderful matte paintings by Peter Ellenshaw.

'Unfortunately, at the time of the shoot, we were in the middle of a National Electricians' Union strike. A go-slow strike. The shop stewards had decided to pull the breakers on us twice a day, and as I would walk across a set, one of the stewards would invariably bump into me and sneer "You don't know when we're gonna shut you down, do you mate?" We survived, but it was very annoying and worrying since they could turn everything to black, and the cast might have been in very dangerous positions – very unnerving. We were worried that it might have scared Disney away from the UK.

'There was one nasty incident I remember on the film. I had just lined up a shot and was about to sit in my chair when something knocked me out. It was an electrician's spanner which came hurtling from the catwalk above and struck me a glancing blow on the right side of my head. My assistant, Clive Reed, grabbed me and told me that I was out cold for a couple of minutes. I came round, bewildered, and wanted to carry on, but was bundled into a car and driven to Uxbridge Hospital. After various checks, and some doping, they let me return to Pinewood. I had minor concussion for three weeks, but we carried on and got a fine movie. Whether the spanner fell accidentally out of the electrician's pocket nobody knows; it could have been accidental as he asserted. We did have some problems with the unions, but you just had to battle on.'

Genevieve

Also, in 1952, Pinewood played host to one of its most enduring and best-loved productions: *Genevieve*. The 39-year-old director Henry Cornelius began his career as an assistant to the famous French director René Clair and later enjoyed a couple of successes at Ealing Studios, particularly with *Passport to Pimlico*. He then took the unusual step of leaving to go independent. He worked on a story idea with Ealing's William Rose about a veteran car race in the hope of setting up the project with Michael Balcon. However, Ealing's schedule was such that Balcon could not bring Cornelius back into the fold. Instead, Balcon suggested that Cornelius go to Pinewood and meet Earl St John.

Cyril Howard, a Pinewood administration clerk who later became managing director of the studio in 1976, recalled the conversation. 'Earl St John asked Cornelius what the film was about and when Cornelius told him it was about a vintage car race with this car called Genevieve, Earl said "Do you want to get me shot? You honestly expect me to put money into a film about an old car race – go on, get out!" That was that … or so it seemed.'

But Cornelius's tenacity paid off and he secured financial support from the National Film Finance Corporation and then succeeded in persuading

2.18 Genevieve, Rank's most fondly remembered film

2.19 Genevieve took some persuading of Rank's top brass that it was a viable film that would find an audience

St John to 'green light' the project. The sterling cast included Kenneth More John Gregson, Kay Kendall, and Dinah Sheridan. 'It really was a wonderful film to work on and we had so much fun,' recalled Sheridan, 'but not with the director I might add – he was awful. I do think he was a very good comedy director, but the way he worked wasn't a pleasant one for us artists. We all loved the story and I think it was really for Bill Rose (the screenwriter) that we strived to make it as good as we possibly could. It was quite funny with Cornelius because Kay and I each had a whistle and when we saw him approach us, or head towards the dressing rooms at the studio, we'd blow our whistles and each head off in different directions so that he couldn't get hold of us!'

Shooting got underway in September 1952. The race was supposedly taking place over a summer weekend, but the weather was anything but summery, said Dinah Sheridan. 'It was freezing cold and one day towards the end of the shoot we were each given a tot of brandy to warm us up. When we asked who we should thank, Cornelius came over and said, "I don't care if you're cold, but when you turn blue it effects my film!" So considerate! As we progressed through the film, I got fatter and fatter with all of the extra clothes I was putting on. I was extra cold with fright too, as John Gregson couldn't drive, and I had the job of telling him what to do out of the corner of my mouth. It was most unnerving.

'Because it was so noisy with the cars, we shot about 80 per cent of the film without sound and came back into the studio after Christmas to dub. That was quite difficult because we'd often be shivering with cold on film and had to try and recreate that in the dubbing theatre.'

The race took place on the London to Brighton road, but the cast and crew rarely strayed more than an hour's drive from Pinewood and never even saw the Brighton Road. 'People always associate Genevieve with Pinewood,' added Sheridan, 'but the truth is we only shot around five per cent of the film at the studio, the rest was location – lots around Pinewood and Denham, and if you look closely you see the gates of Moor Park golf club come into view. The final sequences were to be shot near Westminster Bridge, and so we drove up the Embankment (which is in totally the wrong direction from where the Brighton Road is), where Kenny More was supposed to get his wheels stuck in the tram lines. But would you believe the tram lines had been removed! So, we had to go elsewhere to get that shot.'

Everyone involved thought it was going to be a disaster. Cornelius insisted on numerous takes and often made last-minute changes to the script. The awful weather and budget over-runs understandably led to anxiety, but on the contrary Genevieve was a massive success, primarily through word of mouth, and was voted Best British Film of 1953. Larry Adler's wonderful harmonica score contributes greatly to the overall charm of the film, which was probably the closest Pinewood came to emulating the popularity of the Ealing comedies – but with two of Ealing's geniuses (Cornelius and Rose) on board, perhaps that was only to be expected.

'Adler's score really was very good,' Dinah Sheridan concluded. 'I was so sorry that he wasn't nominated for the Oscar, but he was blacklisted, and Muir Mathieson (the arranger) won the nomination in his place.' But there were compensations for Adler. 'Us artists were paid a few thousand pounds flat fee – no profit share. When Adler was approached, he named a fee, but the producer said, "I'm afraid we don't have any money left." Anyway,

Adler haggled and reduced his price but was still told that there wasn't any money. He really wanted to provide the music so suggested he take 2.5 per-cent of the profits instead of a fee. He made a fortune and didn't fail to remind me whenever I saw him.'

Former Gainsborough Pictures screenwriter Val Guest directed Dirk Bogarde and Yolande Donlan in his first Pinewood film, *Penny Princess*, in which a New York shop girl inherits a tiny European state and boosts its economy by selling cheese and schnapps. 'When I originally brought the story to Earl St John, Yolande and I went to Hollywood to see if we could secure Cary Grant's interest,' Guest reveals, 'and we were also thinking about Michael Wilding. But one day Earl said to me "What's wrong with Dirk Bogarde?" "Well, first of all," I said, "Dirk has always played dramatic parts, and this isn't that kind of part." "Make him funny then!" Earl barked. I must say, Dirk was lovely to work with and we got along very well, but I remember that in one of his books he wrote about the film and said "Poor Val – he wanted Cary Grant and got me!"

'For some reason they decided to launch the film at a big bash in Llandudno [North Wales] and, along with the cast, many of the top Rank executives attended, including John Davis. Someone else who came along, as a friend, was Dinah Sheridan and that was the night that she met JD and danced with him. Soon afterwards they married. I always say to Dinah that she shouldn't blame me!'

Expansion

J Arthur Rank became more involved with the family flour business in 1952, after the death of his brother James Rank, and withdrew from the day-to-day running of the Organisation. John Davis then assumed responsibility for the whole of the Rank Organisation and expanded into other areas which, ultimately, proved far more profitable than film, namely Bush Radio and Rank Precision Industries, which manufactured products such as sound and projection equipment, cameras and lenses.

1953 witnessed the birth of two of Rank's most successful comedies. The diminutive British funny man Norman Wisdom made his début in *Trouble in Store* (he starred in 12 more films at Pinewood), while *Doctor in*

2.20 *The first, and most successful, of the Doctor comedies*

2.21 Production manager Jack Swinburn, director Ralph Thomas, editor Gerald Thomas, and producers Betty Box and Muriel Box in a production meeting.

the House was the first of seven in the successful Betty Box-Ralph Thomas *Doctor* comedies.

Lured to Britain by the Eady Levy, Albert R Broccoli and his producing partner Irving Allen had a major success with *The Red Beret*, directed by Terence Young at Shepperton. For their next picture, *Hell Below Zero*, they moved to Pinewood. Based on The White South by Hammond Innes, the film was directed by Mark Robson. The action was set on whaling ships in Antarctica and that's where the cast and crew – but not the film's star, Alan Ladd – had to go for the location shoot.

Not long after completing *Hell Below Zero*, Broccoli and Allen returned to make *The Black Knight*, another vehicle for Alan Ladd. Ladd wasn't too keen though, according to Euan Lloyd. 'An American friend, whom I'd met during my tenure as joint press officer of the Variety Club of Great Britain, was back in London and asked if I would care to join him for lunch at Pinewood with Alan Ladd. He was shooting *Hell Below Zero* at the time.

2.22 Norman Wisdom – Rank had signed him to a seven year contract but didn't know what to do with him and so it was over a year before he made Trouble in Store

Alan Ladd and I hit it off from the start and our long conversations about the American West sealed a friendship that lasted until his death. He also became my mentor.

'Alan wanted nothing more than to get home to his ranch in California and resisted every effort to keep him here for the third film Broccoli and Allen wanted him to make. At the pool-side in Eden Roc in the South of France (where I had been invited to join the Ladd family), Allen and Broccoli, along with director Tay Garnett, made one final pitch to get Alan's agreement to make *The Black Knight*. It was not a promising script, despite substantial doctoring by Bryan Forbes, but finally Alan relented. There was one condition: that they would get me a production job. Unbelievably, Allen said yes. I think he would have given his wife away to please [Columbia's]

2.23 The Black Knight

Harry Cohn. A deal was made, and I found myself personal assistant to the now legendary duo, who proved to be the finest teachers any student of cinema could hope for. And I was back at Pinewood, working alongside Alan, Peter Cushing, the gorgeous Patricia Medina, and some of the best technicians alive. From there I moved on to become an independent producer.'

Bryan Forbes recalled how he was drafted in to work on the script. 'Early in my screenwriting career I was a contract script doctor, called in to perform emergency surgery on terminal cases … the most famous of these was *The Black Knight*, the brainchild of half a dozen parents. One Saturday afternoon the producers rang me to say that they had reached an impasse. "We've run out of pages," they said. "Could I come up with something by Monday morning?" I was young and hungry, so with the misguided confidence which often goes with these two factors, I agreed and was shown footage of what had already been shot.'

At Broccoli's memorial service in 1996, Forbes told the assembled 2,000 people at the Odeon Leicester Square of one particularly awkward plot complication he had to contend with. 'Sue Ladd, Alan's wife, had script approval – that was in the contract. Every word uttered by Ladd had to first be approved by her. I came up with a few pages in which Ladd dodged a few arrows, vaulted from the castle battlements into a cart of hay, sliced a few of the villains in two with his sword, seized a horse and galloped across the rising drawbridge just in time. What was Mrs Ladd's verdict? "Alan Ladd does not steal horses." She went on to explain that if he did, they would lose the Boy Scouts Association, the Daughters of the American Revolution and probably half his fan club. Everyone was dumbfounded. However, Irving Allen said, "Sue, he's not stealing a horse, he's borrowing one." She was not convinced. So, I came up with a line, when Ladd has done his vaulting and slicing, that he would deliver to a sentry – "Is this the horse I ordered?" He jumps onto it and gallops off. Sue agreed it! And that's what they shot.'

Headlines

Pinewood made the headlines on Monday July 20, 1953 when Rank threatened to close down the studios. All studio employees were given 14 days notice that production would cease unless a dispute with the Film Artistes

Association (FAA) was settled. Thankfully, the dispute was resolved before the two weeks elapsed and production continued.

After Queen Elizabeth II's coronation, the number of people who rented or owned television sets multiplied tenfold. The effects on cinema were painfully obvious – audiences were declining rapidly. One idea to lure people back was to produce three dimensional (3D) films. Another was to develop a new lens system – anamorphic – which produced a picture 2 ½ times as wide as it was high. The process was dubbed CinemaScope and, unlike 3D, proved popular with both audiences and filmmakers. The first film shot in CinemaScope was *The Robe*, a Biblical epic which provoked a massive row between Rank and 20th Century-Fox when the Organisation refused to install stereo sound in all cinemas at which the film played. Things were soon patched up, however, and, as a matter of course, all Odeon cinemas were fitted out with stereophonic sound equipment.

In November, Pinewood made the headlines again, this time over a daring £10,000 robbery. Thieves climbed a ladder across the canteen roof and entered a window on the first floor of the administration block. They broke into the cashiers' room and blew the safe open by putting a charge of gelignite into the keyhole and used cushions to muffle the explosion. Newspapers reported that 'The robbery was discovered shortly after 2.00 am by security officers when they were making an inspection. On each pay-packet was stamped J Arthur Rank Productions Limited.' The studio was in full production at the time, but all 1,500 employees were paid as usual.

Up until 1955, Muriel Box was the only female director to make a film at Pinewood. However, that was set to change with *All for Mary* from director Wendy Toye: 'My contract was originally with Alex Korda and when he died it was transferred to J Arthur Rank and I made the move from Denham to Pinewood – it was quite a shock in some ways because whereas I considered Korda and Denham to be a very creative and interactive partnership, Pinewood seemed much more like a factory. Everyone there was lovely and very helpful, but it was a very business-like atmosphere, perhaps due to John Davis's influence.

'Many people ask if I found it difficult being a female director in those days. "No" is my answer. I never really had any problems, although I know Muriel Box often said she had trouble and didn't get the support she hoped for. I think it may have been because she was Sydney's wife and the fact that she had moved from writing to directing and never really dealt with actors. I myself came into directing films through the theatre and had been directing there since 1949. I'd also choreographed many dances in films, so I knew a lot of British crews through my work on those. I think I was more readily accepted because of that work.

'*All for Mary* was adapted from a stage play and one of the stars – David Tomlinson – had appeared in the stage version. When I heard that he'd been cast in the film with Nigel Green, I insisted he didn't play the same role as he had on stage. I knew David and realised that he'd bring very little freshness to the part. So, Nigel took that role and David took the other leading role. It worked very well, apart from the fact that David insisted on giving Nigel directions! It was Leo McKern's first film, and they weren't really keen on him being cast, but I was. Leo had a glass eye, and at every opportunity Nigel tried to stand on that side of him, to make the camera pick up on it. He was very naughty like that!

'The producer was Paul Soskin and had a very strange sense of humour, so much so we tried to keep him off the set by putting the red light up early. We had one shot where I was shooting through a window, four floors up, at David coming down on a bed sheet. The cardboard boxes were built up to the second floor though, so if he had fallen it wouldn't have been far. David put on a great show of being terrified about this and the sheet was creaking, as though on the point of tearing, and he was saying "Oooh God, Oooh God!" but we did the scene, and it was perfect. The red light went off and in came Paul, insisting we re-take it. I told him it was perfect, but he was adamant. So up we went again. I called "Action" and there was a terrible tearing sound, an awful scream and the body of David Tomlinson went shooting past the window, bounced on the boxes, and hit the floor. The minute it hit the floor, I realised it was a model because of the noise it made. I was in tears by then though, and it turned out to be the crew's idea of a joke! They'd dressed the dummy up in David's clothes and moustache and thought it was hilarious.'

Run-Ins

Lewis Gilbert next brought the Douglas Bader story to the screen with *Reach for the Sky*, which he both adapted and directed. 'When I made *Reach for the*

2.24 Reach for the Sky – the true story of Douglas Bader

Sky there were only seven or eight stages at Pinewood,' said Gilbert, 'but it's grown a lot since then. We needed a couple of large stages for the film and there were only really two studios that could offer them – Pinewood and Shepperton. I much prefer Pinewood, so that's where we went. It was a very enjoyable experience coming to make a film at Pinewood, and Kenny More loved working at the studio, so we were off to a good start. However, the problems came soon afterwards – not with Pinewood, but with two scenes I'd written. The first scene was when a soldier said 'bloody'. Now, this was 1954 and I couldn't get the censor to agree to pass it. I said "How can you have a soldier who doesn't say bloody? They used to say a lot worse." All he said was, "Well, can't he say ruddy instead?" I said no – we really fought for that one.

'Then after that I had a run-in with John Davis over a scene. It was when Kenny More, who played Bader, was trying to get back into the air force without his legs. He went in for his medical and in the outer office a warrant officer told him "You're wasting your time, they'll never let you back in." Having gone in and got his recommendation, Bader came back into the outer office, just looked at the warrant officer and put two fingers up at

2.25 Doctor at Large, filming on location with director Ralph Thomas next to the camera

him. JD was horrified by this. He said he didn't like it and I should cut it. I said, "No, JD, this actually happened – it's the story." No more was said. However, the next day, JD sent his assistant Archibald over to see me. He said, "You've got to take it out." I said, "Please – don't even ask. It's in the story, it's a bit of fun and it will get a laugh." At this point Archibald started to cry. He sobbed, "JD will murder me." I never really saw him around after that! But the scene stayed, and it always got a laugh!'

In 1956 Roy Baker was at Pinewood with *Jacqueline* and *Tiger in the Smoke*; Ralph Thomas directed Anthony Steel, Stanley Baker and Odile Versois in *Checkpoint*, an industrial espionage thriller set in Italy, and Muriel Box directed *Eyewitness* with Donald Sinden and Muriel Pavlow – both of whom also starred in *Tiger in the Smoke* and *Doctor at Large* the same year.

'We became known as the Rank Rep Group,' recalled Muriel Pavlow of her threefold teaming with Donald Sinden, 'but I did so much like working with him. My only regret on *Tiger in the Smoke* was that Donald wasn't in

2.26/2.27 The Prince and the Showgirl, cast and crew

the Tony Wright part – it would have worked so much better if they had switched roles.'

Regarding this contentious piece of casting, Roy Baker remembered *Tiger in the Smoke* as the film in which he first felt the 'interfering' influence of John Davis. 'JD found himself being drawn more and more into production matters partly because of all the criticism the Organisation was getting regarding its film output. I dare say he did have some positive influence to offer, but his involvement in this film was disastrous. It was a wonderful story and a half-good film, but JD insisted that Tony Wright should play the lead. I wanted Jack Hawkins or Stanley Baker: the character was a ruthless and dominating bastard, and Tony didn't have that sort of personality. JD believed that Tony was set to become a massive star and became obsessed about our casting him. We relented and cast him. It didn't do Tony any favours at all – he knew it wasn't working and I don't think his career ever recovered.'

Marilyn

The big film of 1956, however – and one that set the whole of Pinewood buzzing – was *The Prince and the Showgirl* starring Laurence Olivier and,

in her only British film, Marilyn Monroe. Media attention was considerable to say the least, and often proved problematic – as did Marilyn Monroe herself, often causing disruption to the filming, as production manager Teddy Joseph explained. 'It was hopeless. Olivier used to cry every day because we would have to stand around waiting for Marilyn, who he said was so unprofessional. He hated the business of her arriving at 9.00 am and meandering over to the set by 11.00 am, when everyone else had been ready hours before. I know she had some problems in her own life, but it was affecting the film greatly. We loved her but hated the way she was.

'Olivier was totally the opposite. I was asked to meet him at least nine months before shooting was due to start, so I went to 146 Piccadilly – which is no longer there – and I remember that I had to be there at 3.30 pm, and naturally had my best suit on. Olivier said, "You must take tea with me" and a butler arrived wearing white gloves and carrying a silver tray with a marvellous tea service. I was used to roughing it with a mug of tea from the canteen, so this was quite something! For an hour we chatted about the film and he wanted to be absolutely sure that I was the right person. When you consider that I was just the production manager, you realise the tremendous effort and detail Olivier went to in making sure everything was just so.

'Six months later I started setting up the film, which I think I must have then been on for a year. Marilyn arrived with Arthur Miller, her new husband, and the 'black widow' [drama tutor Paula Strasberg] – part of her entourage throughout the shoot. Olivier would be behind the camera and as soon as he'd finished directing the scene, Marilyn would turn to Strasberg and Miller and ask how it went. She never asked the director! They all had their input, every bloody day, and it became ridiculous. It was quite often the case that many of the scenes that could be shot 'around' Marilyn were – including Olivier's close-ups – and when she arrived it was just a case of shooting her cutaways and close-ups to insert with what had been shot around her.'

Norman Wisdom recalled meeting Marilyn when he was filming *Up in the World*. 'I remember that we were shooting on adjacent stages, and one day Marilyn Monroe asked if she could come onto mine and watch some filming. She wore a cream satin dress, strolled onto the set with Laurence Olivier and then sat quietly to watch. It was electric! They then had a little chat with me before returning to their set, and Marilyn winked at me as she left. A few days later, I was walking back to my dressing room on the last day of shooting and met her in the corridor. I said it was my last day, and she then lifted me up and kissed me smack on the gob. I'll never forget that as long as I live and always remember her when I walk down that corridor.'

According to Donald Sinden, 'About a month before Marilyn was due to arrive, the number one dressing room was gutted and completely re-decorated in blue. A new carpet, curtains, couch, armchairs, dressing table were installed – all in blue. Then two weeks before she appeared a man arrived from Hollywood to vet the place and ensure that everything would be to her satisfaction. He pronounced "Miss Monroe does not like blue." Back came the painters, upholsterers, and carpet fitters and in six days everything was made white. My dressing room was in the same block, four doors from hers, so I saw the comings and goings of the entourage. She was still suffering from the effects of the Method and one day I pinned up a notice on my door:

Registered Office of the
  NAZAK ACADEMY*
  Prof. Donald Sinden
  'You too can be inaudible.'

Particularisation:
  NEW EGOS SUPERIMPOSED
  MOTIVATIONS IMMOBILISED
  IMAGINARY STONE KICKING ERADICATED
  UMS & ERS RENDERED OBSOLETE
  FEES: Exorbitant but we can work on your minimum
  Extra pockets provided by the school tailor

MOTTO: 'THOUGH 'TIS METHOD YET THERE'S MADNESS IN IT'
(Bacon)

'I waited inside and eventually heard the footsteps of the entourage. They paused outside my door and from the entire group I only heard one

---

* Kazan, as in Elia Kazan, spelt backwards

laugh, immediately recognisable as Marilyn's. The door burst open and in she came. We introduced ourselves and from that moment she regularly popped in for a natter and a giggle.'

The film, based on Terence Rattigan's light comedy *The Sleeping Prince*, boasted excellent production values, with sets designed by Roger Furse and first-class photography by Jack Cardiff, resulting in a wonderful visual backdrop for the meeting of the two very different, yet arresting, star personalities in 1911 London. It is interesting to note, given tales of her unprofessionalism, that Marilyn Monroe's own company co-financed the picture. She reportedly received a massive 75 per-cent of the profits.

❧ 3 ❧

The John Davis Era – Part 2 – (1956-1962)

1957 – the studios' silver anniversary – was a particularly busy year at Pinewood, with no fewer than 21 productions.

The first film into the studio was *Hell Drivers*, in which rivalry between haulage drivers leads to increasingly dangerous driving in a bid to reduce journey times. Cy Endfield pulled together an accomplished cast which included Stanley Baker, Patrick McGoohan, Herbert Lom, Sid James, Jill Ireland and – some way down the list – the young Sean Connery.

Stanley Baker then starred in Betty Box and Ralph Thomas's *Campbell's Kingdom*, a Canadian drama also starring Dirk Bogarde and Michael Craig. 'We were shooting in Cortina for winter because we couldn't use Canada,' remembered Ralph Thomas, 'and when we arrived there wasn't any snow. We must have bought all the cotton wool in Italy and had men in from Milan to spray everything white. It all worked fine. But when we were finishing the picture, we needed spring weather, and would you believe it started to snow! Well, we sprayed the snow green and all the women in the unit were making paper poppies to stick into the green-sprayed snow.

'We had a première in London and the Canadian High Commissioner attended with his wife. In the middle of the film they squeezed hands – he later said that it was because they recognised the location in Canada as Lake Louise where they spent their honeymoon, and it was a very special place for them. We didn't have the heart to tell him it was shot in Italy!'

Box and Thomas made two further films later in the year, both with Dirk Bogarde. *A Tale of Two Cities* enjoyed a deluxe supporting cast including

Dorothy Tutin, Cecil Parker, Donald Pleasence and an extremely hissable Christopher Lee, while *The Wind Cannot Read* (known around the studio as The Illiterate Fart) saw Bogarde marrying Yoko Tani prior to being tortured in a Burmese POW camp.

Ken Annakin, meanwhile, made *Across the Bridge*, based in part on a Graham Greene novel. 'This is still my favourite movie,' Annakin claimed, 'because of the unique story and the great performances of Rod Steiger, Dolores the dog, Noel Willman, Bernard Lee – in fact, the whole cast. John Davis allowed me to make a most extensive recce in the El Paso area of Texas and across into Northern Mexico. We reproduced all the exteriors in the Granada/Seville area of Southern Spain and returned to Pinewood for the interiors – especially those on the train. Rod was an avid Method actor and used to insist on running round the stage before every shot in the railway carriage. I recall Bernard Lee watching and shaking his head. "Silly bugger," he'd say. "Why can't he just act?" '

The One That Got Away

On the other side of the lot, Roy Baker directed the ground-breaking *The One That Got Away*. 'The film was the first with a German hero,' explained Baker, 'and you must remember that this was only a decade or so after the end of World War II. But I was determined to make the film that way because it was all true, and very dramatic. That's why the casting was so important. Franz von Werra was played brilliantly by Hardy Kruger, but there was tremendous opposition to playing a German actor in the lead, particularly from John Davis. He agreed to us doing the picture, but only if we used a British actor in the lead. Fortunately, we were able to buy some time while having the script rewritten and eventually won him over.'

Peter Manley was Roy Baker's production manager and recollected the initial reconnaissance trip in setting up the film. 'We started thinking about *The One That Got Away* in December 1956, and Roy and I went off to Canada to plot the course of Von Werra. It was a factual story, and we were able to follow all the ground he covered; it was fascinating. But it was minus 50 degrees in Canada and impossible to work: cameras froze up and we froze up! In the beginning of '57 we discovered that the temperatures were more favourable in Sweden, so we shot all the winter scenes there and came back and shot the rest of the film in the Lake District and at Pinewood.'

Hardy Kruger regards this film as the most important in his career. 'The year before I met Roy, my movie career in Germany was in danger as I had rebelled against the low quality of German films. I had seen some wonderful British, French and American films and I dreamt of working in these sorts of films, but I knew it was unlikely that anyone would come to me, a German actor, so soon after the war. I tried my luck in Paris and London but without much success. Having returned to Germany I then thought about going to Hollywood, but a call came through from the Rank Organisation to set up a meeting with Roy Baker in Hamburg. Roy then invited me over to London for the screen test. I was walking on air when I got the job!

'It wasn't all plain sailing, however. When the Rank Organisation finally announced that the film would be made with me, they "paraded" me in front of the press at the Odeon Leicester Square. The press was, on the whole, very kind. There was one journalist, however, Tom Wiseman, who attacked me straight away and asked me if I had been a Nazi. I couldn't tell the press the complicated story of my life, but I had seen – to my disgust – that there were hardly any Germans who admitted to being a Nazi; they would say "I had nothing to do with them" or "I couldn't help it" and so on. I never took that attitude, and so I shocked Wiseman by immediately saying "Yes". It was a little more complicated than that, but I wasn't prepared to go into details and nor was I prepared to lie. The press then boycotted me and the film. The Rank publicity department couldn't get my name or the name of the film into the press anywhere.

'As a result, people at Pinewood had a little problem with me. The stars and executives didn't shun me, but they were never seen with me either and I would always eat with Roy and Julian [Wintle, the producer] – we were always alone, nobody would join us. Then one day Finchie [Peter Finch] came in and said "Hi" to Roy and Julian, and he said to me "Are you that German fellow?" I said "Yes". "You're in deep shit, aren't you?" he said. I said, "Yes I am!" "How about dinner tonight then?" he asked. That started a friendship that lasted until he died.'

The press boycott was deemed so serious that, halfway through location filming in the Lake District, Baker was summoned to Pinewood and told

2.28 J. Arthur Rank at Pinewood's 21ˢᵗ Anniversary Party with contract actresses Belinda Lee (left) and June Laverick

by John Davis and Earl St John that they were cancelling the picture. Baker stuck to his guns and, as Kruger puts it, 'The press and public loved the movie, I got fantastic reviews and my career was made, along with plenty of money for the Rank Organisation. I have to thank Roy twice – first for casting me and then for standing by me.'

2.29 21ˢᵗ Anniversary Logo

Lewis Gilbert, hot on the successful heels of *Reach for the Sky*, next brought the biopic *Carve Her Name With Pride* to the studio. Violette Szabo, the British widow of a French officer who enlisted as a secret agent, was played brilliantly by Virginia McKenna in this highly dramatic film, directed with exquisite objectivity by Gilbert. In preparing for the picture, McKenna learned parachute jumping, judo and how to fire a Sten gun, as well as receiving invaluable guidance from Odette Churchill, as she explained. 'I was acting the part of someone who actually lived, and who died in a concentration camp, and no script or book could tell me what that was like. But Odette had lived through it. The courage of the women behind the enemy lines was remarkable and affected me deeply.'

Coming Of Age

On September 30, the grand 21st anniversary studio party was held at Pinewood. Lord and Lady Rank personally greeted all the guests, including 21 girls – all aged 21 – chosen from different parts of Britain, along with John Davis and his wife, Dinah Sheridan. The lawns were crowded with many of Rank's stars: Stanley Baker, Susan Beaumont, Dirk Bogarde, Phyllis Calvert, Jill Dixon, Anne Heywood, Jill Ireland, Belinda Lee, A E Matthews, David McCallum, John Mills, Kenneth More, Michael Redgrave, Flora Robson, Donald Sinden, Norman Wisdom and Tony Wright. 21-year-old Jill Ireland released hundreds of pigeons in the gardens before assisting Jill Dixon (also 21) and Norman Wisdom to launch 500 balloons – each one carrying an envelope which offered a prize to its finder.

More than 500 guests filled a huge marquee for lunch. The guest of honour was the Canadian High Commissioner, the Hon George Drew. In proposing a toast to Lord Rank, he said that he was 'one of the truly outstanding figures of the film world, whose ideals and integrity of mind and

2.30 J. Arthur Rank, John Davis and star Dirk Bogarde on set A Tale of Two Cities at the time of Pinewood's 21st anniversary celebrations

spirit have shown themselves in the quality of the films produced.' A set of curtains in front of a stage area drew back to reveal a huge birthday cake, complete with the appropriate number of candles. Kenneth More handed Lord Rank the knife to cut the cake – Anne Heywood assisted – while the assembled band played 'Happy Birthday'. Dirk Bogarde then took centre

2.31 Belinda Lee graces the cover of Picturegoer magazine with, 'All your Pinewood favourites inside'

stage, pointing out that 'Lord Rank has a far bigger family than he thought', and drawing Davis and Rank's attention to the two silver statuette cameramen adorning the cake he explained these were specially made for them, as a token of the whole family's appreciation. Deeply touched, and holding his statuette, Lord Rank said how much he appreciated 'this token of affection for us which we shall value all our lives.'

During the day's celebrations Lord Rank also paid tribute to his partner in the Pinewood venture. 'The person really responsible for the building of

2.32 The One That Got Away pressbook

2.33 The One That Got Away was the first British film to portray the German as the hero. Here, star Hardy Kruger, director of photography Eric Cross and director Roy Baker relax between set-ups on location in the Lake District

these studios is the late Mr Charles Boot. He, at the opening of this studio, said that if it had not been for me the project would have fallen down, but he made a mistake. He was responsible for it because I am sure that he would have found some other optimist to find the money.' The assembled guests then went on the studio tour. The Ravensbruck concentration camp, recreated on the backlot for *Carve Her Name With Pride*, was given a wide berth, however, so as not to offend or upset guests.

The celebrations were not just confined to Pinewood, as newspapers ran advertisements stating that anyone celebrating their 21st birthday on Monday September 30, should tell their local Odeon or Gaumont cinema.

2.34 *The definitive drama about the sinking of the Titanic*

2.35 The ship's engine room

They then received a month's free pass to the cinema as 'part of Pinewood's coming of age celebrations.'

Titanic

Production, meanwhile, continued apace and undoubtedly one of the greatest films to come out of Pinewood in 1957 – if not in its whole history – was *A Night to Remember*. Roy Baker's semi-documentary film of the Titanic and its fateful maiden voyage enjoyed much critical acclaim, brought great kudos to the Rank Organisation – which had been accused of only producing bland family films – and survives (James Cameron's 1997 blockbuster *Titanic* notwithstanding) as the definitive Titanic film.

The model sequences were shot in the Pinewood tank, over which the 007 Stage now stands, and many of the water sequences were shot at Ruislip Lido, a few miles from the studio. Half the deck was constructed on

2.36 Kenneth More starred as Charles Lightoller

the backlot under the supervision of art director supreme, Alex Vetchinsky.

'The producer, Bill McQuitty, was very persuasive,' recalled Baker in accounting for Rank's decision to film a subject already handled twice before, in 1929 and 1953. 'He was also emotionally involved, being an Ulsterman, as the ship was built in the Ulster shipyards and his father took him to see the Titanic as it sailed down the river when he was a very young boy. He sold the idea to John Davis as a flag-waving project, with tremendous social issues and prestige at its heart. The society of the time had persuaded itself that a ship could be unsinkable, and this film was to show the dramatic effect its sinking had on that society. We've received a lot of backhanded publicity for the film in the last couple of years after Cameron's Titanic. However, I'm still told by Bill [in the year 2000] that, somehow, our film has yet to go into profit!'

In another attempt to break into the US market, Rank Film Distributors of America was formed in 1957, and enjoyed a high-profile publicity launch. It remained the one elusive missing link in the Organisation's distribution network and would remain so, for the company was wound up after encountering 'considerable losses' (never disclosed) in the space of a year. Despite this setback, J Arthur Rank was ennobled a year later for his services to the British film industry. He became the First Baron Rank of Sutton Scotney.

Rank contract artiste Donald Sinden appeared in Jack Lee's *The Captain's Table* next, co-starring with John Gregson, Peggy Cummins, Reginald Beckwith, Richard Wattis, Joan Sims, and Maurice Denham. Based on a Richard Gordon novel, the screenplay was the work of playwright John Whiting and actors Bryan Forbes and Nicholas Phipps. Recalls Sinden, 'I was in the bar at Pinewood, which is where I got most of my jobs actually, having just finished *Rockets Galore*. I bumped into Joe Janni, the producer, and he started telling me about this script which involved three months' location work cruising around the Greek islands. I said, "Count me in" and didn't even wait to read it.

'A few weeks before shooting, he called to say that, unfortunately, the budget wouldn't stretch to the Greek islands. It was to be the Channel Islands instead. It still sounded good to me. However, a week or so before shooting I went for a costume fitting and the wardrobe man said, "Shame about the Channel Islands, isn't it?" I didn't know what he meant. He then explained that the budget wouldn't stretch: the location was now Tilbury docks! We shot out to sea on one side, turned the ship around and shot the other way, and spent three months in those wretched docks!'

Sinden's reference to the importance of Pinewood's bar area is no exaggeration. 'Betty [Box] and I had our offices directly above the bar and restaurant area,' said Ralph Thomas, 'and you could look out of the window on a summer's evening and cast a whole picture with the people in the patio area! At the end of the day, everyone would gather down there and discuss the day's events, along with what was happening the following day. As we were all working for the same company, and being paid out of the same pot, there was a tremendous sense of co-operation and collaboration; anyone would do anything to help. I recall some producers literally borrowing sets from others when they were in trouble. That would never happen nowadays.'

Just as valuable a studio asset as the bar was the Commissionaire, Sergeant Arthur Munday. An avuncular figure, he knew who and who not to let in and was a veritable mine of information about what was going on around the complex, as Ralph Thomas explained. 'Arthur Munday was a great sorter-out of people and problems. He was in effect a "super prefect". If you needed to know anything, he was the one who knew or, if something needed sorting out, he'd do it – be it rustling up extras from the gardens after their extended lunch breaks or escorting someone around the studio … or out of it!'

Look At Life

With the advent of Independent Television News (ITN) in 1955, cinema newsreel films were often dated before they arrived in cinemas. To replace them, Rank embarked on an ambitious series of documentary-style short films under the banner *Look At Life* to precede the supporting feature.

Produced between 1959 and 1969 by the Special Features Division of the Rank Organisation for Odeon and Gaumont cinemas, over 500 of the 8-minute films were produced.

Shot on 35mm Eastmancolor, the series depicted lighter aspects of life, in both Britain and further afield. With subjects such as 'Letting off Steam' celebrating British Railways' change of technology with the phasing-out of coal-powered steam and their replacement with oil-powered and electrified trains and signalling to bring in the modern age of travel; 'New Roads for Old' examining traffic crisis and a look at tomorrow's roads in the making including the London to Yorkshire motorway, Preston By-pass, Runcorn Bridge and works around London, including the gyratory system at Marble Arch, underpass at Hyde Park Corner, road widening at Elephant and Castle and the new Chiswick Flyover; 'Alpine Rescue' looking at the hazards faced by Swiss glacier pilots; 'City of Air' taking a look at the many aspects of London Airport with a focus on BOAC and BEA airlines; 'Going Places Under Water' following the world's first underwater sightseeing bus; to, 'Channel Tunnel' visiting the trial tunnel and a look at all the scientific research necessary ... the films were always vibrant with an informative narration.

Look at Life cameras were also offered exclusive access behind the Iron Curtain to present life in the Eastern Bloc, particularly in East Berlin and the Soviet Union. Though people who featured in the programmes were seldom heard to speak unless as background sound, their activities and interactions with others generally being commented upon by the narrator.

Initially hailed as an 'exciting venture in film journalism' Rank believed their new innovative series would have 'a more lasting impact than the present ephemeral newsreel content'.

Though its light-hearted presentation and jaunty theme tune had to increasingly compete with more gritty documentaries on television, and after ten years the concept waned just as cinema audiences continued to decline rapidly at the end of the 1960s.

More recently, films in the series were digitally restored from the original film elements, and released on DVD by ITV Studios Global Entertainment, with many having not been seen in full since their original screenings in the cinemas.

In November 2012, the series Britain on Film commissioned by BBC Scotland for broadcast on BBC Four began a twenty-part series providing an insight into life in Britain in the 1960s exclusively featuring footage from the *Look at Life* series.

2.37 Carry On producer Peter Rogers

Carrying On

1958 saw the arrival of another highly successful series at Pinewood, the *Carry On* films.

Initially backed by Anglo-Amalgamated, the series was shepherded by producer Peter Rogers and he took full advantage of Pinewood by filming in virtually every nook and cranny – why go on location if it could be done on the lot?

Country journalist turned playwright; Peter Rogers wrote for radio which led to him being contacted by J Arthur Rank's Religious Films outfit. Joining as a scriptwriter he was then engaged by his wife's brother, Sydney Box, who ran Gainsborough Studios at Islington to come up with scenarios.

Gerald Thomas meanwhile was an editor working with Betty and Sydney Box, with aspirations to direct. When the Children's Film Foundation

2.38 Carry On director Gerald Thomas

commissioned Peter Rogers to produce a picture called *Circus Friends* in 1956, he gave Gerald Thomas a call. The film attracted good notices and so began a partnership that lasted almost 40 years.

Their first *Carry On* film was all about National Service, called *Sergeant* it was released 1958. Based on a play *The Bull Boys* by R. F. Delderfield, the relatively low-budget comedy performed surprisingly well. Taking many of the same cast, Rogers and Thomas set their next film all about the antics in a hospital into production and re-used the *Carry On* prefix. *Carry On Nurse* became the top grossing film of 1959 ... and so began a series of 31 films over four decades.

Anglo-Amalgamated backed the first twelve films until 1966, when Nat Cohen was appointed the new managing director. He disliked the inuendo filled *Carry On* series intensely, leading Peter Rogers to strike a deal with Rank Organisation – on the condition that the *Carry On* prefix be omitted due to its close association to Anglo Amalgamated.

'They were afraid of being sued,' said Rogers, 'but I owned the titles, not the distributor.'

The first two films made under the Rank deal, *Don't Lose Your Head* and *Follow That Camel* were not as successful, and the *Carry On* prefix was added back in, the films re-released and as a result a surge in takings followed; causing the Rank Organisation to relent and agreeing the series-title to be reinstated officially for the 1967 film *Carry On Doctor*.

By 1976 many, not least The Rank Organisation, felt the series was running out of steam. Their main star, Sid James, had died and the proposed *Carry On England* had a new intake of stars, mainly from television. An unpersuaded Rank refused to back the entire budget leaving Peter Rogers and Gerald Thomas to plug the funding shortfall themselves.

2.39 The first of the series

2.40 The last (so far) entry in the Carry On franchise

Two years later, after poor response to *England* and an enforced 'AA' (equivalent to a '15') rating due to nudity, Rank declined to finance any part of the next film in the series. Rogers was then approached by the private investment company Cleves Investments, keen to make another film. The world had moved on from the innocent comedy of *Carry On Sergeant* and racier comedies such as the *Confessions* films were taking over. Cleves Investments invested £349,000 on the new production, titled *Carry On Emmannuelle*.

Again, given an 'AA' certificate in the UK, which excluded anyone under the age of 14, it was a critical and box office disappointment. It was the end of an era, and the end of *Carry On* ... almost.

In 1992 it was announced *Carry On Columbus*, a £2.5 million budget resurrection of the series was underway at Pinewood, to cash in on the anniversary of Columbus discovering America in 1492.

With backing from a mixture of financiers including Twentieth Century Fox a new generation of comedy actors were cast, including Rik Mayall, Keith Allen, Alexei Sayle and Julian Clary. Jim Dale returned to lead the cast and Jack Douglas featured in a small role. Frankie Howerd had been asked to star as the King of Spain but died two days before the start of filming, and Leslie Phillips stepped in.

Royal Visit

Going back to 1958, the Rank Organisation was preparing to produce a film of *Lawrence of Arabia* – Anthony Asquith was to direct, Terence Rattigan script and Dirk Bogarde star – but, after recces in what were then very dangerous countries with volatile political conditions, the viability of the project was brought into question and it was cancelled. Rattigan got over his disappointment by turning his script into a successful stage play, Ross.

In 1959, a new addition was made to the studio's facilities for *Sink the Bismarck!* – the paddock tank, which was the largest in Europe, with the following dimensions: 221 ft (narrowing to 105 ft) wide, 198 ft long and 3 ft 6 in deep, and an inner tank measuring 51 ft by 40 ft by 9 ft. It has a total capacity of 764,000 gallons and a backdrop measuring 240 ft by 60 ft. Extensive model work was required in *Sink the Bismarck!* and all of it was carried out in the paddock tank. Lewis Gilbert's recreation of the sinking in 1941 of Germany's greatest battleship starred Kenneth More, Dana Wynter, Michael Hordern and Maurice Denham, while the set attracted many visitors, not least Her Majesty the Queen and the 12-year-old Prince Charles.

'It was a very low-key visit,' Gilbert maintained, 'and the Queen didn't travel with any entourage or bodyguards – just her and Charles. The young prince was at school in Cheam and had wanted to see a film studio. On arrival, the Royal party came to the paddock tank and watched some shooting. After a while, the Queen asked if there were any other films being made that she might visit. I said that I believed Betty Box and Ralph Thomas were on another stage [with *Conspiracy of Hearts*]. So, we were walking down the corridor towards the stage and walking towards us was a chippie [carpenter] carrying a load of timber. "Alright guv?" he said as he approached. Then he did a double-take. He couldn't work out if it was the Queen or an actress made-up to look like her for a film. Suddenly it registered just who it really was, and the timber fell slowly out of his arms onto the floor in front

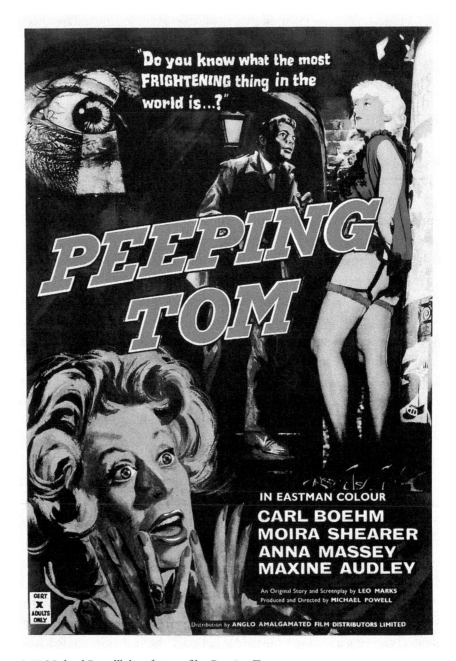

2.41 Michael Powell's last feature film Peeping Tom

2.42 Vilified by critics on its release, but now regarded as a masterpiece, Michael Powell regarded his film as a tragic love story

of the Queen. She found it all very amusing. I finally took her on to the set and that was my greatest moment: the look on Betty's face was priceless. I introduced the Queen to the cast, and she was absolutely delightful.'

'That's absolutely true,' said Ralph Thomas. 'It was just about tea-break time, in fact. I asked Her Majesty if she would care to join us and she said that she would be delighted to, on condition we made no fuss about trays etc – she wanted the same as everyone else. So, she sat on my chair with a cup and saucer in hand and it was a lovely afternoon.'

Peeping Tom

One of the most controversial films ever made also came out of the studio in 1959 – Michael Powell's *Peeping Tom*. The film was berated on its release with one influential critic, Derek Hill, shrieking that it ought to be 'flushed down the nearest sewer.' However, those involved with the film saw it as a sad love story rather than a horrific thriller.

'I received a call from Mickey,' said editor Noreen Ackland, 'and he asked if I would like to cut his new film. I didn't need to think about it! When I read the script, I saw a very sad and tormented man in Carl Boehm's character and, while his methods were perhaps a little gruesome, it was by no means a "bad taste thriller". Mickey was devastated, as were we all, on its release when the reviews came in. They vilified the film. It really did have a severe effect on him, and he never really recovered. Thankfully, the film is now rightly regarded as one of the best he ever made and has become something of a cult classic. I'm always being asked about it and it's always showing somewhere in the world; a remastered print enjoyed considerable success on its re-release in New York, mainly thanks to Martin Scorsese.'

The movie used Pinewood extensively, as part of the story was set in a studio punningly called Chipperfield. E Stage and its surrounding corridors, together with the double-lodge entrance, can be seen quite clearly in the film.

The story, written by Leo Marks, tells of how a photographer uses a spiked tripod to kill young girls while photographing the look of terror on their faces. The tormented Mark Lewis (Boehm) is revealed to have been 'scientifically' tortured and tormented as a child by his cruel father who filmed him day and night. (Powell himself plays Mark's sadistic father in these horrific flashbacks.) In retrospect, the horror content is tame compared with modern films, so one could be forgiven for not fully appreciating just how repugnant the critics of the day considered it.

2.43 The huge backlot set for the abandoned UK production of Cleopatra

Cleopatra

1960 went down in history primarily for the film that wasn't made at Pinewood: *Cleopatra*. Filming commenced on September 28 and, just over six weeks later, only 11 minutes of material was in the can when Elizabeth Taylor was taken seriously ill. It was by no means the film's first setback but proved the final straw for 20th Century-Fox, who decided to pull the plug on the Pinewood filming.

It was in the latter part of 1959 that Fox had agreed a deal with Pinewood, bringing in the biggest American production ever to be staged in Britain. Elizabeth Taylor had insisted on a European base for tax reasons and Fox were lured to Britain (after seriously considering Rome) because of potential Eady money. Peter Finch was cast as Caesar and Stephen Boyd as Mark Antony. The distinguished Russian-born director Rouben Mamoulian was hired and spent a year preparing for the task. However, it is said that he was apprehensive about the choice of Pinewood and appalled to learn that the film's desert scenes were to be shot there too.

Teddy Joseph recalled the early days of setting up the production, and how the shooting of the desert scenes at Pinewood came about. 'Rouben Mamoulian and Walter Wanger [the producer] sent me to Rome to see Dino De Laurentiis to try to reclaim some of the money they had spent on buying chariots and costumes when they were thinking about filming there. When I arrived, De Laurentiis met me and was very curt. He explained that Spyros Skouras at Fox had asked him to build two new stages at his studio six months earlier in order for the film to go to Rome. "There they are," he said. So here was I, not only telling him that the film wasn't going to Rome and we didn't need stages, but that we also wanted our money back!

'I reported back to London, and Wanger instructed me to go to Egypt on a recce with Mamoulian. Our party was met by President Nasser's nephew, who was a stills man, and he was going to look after us during our stay. The next day we were escorted by an Egyptian air crew in a Russian-built aeroplane, which was in fact a cargo-cum- parachute plane without any doors, and in which we had to sit on the floor grasping onto a rope for support! We reached Luxor and Mamoulian started to collect pebbles – large ones, small ones – he just loved pebbles. So, by the time we had finished the day's recce all of our pockets were full of these pebbles he'd collected and made us carry. They were everywhere; he was quite insane!

'I was left behind with Nasser's nephew to look for good desert (and there isn't much good desert in Egypt). We went about 40 miles out and arrived at a very large, empty Egyptian army camp. The only person there was a very old man, who I guess was in charge of security. Our guide went over to him and said, "Do you know who I am, I'm Nasser's nephew." The old man was unfazed and refused us entry. So, Nasser's nephew started beating him with a stick, quite violently. I couldn't stand for that. I reported his actions to the British Consulate and said that we couldn't possibly tolerate behaviour like this if we were going to bring a crew over. Within an hour I found myself ordered back to England and the Egyptian authorities took my passport away, saying that I'd only get it back once I was on my way home. When I arrived back at Pinewood, I was summoned to meet Spyros Skouras in the boardroom. "I remember you," he said. "You were the one who didn't get my money back from Dino De Laurentiis!" He said that I'd messed everything up by upsetting Nassau's nephew, so we couldn't go back to Egypt to shoot. It caused quite a storm. The desert was then recreated on the lot!'

Cleopatra was certainly the most expensive and heavily publicised film ever to move into Pinewood. Sets of previously unheard-of dimensions were constructed on the backlot, but soon came the first of the many problems that dogged the production: a shortage of plasterers. The situation became so desperate that the studio finally resorted to advertising on prime-time TV to fill the vacancies.

The most impressive of all the sets was undoubtedly the harbour of Alexandria, which held one million gallons of water and was topped up further by the English rain. 'The Americans were enthusiastic about the big set on the lot once they had settled for the fact that it wasn't as big as they would have liked,' says Ernie Holding, Fox's man in London. 'They thought it was an excellent job of work and passed on their compliments to Pinewood.'

The size of the production was giving cause for concern. Before a foot of film had been exposed, the cost had easily exceeded £1 million, and there was still a 16-week shoot to get underway. Elizabeth Taylor's arrival also brought problems for the studio, the main one being that she insisted on using her Hollywood hairdresser, Sydney Guilaroff. The British unions were up in arms and a dispute blew up that threatened to reach out to other studios. Eventually, a compromise was struck: Miss Taylor could have Guilaroff but only as supervisor to a British hairdresser.

The imminent arrival of 5,000 extras was the next headache. Pinewood's management laid on 28 extra tube trains from London to Uxbridge and 30 buses to shuttle to and from the station non-stop. Mobile lavatories were hired from Epsom racecourse and massive catering marquees were erected to house the mountain of food for meals. However, all the planning and organisation was wasted – along with 9,000 sausage rolls – when torrential rain forced shooting to be abandoned.

Then real disaster struck. Elizabeth Taylor became dangerously ill and had to undergo an emergency tracheotomy. Production was halted and Joan Collins placed on standby as a replacement. Fox were facing up to the fact that their English sortie was all but over. Miss Taylor's recuperation was a slow one, and what with the miserable British weather raining down on the sets day after day, the decision was made to transfer production, and

2.44 *The first James Bond film adventure, Dr. No in 1962*

2.45 007's Aston Martin DB5 as featured in Goldfinger posing for publicity outside the studio gate

Ancient Egypt, to Italy – where the climate was more conducive to Miss Taylor's health. The Pinewood sets were destroyed.

Joseph Mankiewicz was brought in to rewrite the script and direct the picture, and the result eventually made it to the screen in 1963. Rex Harrison and Richard Burton were re-cast as Caesar and Mark Antony respectively but even then, alas, the film didn't live up to the mass publicity and hype that had surrounded its production. Pinewood didn't receive a credit either.

Bond

In 1962, Terence Young was directing a film for Albert 'Cubby' Broccoli, who by this time was in partnership with fellow producer Harry Saltzman. This lavish spy thriller, featuring a relatively unknown leading man, was called *Dr. No* and budgeted at $1m.

2.46 *The 007 Stage was constructed for the 1977 adventure, The Spy Who Loved Me, but burnt down on two separate occasions in 1985 and 2006 – and was rebuilt twice immediately afterwards*

2.47 The latest, and 25th Bond adventure, No Time to Die

A dream team of production personnel was recruited including vision-ary production design Ken Adam, editor Peter Hunt who pioneered a fast cutting style, director of photography Ted Moore, titles designer Maurice Binder, screenwriters Richard Maibaum and Johanna Harwood, and com-poser of the tune that became 'The James Bond Theme', Monty Norman, as orchestrated by John Barry.

It was the first in a hugely successful series that has, to date, spanned seven decades and produced 24 sequels. All but four (*Moonraker, Licence To Kill, Goldeneye* and *Casino Royale*) were based exclusively out of Pine-wood and, up until the late 1980s, arrived regularly every two years and invariably bailed Pinewood out of a financial crisis.

Many of the film's sets also changed the Pinewood skyline, not least Blofeld's giant volcano lair in *You Only Live Twice* and the biggest silent stage ever constructed, in 1976, for *The Spy Who Loved Me*. Although the stage was destroyed by fire, as was its replacement, the third incarnation stands proud on the Pinewood lot today and is knows as 'The Albert R Broccoli 007 Stage' in tribute to the producer who backed its construction.

The 25th Bond, *No Time To Die,* with the sixth actor to play James Bond in the Eon series – Daniel Craig – is poised for release at the time of writing.

Call Me Bwana

Also, in 1962, Janet Munro starred as a Welsh girl who sets off in search of wealth and success in *Bitter Harvest*, while Oliver Reed took the lead in *The Party's Over*, which was later disowned by backers the Rank Organisation because of a necrophiliac sequence. Less controversially, 'Cubby' Broccoli and Harry Saltzman made their only non-Bond film for Eon Productions, *Call Me Bwana*, with Bob Hope, Anita Ekberg and Lionel Jeffries in a far-cical tale set in the African jungle.

'We didn't get quite as far as Africa,' said Lionel Jeffries. 'More like Ger-rards Cross golf course [a mile or so from the studio] and we shot it for Africa. They planted plastic palm trees and imported three giraffes, an elephant, and a zebra. They used to let the animals out at night to roam around the course and just close the gate. Then we returned to the studio

2.48 *Broccoli and Saltzman only made one non-Bond film together, Call Me Bwana.*

backlot in the freezing winter, knocked the snow off the potted palms and pretended it was Africa. It was crazy – I mean, it was so cold you could see our breath. But it was wonderful fun all the same.'

'The original intention,' recalled Clive Reed, first assistant director on the movie, 'was to shoot the entire film on location in Kenya, but the fun of the film was in the gags and facial reactions, which did not require the cast to be in an actual African location. A second unit shot various convoy shots travelling through the bush: actual jungle is not very plentiful in Kenya. The exterior camp sequences were shot on a large stage, the "jungle" sequences in Black Park with the addition of a few creepers and banana plants.' An in-joke followed in Eon's *From Russia With Love* (1963), where a hoarding concealing an escape route for one of the villains centres on Anita Ekberg's mouth in the poster for *Call Me Bwana*.

The period from 1952 to 1962 had seen a turnaround at Pinewood. No longer was the studio solely dependent upon Rank Organisation films to fill the stages; indeed, there were just as many 'renters' as Rank films coming in. The press, meanwhile, predicted an imminent upturn in cinema attendance and brought into question the Organisation's closure of over half its cinema screens. Davis retorted that far from closing too many, he had not closed enough. But only 374 screens remained. Audiences were declining at an alarming rate and Rank films were not making the returns on investment that they once had.

Had it not been for John Davis making an investment in a new technology, the Organisation would have folded.

Xerox

Hopping back to 1956, the Rank Organisation's head of business, Thomas Law, reportedly picked up a scientific magazine by chance and read an article about an invention that could produce copies of documents as good as the original.

Rank had a small business making camera lenses and Law saw a potential addition to the vision. He tracked down a photographic-supply company in Rochester, New York, named Haloid who had invested a dry print process they called Xeroxgraphy.

2.49 The XERONIC machine (Rank Xerox)

Haloid and Rank subsequently formed an affiliate called Rank-Xerox (Rank put up £600,000 for a 50per-cent stake) and paved the way for Xerox factories in Great Britain and a sales and distribution system that brought Xerox machines to the European market.

As photocopying took the world by storm, so did Rank's profits.

John Davis's investment in Xerox was not the calculated business move he often claimed, but more a stroke of tremendous, good fortune, according to Cyril Howard. 'Xerox was basically a dry printing process and consisted of very basic technology at the time. Davis got on well with the man behind the idea [Joe Wilson] and decided to take a punt. He had no real idea of how successful it might become. I mean, would you – as a seasoned accountant and businessman – say that a dry printing process would

2.50 Rank's John Davis with the Rank-Xerox 813 machine

provide more profit than a vast entertainment and leisure conglomerate? As luck would have it, it did.'

'Cyril is right about it being pure luck,' confirmed Davis's ex-wife Dinah Sheridan, 'as I was in on the Xerox thing with JD and it was decided on the flip of a half crown coin – he couldn't decide whether to go in or not, and that decided it.

Top Rank Records

With the advent of rock and roll in 1956, the Rank Organisation decided to get in on the act and set up Rank Records Ltd. (the label was named Top Rank) and Jaro Records (a US subsidiary). Artists included Gary U.S. Bonds, the Shirelles, B. Bumble and the Stingers, Wilbert Harrison, Skip &

I'll use a copier, I'll use a duplicator, a copier, a duplicatoracopier, a duplicatoracopiera . . .

Stop! use <u>one</u> machine.
The New Rank Xerox 420.

It's a copier duplicator.

A single machine, developed by Rank Xerox* to bridge the gap between copiers and duplicators.

What is this gap?

Well, think of your present choice if you want, for example, 25 copies of a document, what do you do? You choose.

Either a copier because it's convenient, since it works directly from the original. But the cost-per-copy remains the same through the run.

Or a duplicator, with all the trouble of making a master or stencil first. However, the cost-per-copy reduces through a run.

In other words, a choice of convenience or economy.

Or was. Now you can have the penny and the bun.

The Rank Xerox 420 reproduces from an original and the cost-per-copy reduces through the run.

So you get both economy and convenience.

Take the original. Dial the number of copies. Press a button. Out come sharp, permanent copies made directly on ordinary paper. As they come they get cheaper. The cost of the fourth copy is about half the cost of the first, the eleventh about half the cost of the fourth.

It's called xeroduplicating.

And it's worth finding out about. Right now.

Rank Xerox Ltd., 84-86 Great Portland St., London W.1.

*Xerox is a registered trade mark of Rank Xerox Ltd.

A DIVISION WITHIN THE RANK ORGANISATION
JOINTLY OWNED WITH XEROX CORPORATION

Telephone at once for a demonstration: MUSeum 5010

2.51 Further Xerox publicity

Flip, Andy Stewart, Craig Douglas and John Leyton; the US featured artists including Jack Scott, Dorothy Collins, and The Fireballs. They never really had the chart success of other recording labels however, and the division quickly became loss-making. It was put up for sale.

In 1960, Top Rank Records Ltd, was taken over by the ambitious and expanding EMI Records Ltd, which had labels such as The Gramophone Co. Ltd., Columbia Graphophone Company, and Parlophone Co. Ltd.

Visual

Rank Audio Visual was created in 1960, bringing together Rank's acquisitions in multimedia, including Bell & Howell (acquired with Gaumont British in 1941), Andrew Smith Harkness Ltd (1952) and Wharfedale Ltd (1958). Subsequent acquisitions included Strand Electric Holdings (1968) and H.J. Leak & Co. (1969)

Retirement

On June 6, 1962, Lord Rank announced his intended retirement as chairman and that he was to become the first Life President of the company.

All Rank's employees signed a special commemorative book of thanks, totalling 28,066 signatures in all.

Lord Rank was held in tremendously high regard by each and every member of his staff, especially John Davis, who succeeded him as chairman. Davis was consciously moving the Organisation, of which he now had almost total control, away from film production and was keen to concentrate instead on its more profitable divisions, including bingo and holidays. Lord Rank never interfered with Davis' running of the Organisation but did keep in daily touch and always lent support and advice when required. The Organisation was now a very profitable proposition, worth almost £90 million.

John Davis had certainly achieved what he was charged to do.

4

Film Boom (1962-1969)

Rank Bush Murphy Group & Motorways

In 1962 with Bush Radio Ltd already under its ownership, the Rank Organisation acquired Murphy Radio and amalgamated the radio and television manufacturers into Rank Bush Murphy Group. (The company was later sold to Great Universal Stores in 1978).

In further diversification, in 1963, Top Rank was one of the early operators of motorway service areas in the UK, opening its first services at Farthing Corner on the M2 in Kent. It cost £350,000 to build – almost four times as much as the government suggested they spend.

Upon opening, Rank described it as 'gay and colourful', and intended its blue and yellow colours to offer a warm welcome to visitors to England (from Dover port). In reality it became known for being particularly dirty and described by inspectors as 'sleazy'

They were the first operator to introduce showers, claiming that the image of lorry drivers was changing.

In 1967 they dropped the phrase 'service area', and insisted on using the grand title 'Motorports'. Rank's futuristic ambitions gave rise to elaborate architecture and facilities, with restaurants filled with potted plants, 'Wimpy Express' takeaways and even a Lyons ice cream van. They later had a restaurant called Country In.

Following Forte's creation of Forte Travelodge and Granada's creation of Granada Lodge, Rank wanted a piece of the budget accommodation

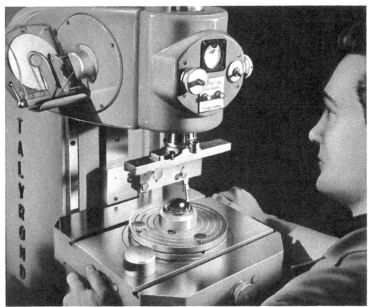

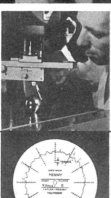

WHEN IS A MILLIONTH OF AN INCH NINE MILES?

By ordinary standards, a millionth of an inch seems pretty small beer. But in the exacting world of science and technology, it takes on a very different meaning. An error of a millionth of an inch could mean a rocket missing the moon by nine miles. The smoothness of tubes carrying blood in heart-lung machines must be measured in millionths of an inch to avoid minute surface irregularities which make blood congeal. Certain bearings in huge jet engines must be round to within millionths of an inch to prevent highly destructive vibration. Talysurf, Talyrond, Talylin, these are the names of three remarkable instruments made by Rank Taylor Hobson to measure surface smoothness, roundness and straightness within such fantastically small limits. They are at the heart of the research and industry that strives to increase our knowledge and achieve better products.

MEASURING IN MILLIONTHS

RANK TAYLOR HOBSON

A Division of The Rank Organisation
LEICESTER HOUSE, LEE CIRCLE, LEICESTER.
Telephone : Leicester 23801

2.52 Rank Taylor Hobson won the Queen's Award to Industry over three consecutive years

with their own Motor Lodge. This opened at some of their motorway and One Stop sites but although well-maintained and tidy, their services were known for being expensive and returns never caught up with their initial investments.

2.53 The Rank Car Park!

Decline of the service stations

After an initial couple of years of building bold and distinctive services, Rank quickly learned that such buildings were expensive to maintain and difficult to make a profit out of. As such, the rate of their construction slowed down significantly and in the following 20 years saw no expansion at all, but rather exercised extreme caution which was perhaps not surprising when in 1966 the motorway service area division reported a loss of £625,000. Rank reached out to the Ministry of Transport to have their rent arrangements renegotiated, arguing that this was an emerging industry and a lot had been learned. The Organisation wanted to introduce a news theatre, conference room and grocery shop to their services to attract more custom. When this was declined, Rank warned that the whole industry could unite to fight the government's regulations.

The division began to turn a profit in 1971 and by 1978 confidence was such they started building new service areas again, albeit smaller in scale, and their existing sites were all refurbished and Motor Lodges were added. New petrol filling areas were also opened in partnership with Esso.

In 1986, Rank made an ambitious bid for Granada's parent company – valuing it at around $1.06 billion – which could have seen its services, hotels, entertainment and television facilities merged with Rank's leisure and film empire. Granada said the offer was 'unacceptable in every respect' and urged its shareholders to ignore it.

Five years later, following the takeover of Mecca, the wider Rank business encountered a mountain of debt which they blamed on the (then) recession. As a result they decided to sell off some of their 'non-core activities', the first of which was the motorway services. These were sold to Michael Guthrie, former CEO of Mecca, in December 1991 for £86million. As a result the Rank services were all rebranded Pavilion a few months later. Rank also sold him Pizzaland and Prima Pasta. Two brand new services were included in the deal, which Rank said had not reached their full potential – one of which, Swansea, had only been open four months. Rank eventually operated a portfolio of 11 service areas, ahead of the disposal with four others planned – Leicester Forest East (M1), Taunton Deane (M5), Toddington (M1), Trowell (M1) but not built.

TV arrives

The sixties were buoyant years for Pinewood, with more and more big American pictures renting space in the wake of Bond and Disney, and television production creating its first major impact, ultimately leading to new stages being constructed specifically for TV.

TV series *Court Martial* was the first to move into the 89 x 37 x 28 foot space of H-stage, as producer Bill Hill explained.

'The people at Pinewood built us our requirements as a self-contained unit. They gutted a whole block and reconstructed it, creating an admin block, completely self-contained and inter-communicating, plus dressing rooms, make-up, hairdressing, and wardrobe departments. They modified three stages for our production. This went on during July and August. The

As the ribbons of new trunk roads push out across the countryside, the Top Rank Motor Inns and Motorway Services Division is expanding to meet the needs of the growing motoring public. This aerial photograph shows the Top Rank Motorway Service Area on the M6 at Knutsford, Cheshire, which opened on 15th November, 1963.

2.54 *The M6 Knutsford Rank Motorway service area*

unit of 150 people started to arrive ready to shoot on September 7. When the first four 48-minute episodes were sent over to New York, back came the order "Double the number, let's have 26." Each film was made in an average of 9 1/2 days, and that's not bad going.'

Epics

Those Magnificent Men in Their Flying Machines boasted an all-star cast, including Stuart Whitman, Sarah Miles, James Fox, Robert Morley, Gert Fröbe, Eric Sykes and Terry-Thomas, in a rip-roaring comedy set in 1910. Press mogul Lord Rawnsley (Robert Morley) puts up a £10,000 prize for a London to Paris air race. All manner of contraptions are entered, piloted by one of the most international (and funniest) casts ever to come together at Pinewood. The script (co-written by director Ken Annakin) was nominated for an Academy Award.

'The film was wonderfully serviced by Pinewood and every technical department attached to it,' recalled Annakin. 'We shot an amazing number of flying sequences against blue screen and the crews worked skilfully and patiently to get it right. Some people say it launched my "Hollywood career". Well, I never really had one, as most of my films were shot on locations all around the world. But I have been based in Hollywood since the 1970s, so I guess in that sense it did.'

The last film to shoot in 1964 was another Hollywood epic, but one that attracted some unwelcome attention from the press, thanks to the rivalry that existed between its two stars Kirk Douglas and Richard Harris. 'After working for Disney for many years,' recalled John Willis, 'I decided to become a freelance publicist and *The Heroes of Telemark* was my first. Talk about a baptism of fire!

'The film's director, Anthony Mann, had originally been signed to direct *Spartacus* but he and Douglas didn't get on and Mann was replaced by Stanley Kubrick. He'd also made a film with Richard Harris and didn't get along too well there, so bringing them all together wasn't perhaps the best idea. Douglas and Harris were very jealous of each other and were always bitching about who the 'star' was. Their demands became silly and seriously affected the running of the production. For instance, Harris rolled up at the studio one day with a tape measure, measured Douglas' trailer and then announced he was going home. Apparently, it was a little bigger than his own trailer. Another day, Douglas fired his chauffeur and Harris immediately turned round and hired him.

'It got worse. We were on location in Rome, and one evening we all attended a film première. Earlier in the day, the British papers ran a story

2.56 Bush Murphy Ad

about all the childish behaviour and petty rivalry between the two leads and Richard Harris was furious. He saw me in the foyer of the cinema, pushed everyone else out of the way and demanded to know who leaked the story. I said nothing! He threatened to hit me – and I wish he had done – but we were pulled apart. The most annoying thing for me was when, on the last day at Pinewood, both of them were in the corridor walking towards each

2.57 Inside one of the Top Rank TV rental shops

other – it was a bit like High Noon – and I couldn't believe my eyes: as they met, they shook each other's hands like they were old friends!'

Taking stock

With the film division of the Rank Organisation booming, it was also a highly productive time for other divisions. Here is a summary of everything Rank was involved with:

- **Film production**
  Principally at Pinewood Studios.
- **Advertising film division**
  Producing and distributing cinema and television commercials.
- **Film processing**
  Rank Film Laboratories in Denham processing feature prints and amateur film-maker prints
  Top Rank Film Processing of colour stills for amateurs and professionals.

2.58 The shop front

- **Rank Audio Visual**
  Equipping cinemas with screens (by Andrew Smith Harkness division), projectors, sound equipment and furnishings (such as drapes, floor coverings, stage accessories and seating).
- **Rank film library**, a unit of Rank Audio Visual, leading distributor of 16mm educational and training films.
- **Rank Film Distributors**, the leading European distributor of entertainment films in the UK and throughout Europe, including American and foreign titles.
- **Photographic equipment** marketed by Rank included Bell & Howell 8mm amateur cine cameras and projectors, Asahi Pentax cameras, Mamiya cameras, slide projectors, screens and accessories.
- **Laboratory equipment and instruments** (including oscilloscopes, and demonstration tubes such as radar cathode ray tubes, scanning cathode ray tubes, precision cathode ray tubes), photo-electric cells, photo-conductive cells, photo-diodes, photo-switches, delay lines, school television receivers and loudspeakers.

2.59 Kirk Douglas and Richard Harris made uneasy co-stars in The Heroes of Telemark

- **Rank-Bush-Murphy**
  Manufacturing radios, record players and radiograms,
  Tape recorders by Bush Radio;
  Flying aids – for visual flight simulators, radar transponder beacons, and auto-land cable equipment
  Wharfdale Wireless division manufacturing hi-fi speakers;
  Closed-circuit television systems – monitors and cameras.
  Television studio equipment.
  Telecine equipment (16mm and 35mm).
  Communications equipment for all armed forces.
  Missile telemetry and destruct equipment.
  Airborne electronic countermeasures and anti-submarine equipment.
  Microwave systems and aerials.
  Ultrasonic, magnetic, penetrant and Eddy current testing equipment.
  X-Ray and Gamma-ray radiography equipment.
  Wall thickness measurement equipment.
  Nuclear reactor control instruments.

Radiation measuring instruments.

Nuclear fallout monitoring equipment.

Monitors for the military.

Traffic control equipment.

Traffic monitoring systems.

- **Theatres & Clubs**

336 theatres in the UK (owned or controlled by Rank), and over 500 theatres overseas.

Catering of all kinds ranging from theatre restaurants to banqueting suites.

Top Rank Bingo and Social clubs: 38 full-time bingo clubs in addition to part-time operations.

25 Top Rank Studios and Dance Clubs.

15 Top Rank coin operated laundries.

- **Top Rank Dancing and Bowling**

29 ballrooms.

18 bowling centres.

- **Top Rank Home & Leisure**

183 retail outlets selling and renting radio and televisions, and consumer durables.

Operated wired relay services to 34 towns.

- **Top Rank Motor Inns and Motorway Services**

Managed Motor Inns in UK and Ireland, with catering, petrol, and servicing facilities.

8 Top Rank Service Stations in operation.

- **Television**

Independent Television – The Rank Organisation held a 37.6 per-cent interest in Southern Television Ltd

Pay-TV – developing and promoting the Choiceview system in partnership with Rediffusion Ltd (since 1961).

- **Rank Taylor Hobson And Kershaw**

Developed Varotal television zoom, Ortal, Kinetal, Ental and Vidital lenses.

Aerial reconnaissance lenses.

Intro periscopes.

Periscopes for armoured fighting vehicles.

Peri-binoculars.

Prism paralleloscopes.

Radar telescopes.

Sights for artillery.

Pantograph engraving machines.

Cutter grinders.

Portable X-ray units.

Ward X-ray units.

X-ray tables.

Protective aprons.

X-ray tubes.

Radiographic accessories, darkroom equipment.

Electro-cardiographs and accessories.

Electro-medical apparatus, diagnostic and therapeutic.

'Talyrond' engineers' roundness measuring instrument.

'Talysurf' surface finish measuring instrument.

'Talymin' comparator gauges.

Micro-alignment telescopes.

'Talyden' workshop microscopes.

'Talyvel' electronic level.

- **Data Systems**
  Marketed and manufactured the Xeronic High Speed Computer Output printer.
- **Rank Research Laboratories**
  Fundamental research for all divisions of The Rank Organisation and sponsored research for outside companies.
- **Xerography**
  Manufactured Xerox 914 and 813 office copiers.
  Copyflo continuous printer.
  University micro-films.
  Xerography equipment for high speed copying.

The epics continue

At Pinewood, 1965 kicked off with epics from Terence Young returning to the Bond fold for the fourth 007 adventure, *Thunderball*. Meanwhile, Basil

Dearden directed Charlton Heston, Laurence Olivier, and Ralph Richardson in *Khartoum*. 'That wasn't my first time at Pinewood,' said Heston, 'because we stopped off there for costume fittings on *Ben-Hur*, and I thought it a wonderful place then. And in my opinion the restaurant was (and still is) the best of any film studio in the world!

'I had a wonderful new Jaguar at the time of *Khartoum* and used to drive myself into the studio. I'll forever remember pulling into my space on one of the first few days, and seeing the great Ralph Richardson pull up in a new Bentley. We hadn't met at this point, so as I was pondering whether or not to go over. I saw him close the door ever so gently, pat the car on the roof and say, "Farewell old dear," before trotting off to the stage. I'll never forget that moment!'

Meanwhile, John Mills made his directorial début with *Sky West and Crooked*, which starred Hayley Mills and Ian McShane. 'I took the book to Arthur [Rank] and he agreed to the film on the strength of that alone,' claims Sir John. 'I was very close to Arthur and he was a great personal friend of Mary [Lady Mills] and I. Making the film was an interesting experience and working with Hayley was sheer joy – she's such a perfectionist. The arguments started, though, when the Rank Organisation wanted the title Sky West and Crooked; the story was called Bats With Baby Faces and I couldn't understand what Sky West and Crooked meant. Anyway, that's the title they insisted on. I rather thought I'd stick to acting thereafter – it's much easier!'

Birthday

The studio's 30th birthday was celebrated in 1966, and a publicity brochure of the time proudly proclaimed that 'There are 1,300 people at Pinewood.' Busy times indeed. Work started on two more new stages, to become known as J and K, which were particularly important additions as they provided facilities for both television and feature production. Kip Herren, managing director at the time, explained the evolution of the stages in an article written at the time of the 30th Anniversary. 'We have toured Europe both in front of and behind the Iron Curtain to look at new methods not only of shooting, but even of the initial construction of studios of the future. We have evolved, with our technical friends, stages which will have a completely dual role; stages in which we can continue feature production and also take our place as television film series producers.'

The stages were designed to 'have a carefully landscaped setting in the green acres of the Rank Film Production Division, so that they will skilfully blend in with the current studios and surrounding countryside' and to be the most modern in Europe. However, there was one major difference between film and TV stages of the day – the floors. Kip Herren continued: 'When it came to the problem of the floor of the stages it proved a very tough nut indeed. It is simple to provide a floor for television to allow free rein to their equipment. The floor for feature production is traditionally wood, and the heavy set construction requires braces nailed to the floor. Nails damage the smooth surfaces required for television type mobility. The staff involved in Pinewood came up with many ideas after a great deal of hard work and research, and we think we can combine the benefits of both systems in one type of floor surface.'

The design incorporated the traditional wooden 'feature' floors but underneath lay wonderfully smooth TV production floors which could be accessed very easily. TV productions which took advantage of the new facility later in the year included The David Niven Story and Man in a Suitcase. The design was adhered to again with the construction of L and M Stages later in the decade.

Other new buildings included an engineering workshop, vehicle maintenance workshops, an extension to the stills department and a new central canteen for the staff. John Davis described Pinewood as 'the finest and most forward-looking studios anywhere. And by enabling television and feature production to share both studios and technicians, they will be more fully employed and offer the best opportunities for modern and economic production.'

Award

In April 1966 the Prime Minister announced The Queen's Award For Industry had been bestowed upon the Rank Organisation, in recognition of the export achievement of Rank Xerox Ltd, and the Rank Taylor Hobson's technological advancements. It was noted RTH was the biggest British exporter of optical goods. The presentation took place on July 18.

Whilst its true the Rank Organisation achieved substantial increases in sales, exports and profits, John Davis reported he was, 'Disappointed that even better results were not realised, largely due to circumstances beyond our control. The unsatisfactory conditions prevailing in television and radio manufacturing industries are well known and this factor has slowed down the recovery of our Bush Murphy Division. The pressure on margins in relation to steadily increasing costs is a common factor to all businesses and so far the efforts of the Prices and Incomes Board appear to have been to restrict prices. The added burden of the Selective Employment Tax which bears unfavourably on a large section of our activities will add to these problems as from September 1966.'

But he stated management was well geared to meet the various difficulties as they arose.

The Pennine Hotel in Derby was officially opened by the Mayor of the city and marked the fifth city-centre hotel to be opened by The Rank Organisation in 1966.

On another more positive note, and following developing interests in the educational field, such as the 'learning to read by machine', the latest Bell and Howell Language Master equipment as marketed by Rank Audio Visual, Rank announced it would provide funds for the establishment of Chairs at Universities. Specifically for the 'furtherance of education in fields related to our activities', with the result they endowed Chairs for: Catering at the University of Strathclyde, and the University of Surrey (in the course of formation) and Audio Visual Education at the University of Sussex, plus University of Reading in a Chair of Applied Optics.

Chaplin & 007 (unofficial)

Meanwhile, over at Pinewood Studios, the great star of silent cinema, Charlie Chaplin, unexpectedly returned to features with *A Countess From Hong Kong*, which he wrote, directed, and composed the music for. It was an unmitigated disaster. Marlon Brando starred with Sophia Loren but could do little to help save the film that Chaplin was so passionate about making. When asked why he agreed to appear in it, he replied 'How could you not want to work with Chaplin?' It turned out to be Chaplin's last film and

a very uncomfortable and tiring experience for the artists involved, mainly due to the fact that their director insisted on playing every part in rehearsal to show how he wanted them to perform.

Casino Royale was the first of Ian Fleming's Bond novels. The screen rights had been sold at an early stage and thus were not controlled by Broccoli and Saltzman's Eon Productions. The rights ultimately found their way to producer Charles K Feldman at what was the height of Bondmania. Realising that he couldn't emulate Eon's success without Sean Connery, Feldman opted to make a spoof Bond film instead.

'Oh God!' said the film's production accountant, John Collingwood, at the mention of *Casino Royale*. 'You know, I've been involved in hundreds of films in my career and that was the only one ever to go over-budget – but with five directors, three studios and a cast that multiplied daily, it was hardly surprising.'

The production sprawled across several studios, including Pinewood: there were so many sets spread over such a long shoot that no one studio could cope. 'I

2.60 Rank Screen Advertising

2.61 Taylor Hobson invented the world's first roundness measuring instrument, the Talyrond 1

remember being at MGM, Shepperton, Elstree and Pinewood,' added Val Guest, one of the film's directors. "We were all over the place! It's difficult to remember what was done where really, but I'm sure I did some of the casino scenes at Pinewood. That film is a book in itself!'

'I went on to *Casino Royale* and stayed for 11 months,' said publicist John Willis. 'I'd only usually be on a picture for three or four months. We shot most of the John Huston parts at Pinewood – it was quite crazy! Feldman would phone and say, "I've got William Holden for a couple of days next week" and we'd have to change everything – and write new scenes – to bring him in. The script was rewritten almost every day. It didn't matter that a part might not make sense, we just had people who were in town. The publicity side was actually terrific fun because it centred around who was James Bond – was it Woody Allen, Terence Cooper, David Niven? etc – and that was marvellous for someone like me.'

The cast list was indeed a veritable Who's Who. In addition to the above-mentioned were Ursula Andress, Jacqueline Bisset, Charles Boyer, John Huston, Deborah Kerr, Derek Nimmo, Peter Sellers, Peter O'Toole, George Raft, Orson Welles … The list goes on. The five credited directors were Val Guest, Ken Hughes, John Huston, Robert Parrish, and Joe McGrath. The film's saving grace was the superb score by Burt Bacharach, which included the Oscar-nominated 'The Look of Love' performed by Dusty Springfield. Although the film was a box-office success, it came nowhere near to rivalling the business generated by Eon's continuing series. The film rights to *Casino Royale* were eventually transferred to MGM/UA (Eon's distributor) as part of the resolution of a lawsuit with Sony Pictures in February 1999, and in 2006 a new version – launching Daniel Craig's tenure as 007 – was produced.

Chitty

Producer Albert R 'Cubby' Broccoli – fresh from making *You Only Twice* – arrived with another of Ian Fleming's stories. Only this was a children's story: *Chitty Chitty Bang Bang*. Fleming wrote this tale of a phantasmagorical flying car with magical powers while in hospital recuperating from a heart attack. Dick Van Dyke, Sally Ann Howes, Gert Fröbe and Lionel

2.62 Rank Hotel publicity

Jeffries starred, while Irwin Kostal's music was complimented by songs from the Sherman Brothers. The title song, in fact, gained an Academy Award nomination.

Production designer Ken Adam came up with some interesting ideas, not least for the car itself. 'When we had to design the airship for the

BUILDING FOR THE FUTURE – TODAY'S CINEMA

The cinema screen will always be a world of wonder for millions of people. But how does the cinema itself look? New film techniques are evolved in a matter of months. New themes produced almost overnight to satisfy changing public tastes. Can bricks and mortar keep pace?

One look at the Rank cinemas tells you that they not only reflect the spirit of our own age, but also look forward to exciting developments in the years to come. And at the heart of these forward looking designs and decor, there lies the advanced equipment that can meet all conceivable needs for many years ahead. This is the Rank cinema of the 60's—a cinema designed and equipped to satisfy millions of people—and to keep them satisfied.

ODEON MERRION CENTRE, LEEDS

ODEON LEICESTER – AUDITORIUM

ODEON PRESTON – FOYER

GAUMONT BIRMINGHAM – AUDITORIUM

THE RANK ORGANISATION— THEATRE DIVISION

11 BELGRAVE ROAD, LONDON, S.W.1 – TELEPHONE VICtoria 6633

2.63 Rank Theatres publicity

Baron – the Gert Fröbe character – I was quite prepared to design a model which in those days would have cost about £6,000. However, two gentlemen walked into my office – they were balloonists – and they said that they wanted to build us a full-sized airship. I said, 'You're joking,' but they came up with some designs and an estimate for about £9,000 – so it wasn't

2.64 Rank Taylor Hobson innovated in all areas, including teaching aids

that much more than the model. United Artists and Cubby said that they should go ahead. What we didn't realise, however, was that my original design was based on a French airship – one that never flew! The balloonists were a little nervous about using the engine and one day they crashed into some power lines while on a test flight and cut off all the electricity in the Hampshire countryside. The farmers were most irate as they couldn't milk their cows and so threatened to sue United Artists!

'It was almost like a period Bond film in many ways because we had so many gadgets. I designed the car, and we built a complete mock-up, which we kept changing, and I found that the period car concept wasn't as easy as I thought it would be. There were in fact five cars built, by the same people who built the Ford GT, and Cubby had done a deal with Ford to supply the power unit. Other people were called in to build the body, and each car had a specific purpose: for flying sequences, water scenes and ordinary road use. They worked very well.'

2.65 *Can't come to us? We'll come to you! Rank-Xerox on the road.*

2.66 *The Odeon Cinema, Marble Arch, London*

2.67 A Top Rank Skating Rink

'Chitty Chitty Bang Bang is my favourite picture,' recalled Lionel Jeffries, 'mainly due to the director Ken Hughes. He was great fun and had the secret of making good movies – that was to tell the story and make sure there were no tensions on the floor: I don't remember anyone's voice ever being raised. It was a tough shoot though and wasn't helped by Dick Van Dyke deciding not to turn up sometimes. In fact, at one point, we all sat on the backlot for two solid weeks as he'd disappeared, and we'd run out of things to shoot around him! We found out later that he'd gone to live on the Thames embankment for a week and grown a beard, and the following

2.68 The 'other' Bond(s) in, Casino Royale

2.69 Orson Welles and Peter Sellers in one of the few scenes they appeared in together after Sellers took against him

week he'd gone off to Hollywood to be with Mary Tyler Moore. Meanwhile, the rest of us played darts in our caravans!'

Trading

Despite being awarded their second Queen's Award to Industry in April 1967 – in recognition of the export achievement of Rank Taylor Hobson Division with year-on-year export sales increasing by 36per-cent – John Davis reported 1967 had been a 'rough year from a trading point of view'.

Government financial and economic policies were to blame. The Six-day war raised the cost of petrol and the UK had to spend more on imports and the UK government of Harold Wilson devalued the Pound from $2.80 to $2.40 (14 per-cent), because of a trade deficit, a weak domestic economy and

2.70 Ian Fleming's other literary creation, also turned into a film by Albert R Broccoli – Chitty Chitty Bang Bang

external pressures from creditors. The year witnessed a rise in unemployment from 280,000 to 540,000 and marked a year of lower global economic growth.

However, Davis reported an improvement in turnover and profits as a result of the 'continued spectacular advance of Rank Xerox [and] our manufacturing activities in Rank Taylor Hobson'. Rank's other businesses – mainly in the leisure sector – were amongst the hardest hit prompting him to say, '…all divisions will be reviewed with this in mind'.

He continued, 'I would comment on the effect of Government policy on our Hotel operation. We would not expect that all our leisure activities should be shielded, and indeed the Cinema, Bowling and Dancing and also Television Production, Hire Purchase and Rental all suffered from the severe credit restrictions imposed last year, but we cannot understand the Government's attitude towards hotels. The hotel industry can clearly be an important contributor to rectifying the Country's present balance of payments problems by attracting overseas visitors, but it seems obvious that this fact has not been recognised by the Government.'

In fact, for the second year running, the Rank Hotels operation incurred a substantial loss and in an attempt to streamline running costs the activities of the Hotel Division and the Dancing and Bowling Division were merged under the new title of 'Leisure Services Division'.

The Bridgford Hotel, Nottingham, was the latest Rank hotel to open providing first-class accommodation for 177 Guests – and some feared it would be the last new hotel Rank would open for some time. Though The Royal Lancaster, The Rank Organisation's seventeenth and largest hotel and its first in London, was already under construction and made its debut on the British travel trade scene with a special presentation for leading representatives of the British Travel Association on August 1, 1967.

Meanwhile the Tenpin Bowling division had been 'aggravated' by the general economic conditions and resulted in it making a loss. Whilst its Ice Rink in Brighton opened during October 1966 and had proven successful from the day of opening, it prompted Rank to carry out a modernisation scheme at its only other venue, the Southampton ice rink.

It's Ballrooms now consisted of 13 suites and nine ballrooms with a further four opened in 1967 – and ending what was described as the current expansion programme.

Hammer

In spring 1968, director Freddie Francis returned to Pinewood to helm a horror film for Hammer, the company's first full-length shoot at the studio. *Dracula Has Risen From the Grave* was the third incarnation of Christopher Lee's red-eyed vampire and a proud moment for Hammer: during filming the company was presented with the Queen's Award to Industry on the steps of Pinewood's Castle Dracula.

Guy Hamilton, meanwhile, directed *Battle of Britain* for producer Harry Saltzman. Laurence Olivier, Robert Shaw, Michael Caine, Christopher Plummer, and Susannah York headed a star-packed retelling of the famous wartime air battle. The real stars, however, were the historic aeroplanes – Spitfires, Hurricanes, Spanish built Heinkel bombers and Me109 fighters, and an American Mitchell bomber as camera ship. 'My lingering memory of that film,' unit publicist John Willis pointed out, 'was seeing literally scores of fibreglass Spitfires pouring out of the workshops at Pinewood. They were all sent down to the airfields and it's amazing to think that only a few of the planes you see on the fields were actually real!'

Little Red Book

One of the last films to shoot in 1968 also proved one of the most controversial: J Lee Thompson's *The Most Dangerous Man in the World*, in which Gregory Peck played an American scientist, recruited by Western intelligence, to go into China and meet Chairman Mao, with a bomb secretly implanted in his head. 'It was probably my biggest film at Pinewood,' said Thompson, 'and was quite a unique story; the idea of an implant was very novel. Greg Peck was very keen on the storyline and was an absolute joy to work with. I think it was his third picture at the studio. We did all of the interiors there, but locations were mainly in Wales and Hong Kong.'

On November 28, the Daily Express reported that 'Chairman Mao let it be known yesterday that he is very definitely not thinking beautiful

2.71 Gregory Peck during production of The Chairman

thoughts about his début as a ping-pong playing decadent Western film star. An official Communist China newspaper warned that if anybody tried to take shots for the film in Hong Kong there would be "grave conse-quences". But last night the film company and Gregory Peck were airborne and on their way. Chairman Mao was being "attacked" and the film was highly "anti China" said the Wen Wei Pai editorial.'

Twentieth Century-Fox's Arthur P Jacobs said in response: 'We sent a script to the Hong Kong government and had their, and police, approval. There are shots we must have and are going ahead to get them. There are plenty of opportunities for the Chairman to express pro-Chinese views. It is a thriller – not political at all.'

Hong Kong was a free port at the time, without restrictions on the import of film or cameras, so the Hong Kong government vowed not to interfere.

Having overcome those problems, however, there were difficulties back at Pinewood in recruiting the many Chinese extras required. Some sequences in the 'House of Exotic Pleasure' called for clusters of nude Chinese girls, but very few of those gathered were prepared to strip off. On top of all that, cinematographer Ted Moore had to be replaced towards the end of shooting by John Wilcox, after one of the large studio lamps hit Moore on the head, rendering him unconscious.

Cinema downturn

1968 saw Rank report a net increase in profit of £3.3 million after tax, from which £1.4 million came from non-Rank Xerox activities.

There was also substantial publicity generated when Rank sought to acquire Cambridge Instrument Company Limited as part of a planned expansion of Rank-Taylor-Hobson activities. After approaching the Cambridge board, and making two offers, Rank's overtures were rejected flat. This was on the back of the Queen's Award For Industry being bestowed for an impressive third consecutive year.

In a more quirky press story, the question was asked: 'How far and how fast is the Tower of Pisa leaning over?' The answer was soon to be discovered after investigations by the Taylor Hobson Division, who have installed precision measuring equipment in the Tower at the request of the Italian authorities! [It was 5.5 degrees!]

Meanwhile, John Davis sounded a sombre note about film production.

'The Rank Organisation has been since its formation, and still is, vitally interested in the Film Industry. Our interest is not only for historic reasons, but because we have a very substantial investment in the Industry.

'We still believe, and in my view have shown by our actions our belief, that the cinema is the best and most satisfying entertainment for the mass audience. In our further reappraisal of our activities we reluctantly came to the conclusion that under present conditions, after taking into account the markets available to us, we had materially to curtail our film production programme. Whilst this decision is not reflected in the accounts under review, it will become noticeable in the year ahead.'

Domestic film distribution was on the downturn with a significant number of cinemas having closed – 1,739 were open in 1968 as opposed to 2,047 in 1963.

'[We need to] continue to adjust our distribution organisation so that we can efficiently service the reduced market. This we have done,' added Davis, 'and I am pleased to report that we have negotiated a further five-year agreement with our friends at Universal Pictures, for the distribution of their films in this country. This extends a happy and successful relationship which has existed for over 30 years.'

Modernising remaining cinemas was seen as apriority to hold on to, and attract new, audiences.

'We are spending in excess of £2 million per annum. During 1966/67 we modernised ten theatres and built three new ones. In 1967/68 the programme was accelerated, resulting in thirteen theatres being modernised and two new ones built. We are currently committed to seven 'twinning' schemes (transforming a single theatre into two), seven major modernisations, one new theatre, and three new theatres replacing old theatres,' added Davis.

Butlins

Also, in 1968, holiday camp entrepreneur Billy Butlin appointed his son Bobby to take over the management of Butlins. Four years later, in 1972, the business was sold to the Rank Organisation for £43 million. The number of camps peaked at ten between 1966 and 1980, but the business experienced the problems that were being faced by the British seaside holiday industry at large, with the introduction of cheap package holidays to Mediterranean resorts from the 1960s onwards. It also had a specific image problem of being seen as providing regimented holidays, which caused it to all but abandon the Butlins name at its remaining resorts between 1987 and 1990.

Elementary

Meanwhile in 1969 director Billy Wilder arrived at Pinewood to shoot *The Private Life of Sherlock Holmes*. He cast Robert Stephens as the consulting

2.72 Baker Street was recreated on the Pinewood backlot for The Private Life of Sherlock Holmes and remained for many years afterwards, used in other films particularly the Carry Ons

detective, Colin Blakely as his faithful chronicler Dr Watson and Christopher Lee as Holmes' mysterious brother Mycroft. It was a very personal project for Wilder and proved to be a very ambitious and elaborate undertaking.

The troubles on the shoot grew in scale as it progressed, with filming suspended at one point when Stephens was suddenly taken ill. An impressive Baker Street set was built on the backlot, costing around £80,000 to construct. No expense was spared, according to production runner Gordon Thomsen. 'All the cobbles on that street were real cobbles. They found a street somewhere in the north of England, which was being demolished, a real cobbled street, and they brought down lorry-loads of cobbles and actually laid them one by one on the set. Each one of those houses had real cellars too. It was dug out so you could walk downstairs below street level. The sash windows weren't made out of cheap wood, they were all proper windows. There were some tremendously good quality materials used in the set building. In fact, I remember one person in the art department saying that Alex Trauner, the production designer, was the last of the Vincent Kordas.'

In fact, Trauner earned the disapproval of some crew members over his extravagant set designs, which were causing practical problems while filming. The director of photography, Christopher Challis, had some arguments with Trauner and later called the designer a 'builder of houses, not sets' who 'didn't know what was required for front projection.'

And Trauner's elaborate and expensive ideas were not confined to the Baker Street set. 'One of the biggest sets was the Diogenes Club,' said Thomsen. 'That was built on E Stage in the north tunnel. It was built for just one shot where they go to see Mycroft Holmes. It was all one composite set on E Stage, but to get extra length they built out into the old projection tunnel, which was left over from the days of Independent Frame. It seemed to take weeks and weeks to build it, just for one walk-through shot!'

Over schedule and over budget, the movie performed badly at the box-office and has since become notorious for the many scenes that United Artists executives demanded cut. The Baker Street set, however, remained a feature of Pinewood's lot for several years (ingeniously recycled in *Carry On At Your Convenience* for example), before being struck after severe flooding in 1973.

Next, Val Guest jetted back to the studio with the barely seen Olivia Newton-John vehicle, *Toomorrow*. 'Aaggh! That was an awful experience!' Guest groaned. 'Nobody ever got paid! Harry Saltzman was behind it, and we later discovered that he put up his interests in the Bond films as security on the finance. But he came a cropper with it. He did the same with other projects, and then with his purchase of Technicolor ... That last one went a bit too far, and it led to him and Cubby parting company.'

End Of Decade

1969 saw record net-profits for The Rank Organisation of £11,258,000 – an increase of 30 per-cent over the previous year.

Profits from Rank Xerox had increased 50 per-cent.

The most important development of the past year was the establishment of the Scientific Instrument Division when Rank-Taylor-Hobson merged with the Hilger & Watts Group (acquired in July, 1968). Also absorbed into the new division were Rank Bush Murphy and Rank Electronic Tubes. Negotiations to acquire the Scientific Apparatus Division of G.E.C. sadly didn't materialise in a deal which would have further expanded activities.

The Audio Visual Division was augmented by the acquisition of the Strand Electric Group, H J Leak & Company Ltd and A C Vallance Ltd.

Strand was one of the largest theatre lighting contractors in the country with additional interests overseas; Leak, manufactured high quality amplifiers and other sound reproduction equipment; whilst Vallance was a leading name in Amateur Film Processing covering the Midlands and the northern home counties.

Rank employees now totalled 39,947(including 1,024 part-time) and 11,716 overseas, totalling 51,663.

~ 5 ~

Film Bust (The 1970s)

An influenza epidemic took hold in early 1970, affecting many of Rank's leisure activities – especially at a time when cinemas and clubs are normally at a peak. That coupled with, for the second year running, an exceptionally hot summer and the World Cup football series has a seriously negative impact.

Cinema admissions continued to decline. In the year to October 1970, there was a 10 per-cent reduction.

John Davis cautioned, 'Unfortunately, as I have said before, many of the films which are produced today do not contain the ingredients of entertainment which the public will pay to see as unfortunately many producers continue to ignore the disciplines of the market place, often with disastrous results.

'In my view, this is a highly dangerous situation as the Industry is creating an image with the public which, long-term, can have only a harmful effect.'

But Rank continued their policy of modernisation, re-building and converting cinemas into twin and triple screens – including the Odeon, Glasgow into a triple and Bournemouth, Bradford, Sheffield, Shepherds Bush and Southend into twins.

Tenpin Bowling also saw declined attendance and rising costs – consequently Rank decided to close the remainder of the bowling alleys operating and converted them to other uses (such as bingo)or disposed of them.

Thankfully there was better news for the hotel division which moved into profit.

2.73 One of the Rank Film Distributors acquired TV films from Universal, directed by a young Steven Spielberg

Meanwhile at Pinewood there was what was described as 'a slack period' until May 1970 when production started to pick up again, although the size and scale of the productions was smaller than in the previous year. The Rank Organisation financed 8 first and 6 second features during the period at a cost of £1,500,000.

'A garish glossary of sado-masochism … a taste for visual sensation that makes scene after scene look like the masturbatory fantasies of Roman Catholic boyhood,' was critic Alexander Walker's verdict on Ken Russell's *The Devils*, which shot at Pinewood and starred Vanessa Redgrave and Oliver Reed. With masturbating nuns, demonic possession, burning at the stake, sacrilegious dream sequences – not to mention an abundance of rotting skulls, rats and running sores – the film was pounced on by the Festival of Light and was one of the main 'exhibits' in the censorship controversies which marked the early 1970s. What the devout J Arthur Rank thought is unrecorded.

More and more television productions were based at the studio. There were five in 1970 including Gerry and Sylvia Anderson's *UFO* – starring Ed Bishop, George Sewell, Michael Billington and Wanda Ventham – and *The*

2.74 The Persuaders! with stars Roger Moore and Tony Curtis flanking producer Lord Lew Grade

Persuaders! with Tony Curtis and Roger Moore. 'What you must remember about Pinewood,' said Robert Baker, creator, and producer of *The Persuaders!* 'is that as well as being a first-class facility, there are also some wonderful locations right on the doorstep. We used Black Park [which backs on to the lot] to double for everything from Red China to the south of

France and grand country estates back in England. Apart from the necessary establishing shots we hardly left the locale and used areas around the studio extensively – particularly the house and gardens.'

Rank Film Distributors also did a deal with Universal Television around this time. Universal made a series of TV 'movies of the week' – a format the studio pioneered and steadily refined for the NBC network – running between 75 and 90 minutes, with budgets of under $500,000. Rank bought the UK rights to release the films theatrically. One of the most notable was Steven Spielberg's debut, *Duel*, which actually had some added scenes specifically for the theatrical version to lengthen its running time. Generally, the films had one name, such as Olivia de Havilland, Lorne Green, Robert Culp, Sandra Dee and Stewart Granger. RFD picked up the titles pretty inexpensively, reducing financial risk, whilst having product to feed their cinema chains.

Meanwhile RFD also picked up UK rights on director Alfred Hitchcock's return to the UK, and in particular Pinewood, in 1971. *Frenzy* starring Alec McCowen, Jon Finch and Barry Foster was the brutal story of a man framed for rape and murder. The 34 years since *Young and Innocent* was made at Pinewood had seen Hitchcock achieve incredible success in Hollywood with such movies as *Vertigo, Psycho* and *The Birds*. Understandably, his return to British shores was met with excitement and great anticipation, especially given the top-notch cast and the superior script by Anthony Shaffer, adapted from Arthur La Bern's novel *Goodbye Piccadilly, Farewell Leicester Square*. But *Frenzy* met with mixed critical reactions and still makes for uncomfortable viewing today.

In 1971 plans for a high-end luxury hotel in London's West End were underway when The Rank Organisation purchased Hope House at 116 Piccadilly, overlooking Green Park, with it by then having been converted into an art deco apartment block known as The Athenaeum. After a two-year refurbishment, and with Rank's PR machine swinging into action, the five-star hotel attracted a huge number of guests from the showbiz world, including Elizabeth Taylor, Joan Collins, Marlon Brando, Harrison Ford, Lauren Bacall, Liza Minnelli, Warren Beatty, Charlton Heston and Steven Spielberg amongst them. Rank encouraged stars filming at Pinewood to take up residence and The Hollywood Reporter trade newspaper said 'there were more movie stars to be seen in London's Athenaeum than in the Polo Lounge of the Beverly Hills Hotel'.

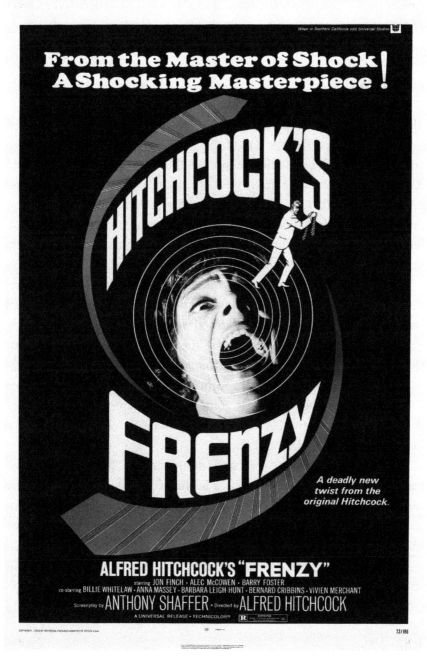

2.75 Hitchcock's return to Pinewood came with Frenzy

Also, in 1971, Rank's formidable John Davis was Knighted by the Queen in her birthday honours list, becoming Sir John Davis.

Lord Rank

The following year was marred with the news of Lord J Arthur Rank's death.

On March 29, 1972, the day of the Rank Organisation's AGM, it was announced that flour and film mogul J Arthur Rank had died. He was 83. Although he had said he didn't want a memorial service, the demand for one was so great that the family organised one at Westminster Central Hall on April 24. Lords, ladies, politicians, staff from all divisions of his many business empires, and senior Methodist Church officials were among the many who gathered to pay homage to the great businessman and visionary.

Like his father, he was as canny in death as he was in life. Fifty-three per-cent of the original shareholdings of Lord Rank and the late Lady Rank (who passed away in 1971), was transferred to Rank Group Holdings Limited – which was ultimately owned by The Rank Foundation Limited and the Trustees of the J. Arthur Rank Group Charity.

The Rank Organisation itself was in a healthy state, the flour business Rank Hovis MacDougal Ltd was going from strength to strength, as was the Lord Rank Research Centre at High Wycombe to which, just before his death, he had donated £1 million.

John Davis wrote in the company's annual report: 'It was my good fortune to know Arthur Rank, both as a business colleague and friend, spanning nearly forty years; my relationship with him was both an inspiration and a source of great personal privilege. We have lost the wisdom, friendship and advice of a great and unusual man.'

J Arthur Rank's legacy lived on through his philanthropic work – and still does so today.

Board Room

In June 1972 The Rank Organisation withdrew a takeover bid of £425 million for Watney Mann, a multinational brewing distilling and pub group. It

2.76/2.77 Comedy-horror The House in Nightmare Park

2.76/2.77 Comedy-horror The House in Nightmare Park

was the largest bid ever made in the UK and Sir John Davis made it clear in a statement that stockholders' revolt was behind the withdrawal.

'We have taken carefully into account the opinions expressed both to us and publicly by many of our shareholders, and in view of the lack of support and, indeed, opposition to our offer, we have decided it would not be right to continue.'

Though the majority of voting shares were actually controlled by The Rank Foundation established by the late Lord Rank, who felt uneasy about the move – one which they felt overvalued the company – and the increasingly autocratic style of Davis, after Lord Rank's death.

Sleuthing

Pinewood remained very busy. The first production of 1972 was *Sleuth*, with Laurence Olivier and Michael Caine delivering extraordinary,

Oscar-nominated performances in Anthony Shaffer's cat-and-mouse mystery thriller. Director Joseph Mankiewicz and composer John Addison also received nominations.

'We had to make the film in a studio,' says production designer Ken Adam. 'We couldn't have done it any other way. We went all over England looking at stately homes, but the geography of the required set was so intimate that we could never have found it – it had to be a set. The whole ground floor of the house was built in one of the wonderful big stages – the cellar and some of the bedrooms were on different stages – and I remember when the director Joseph Mankiewicz arrived to shoot, he said, "Ken you have to allow me two days to live in the set, and I don't want anyone around – just a propman in case I want to change anything around. After that, I'll be ready to shoot." And he was!'

Fifties sex goddess and blonde bombshell Diana Dors returned to Pinewood for two of the year's productions. *Nothing But the Night* starred Christopher Lee and Peter Cushing and was the one-and-only production from Lee's company Charlemagne. Dors stayed on afterwards for Lionel Jeffries' *The Amazing Mr Blunden* with Laurence Naismith and James Villiers, which was adapted by Jeffries himself from Antonia Barber's novel The Ghosts. 'We nearly set fire to the admin block on that picture,' observed Jeffries, 'as we double-cladded the back of the building, to tie in with the period, which the management weren't too keen on, and it caught fire! Thankfully, it was brought under control in time.'

Comedy remained a staple ingredient of Pinewood's output – the *Carry Ons* continued and the big screen treatment was given to TV's popular Hylda Baker vehicle *Nearest and Dearest* and the Jewish sweat-shop hit *Never Mind the Quality, Feel the Width*. 'We used the Baker Street set on that film for one of our main streets,' remembered producer Martin Cahill, 'but dressed it up and modernised it with pubs and bookmakers etc. A wonderful panning shot of the street was going to be used to play the titles and credits over, but when we ran the sequence in rushes, I felt it was a little too short, as it didn't quite extend the full length of the street as I imagined it would. The editor and cameraman told me not to worry, they'd fix it. That was the last I saw of it until the film was completed. The buggers had indeed shot a longer sequence, ending up at the bookmakers. My credit appeared as that shop came into frame, and to my horror I saw the shop front announcing 'Cahill Bookmakers'. They had it planned right from the start!'

Screaming

Still with comedy, Frankie Howerd's return to Pinewood came with *The House in Nightmare Park*, which co-starred Ray Milland, Hugh Burden and Kenneth Griffith. Set in 1907, Howerd plays Foster Twelvetrees, a struggling actor engaged for a private performance in a sinister country house. Again, extensive use was made of Black Park while the house itself was the famous Oakley Court next to Bray Studios, immortalised in numerous Hammer horror films and now a luxury hotel.

'I was executive producer on the film,' said Beryl Vertue, 'as well as being agent for both Terry Nation [the writer-producer] and Frankie himself, so I earned my fee plus 10 per-cent of theirs. It was very much written with Frankie in mind and he was a real attraction for the other artistes, especially Ray Milland! We didn't have a tremendous amount of money, so Pinewood became everything and everywhere, and what we couldn't do at the studio we did in the near vicinity.'

Teddy Francis was production supervisor on the film and vividly recalls the final sequence, in which Howerd is seen digging up a meadow in search of buried treasure. 'We used Langley Park [adjacent to Black Park, but minus the trees], and had use of a helicopter to achieve the effect of pulling away and revealing just how vast the meadow was. We cleared things with Heathrow, and all was set. However, Frankie came over to me, looking quite worried. "Teddy," he said, "nobody knows this, but I wear a toupée." Well, everybody knew that the damn nest on his head was a wig, but he sincerely believed he'd succeeded in keeping it a secret. Anyway, rather than upset him, I feigned ignorance. "I'm a bit concerned about this helicopter," he continued. "It'll be going up and down, in and out, and creating a fair bit of wind." "Yes…" I said. "Well, my toupée might blow off." By now I was biting my tongue, and my young son and his friends, who were watching the shooting that day, were in hysterics. But we arranged things so that the helicopter took off downwind, limiting the "effects" around Frankie.

Secretly, though, we were all hoping his piece would blow off and even taking bets on it!'

New arrangements

Rank Film Distributors' deal to handle Universal Studios' releases terminated on December 3, 1972, (but they continued to distribute all pictures delivered until 3rd June 1973). Meanwhile it was announced a merger of RFD's UK operation with Twentieth Century Fox, effective in December 1972. The new jointly-owned company entitled Fox-Rank Distributors Limited, would handle the distribution of films made by the two companies.

In a further acquisition move, Rank agreed to buy Oddenino's Property and Investment Co. Ltd on April 13, 1973. The company owned five hotels in the United Kingdom, two in Europe along with a number of uncompleted property developments in the United Kingdom, Canada and the USA and in Australia through a 50per-cent-owned associated company.

TV

Into 1973 at Pinewood, and television continued to play an increasingly important role, the studio playing host to Peter Hunt's *Gulliver's Travels*, in which Richard Harris shared the screen with cartoon Lilliputians; *Applause*, which teamed American stars Lauren Bacall and Larry Hagman; the ambitious *QB VII*, directed by Tom Gries with an all-star cast including Anthony Hopkins, Ben Gazzara, Leslie Caron, Anthony Quayle and Lee Remick; *Frankenstein: The True Story*, an epic reinterpretation of the horror classic by Christopher Isherwood which played theatrically in the UK, and *The Zoo Gang* series with John Mills, Lilli Palmer, Brian Keith and Barry Morse.

Gatsby

Jack Clayton, meanwhile, was busy preparing *The Great Gatsby*, starring Robert Redford and (substituting for Farrah Fawcett) Mia Farrow. With

location shooting in Newport Rhode Island completed, the unit moved to
Pinewood on July 20 for interior sequences. The film had been two years in
preparation and Vogue said the movie 'caused the greatest pre-production
excitement since *Gone With the Wind*.'

Sets created at Pinewood by the Oscar-laden production designer John
Box included Myrtle's Riverside Drive, her room over the top of her husband's garage, Gatsby's study and bedroom, the interior of the Buchanan
home, and Gatsby's cabana and pool – which survives to this day, aptly
dubbed 'The Gatsby Suite'. Attention to detail was minute. A wealth of
documents on clothing, furniture, homes, hair styles and jewellery to help
create the 'Gatsby look' had been accumulated over the two-year preparation period. The most publicised item was a collection of Cartier jewellery
valued at $900,000.

Ten weeks of studio work were completed in October 1973, although the
producers were keen that it shouldn't be apparent that a British studio had
been utilised for this very American story, hence the omission of the usual
'Made at Pinewood Studios' credit. The film was not well received ('pays
its creator the regrettable tribute of erecting a mausoleum over his work',
was one choice response), but Nelson Riddle won an Academy Award for
his score.

Losses

John Davis reported the company's profits in 1974 showed a significant
down-turn from £34,116,000 the year prior to £31,153,000. Much of the
loss was blamed on the Hotels Division and in less demand for Television
and Hi-Fi equipment.

With falling attendance numbers at Odeon sites in Northern Ireland,
plus 'the troubles', causing business uncertainty, Rank accepted an offer of
£467,000 to purchase the company by a group of local investors.

Over at Pinewood, Freddie Francis kicked off 1974 with *The Ghoul*, a
1920s-set shocker starring Peter Cushing, John Hurt and Alexandra Bastedo
which picked up some of the properties left behind by Gatsby. Francis followed a few months later with *The Legend of the Werewolf*, again with Peter
Cushing. 'I'd made a very successful horror film for Hammer', said Francis,

2.78 Gold – star Roger Moore talks with director Peter Hunt

referring to *Dracula Has Risen From the Grave*, 'and after that all the films I directed were horror! They weren't necessarily brilliant films, but the finished pictures always transcended the script. And that I remain very proud of. Peter Cushing was an absolute joy to work with – such a gentleman. I'll forever remember that I used to meet him at a lovely little tearoom in Charing Cross to talk about the films, and they were often quite gory subjects. Such civilised surroundings for such horrific talk!'

It was a particularly busy year for Roger Moore too. Peter Hunt directed Moore and Susannah York in *Gold*, based on the novel *Goldmine* by Wilbur Smith. Ray Milland, Bradford Dillman and John Gielgud lent support in this spectacular action-thriller with heart-stopping underground sequences. Moore then did a quick change into his tuxedo for his second 007 outing, *The Man With the Golden Gun*, before once again starring with Susannah York, this time in *That Lucky Touch*, a romantic comedy set in Belgium.

Michael Tuchner directed *Mister Quilp*, a musical adaptation of The Old Curiosity Shop that brought Anthony Newley back to Pinewood with a Dickens classic 27 years after Oliver Twist, while Norman Jewison's choice for his next project couldn't have been more different from his previous

Pinewood film *Fiddler on the Roof.* The advertising campaign for *Rollerball* stated that 'In the not too distant future, wars will no longer exist. But there will be *Rollerball.*' A grim fantasy about major corporations controlling the world in the year 2018 and channelling the public's frustrations into a brutal spectator sport, the film starred James Caan, Ralph Richardson and Maud Adams and went straight to the top of the British box-office charts, where it remained for three weeks before being supplanted by the Robert Redford vehicle *Three Days of the Condor.*

Perhaps inspired by the physical exertion involved in *Rollerball,* the more energetic residents of the studio joined forces in forming a Pinewood football club. Modestly successful, the club became part of the Slough Saturday League and was always cheered on from the touchline by future managing director, Cyril Howard.

Lunchtime

Alan Parker meanwhile remembered his arrival at Pinewood.

'One of the things that amused us no end when we first arrived at Pinewood was Rank's "Studio Management" table in the restaurant. At this table sat Kip Herren, a huge Mr Bumble figure, whom we younger film-makers despised.' [A contentious point, incidentally, as Herren's popularity was formidable.] 'The table was turned around so that it faced the rest of us, like the "high table" in a pompous University dining hall. Anyway, we rented the restaurant for a ballroom set one Sunday when they weren't dining and had the run of the place for the whole day – the lunatics in charge of the asylum. At the end of the day's filming, a gaffer taped a very large Camembert cheese to the underside of the aforementioned table. For many weeks we could all smell it. People would give a wide berth to the top table as they looked towards the puzzled occupants, wondering why these gentlemen all ponged in such elegant surroundings!

'It was a marvellous restaurant though, and I have wonderful memories of lunching there with people in powdered wigs and crinolines, Christopher Reeve in his Superman costume with a napkin at his neck sitting at my table for a chat after lunch, and David Lean coming up and wondering "Alan, why do you keep making films in America?' He always articulated

2.79 The famous glass slipper from The Slipper and the Rose

the word "America" with such disdain, like someone describing the emanation of a leaking sewer.'

Parker's production outfit, The Alan Parker Film Company, based itself at the studio for 10 years – in one of the bungalows in the gardens, originally built as a schoolroom. 'Outside it resembled a rather ugly 1950s public lavatory,' Parker recalls, 'but inside we had wonderful views of the gardens and, most importantly, we were completely self-contained. We had, in effect, the equivalent of a bungalow at a Hollywood studio. In fact, the only one in the entire British film industry! Pinewood is a wonderful studio. It's the best studio we've ever had in the UK and hopefully will continue to be so in the future. Every time I drive through the gates, I get a tingle. I had many happy years there.'

Fairy-tale

The Slipper and the Rose was a modern re-telling of the Cinderella story, produced by Stuart Lyons and David Frost, and directed by Bryan Forbes. According to production supervisor Peter Manley, 'The picture was set up at Pinewood (after initially starting out at Shepperton) because that was the best situation and studio for a musical of this scale. When the Sherman Brothers first came over with the story outline and the music demo tracks, we spent a long time in development and preparation at the studio. The first location scenes were shot in the winter over in Austria, for about three weeks, and we then came back to Pinewood for some of the interiors, music work etc. When the weather improved, we returned to Austria for some spring sequences. It was then back to the studio and those lovely sets designed by Ray Simm. One of the largest of which was on E Stage, and you must remember the cast were wearing rather heavy period costumes, and under the intense lights it became rather hot to say the least! In fact, it became quite unbearable and we had to arrange to bring in air conditioning.'

It was a particularly memorable film for Bryan Forbes, as it was not only his one and only musical but was also the occasion, while shooting the snow sequences in the Austrian Alps, of a major health scare. Back in London, he had been told that he had multiple sclerosis. The very next day he was scheduled to shoot one of the film's musical numbers in the presence of a Royal party consisting of Her Majesty Queen Elizabeth the Queen Mother, Princess Margaret, and her children. The day went without a hitch and Forbes himself refused to accept the inevitable. He battled on and a self-administered treatment – a special diet – saw him enjoy a period of remission for decades. He continued his work on *The Slipper and the Rose* and was rewarded with the honour of the film being selected as the Royal Film Performance.

2.80 *Scandal in the boardroom – Graham Dowson was being groomed to take over from John Davis, until he dared to speak up against Rank's feared boss*

Scandal

Rank Organisation profits, after taxation, for 1975 had fallen again, to £24,438,000. Furthermore, cinema attendances were down 8.4 per-cent.

It was the least of Rank's worries though as in September a boardroom battle made headlines in the British press. Fifty-two year old Graham Dowson, a protégé of Sir John Davis and only recently installed as Chief Executive, was dismissed by Rank's board – at the instigation of Davis – and given a £100,000 golden handshake.

In a statement, the board said it was also considering the 'division of senior responsibility and plans for succession in senior posts.'

In other words, the writing was on the wall for Sir John Davis too.

But why?

Press disclosures of what became known as 'the problem' within Rank involved the marriages and girlfriends of both Dowson and Davis, as well as claims against Davis of 'one-man rule'.

It seemed one-time saviour of The Rank Organisation was now fast becoming its biggest problem and embarrassment.

2.81 John Davis put a brave face on, but knew his days at the head of the Boardroom table were numbered

Fearing Xerox sales growth would level off, Davis' attempts to diversify into other fields, including the aforementioned costly attempt to buy leading British brewery Watney Mann, hadn't produced the rewards Davis and the board had sought in the early 1970s; and it hugely frustrated Dowson who claimed Davis remained in absolute control despite supposedly relinquishing day-to-day running of the organisation to him in 1974. He'd also discovered Davis had excluded him from important meetings.

'I have been trying to get John to do things in a modern way,' Dowson said on September 18, 1975. 'I have been chief executive for eight months and I have not been allowed to do anything, so I cannot see how they [the board] should reach the conclusion that I should be dismissed.'

In fact, two weeks earlier Davis had privately told his confrontational Chief Executive to resign and warned, 'You are damaging Rank's image by being associated with a girl half your age'. Davis had seemingly been the one to tip off the press too, as Dowson claimed one of the accusations levelled at him by the tabloids was that his recent behaviour had been deemed 'erratic' and that they singled out his marriage in August 1975 to 26-year-old Denise Shurman after, only a few weeks before, announcing his engagement to a different woman — his former secretary and long-time friend Pamela Awbery.

Sensing there was more to the story the press began to investigate further – and actually discovered Sir John Davis had had five wives to date, not three as his own entry in the British Who's Who said, and that Dowson had had four, rather than the two he claimed.

Pictures of many of the men's former wives and girlfriends, plus interviews with them, started appearing daily. John Davis – then aged 68 – was also reported as living with 35-year-old Felicity Rutland, debutante of the year in 1956.

This wide public airing of the executive clash, plus the marital disclosures, aroused concern among investors about Rank's management.

John Davis announced his own future, no doubt upon the suggestion of the Board:

'I had several discussions with the late Lord Rank before he died in regard to succession after my retirement from active office. Lord Rank was concerned that the management should be continued on the lines and principles he had himself followed. I assured him that before deciding upon

2.82 Boys' own adventure At the Earth's Core came from director Kevin Connor, director of photography Alan Hume and producer John Dark

resignation from my executive duties, which I hoped to do upon reaching the age of seventy, I would fully satisfy myself as to the succession.

'It is therefore my intention to retire as Chairman at the conclusion of the Annual General Meeting in 1977. I proposed to my colleagues in April last that we should create a new office of Deputy Chairman, which was agreed. In June, I approached Mr. Harry Smith, an eminent and successful industrialist, to see if he would accept this appointment. Mr. Harry Smith will be appointed Deputy Chairman to take effect from March 30, 1976, with the understanding that he would be appointed Chairman following my retirement as Chairman in March 1977.'

Meanwhile...

Production continued over at Pinewood with renters taking space, and *At The Earth's Core* came from the producer-director team of John Dark and

2.83 The second incarnation of the 007 Stage being opened

Kevin Connor and kicked off in 1976. Peter Cushing re-teamed with the duo – their first film together had been *From Beyond the Grave* at Shepperton – and Doug McClure was cast in the first of several adventures he would make with the filmmakers at Pinewood. Based on Edgar Rice Burroughs's novel of the same name, and adapted by Milton Subotsky, the Boy's Own-style adventure takes us, appropriately enough, to the centre of the earth by means of a miraculous giant drill, or geological excavator to give it its technical title. There the intrepid explorers encounter prehistoric people and monsters. Peter Cushing's umbrella helps save the day.

'I first worked at Pinewood as a second assistant editor, on two pictures – *An Alligator Named Daisy* and *Jumping For Joy* – back in 1952,' recalled Kevin Connor, 'and, to be honest, it wasn't a particularly happy experience as the cutting rooms had a very snobbish "old boys" atmosphere and attitude. When I returned to direct my first feature at Pinewood, having moved over from Shepperton (which was being asset-stripped at the time), that atmosphere had gone; mainly, I guess, due to the fact that it wasn't just Rank product and Rank staff anymore; the renters had changed

2.84 The New Avengers had pretty much the whole of Pinewood to itself

all that. It was a delightful experience this time round and it was the first of many times I returned with a picture.'

By this time, the Pinewood-based *Carry On* films were running out of steam. There was also a question mark hanging over the studio's other successful franchise, 007. After lengthy negotiations and legal wrangles over the ownership of Bond – not to mention a couple of years' absence from the big screen – Cubby Broccoli returned to Pinewood with his most ambitious Bond yet, minus his old partner Harry Saltzman. *The Spy Who Loved Me* was Roger Moore's third, and some say definitive, 007 adventure and also changed the landscape of the studio with the construction of the huge 007 Stage.

Avenging

Classic television next came to Pinewood in the shape of *The New Avengers*. One of the most popular series of the 1960s, *The Avengers* had seen Patrick Macnee's sophisticated John Steed partnered in turn by Ian Hendry, Honor Blackman, Diana Rigg and Linda Thorson. The last episode was broadcast in 1969, with Steed and Tara King (Thorson) being unwittingly blasted into outer space. Their boss – known as 'Mother' – turned to camera and said, 'They'll be back … you can depend on it!'

The new series came about following a French TV commercial for champagne, for which Macnee and Thorson were engaged to resurrect their Avengers characters. The commercial's producer, Rudolph Raffi, then struck a deal with the show's producers, Brian Clemens and Albert Fennell, to make a new series. The original series had been shot at Elstree Studios, and the choice of Pinewood for the new project may well have been influenced by the fact that Fennell's brother Jack was studio manager.

This time, Macnee was to have two assistants; he was now 53 and the producers accordingly introduced a younger male colleague alongside the traditional female. Auditions for the two parts took place at Pinewood on 20 January 1976, with further tests for the short-listed applicants a week later. Among the many hopefuls were Cassandra Harris (later to marry Pierce Brosnan), Jan Harvey, Jan Francis and Diana Quick. The role finally went to Joanna Lumley, who suggested that her character's name be changed from Charlie to Purdey. Gareth Hunt, meanwhile, withstood stiff competition from Lewis Collins, Michael Elphick and John Nettles for the part of Mike Gambit. In the book The Ultimate Avengers, Brian Clemens commented, 'The interesting thing about the auditions is that we put a girl and boy opposite each other, and it was purely coincidental that Gareth tested opposite Jo. We took them both.'

Filming commenced in April 1976. The series was to run for 26 episodes, filmed in batches of 13. After the first 13 were completed, a short

2.85 New Managing Director Cyril Howard (left), seen here with Bond producer Albert R. Broccoli

break was taken during which time the show's French backers indicated that they were not entirely happy. They complained that Joanna Lumley's character wasn't sexy enough. As fashion and style were an important part of the Avengers appeal, Lumley had created the now famous 'Purdey bob' hairstyle, but the French wanted a sultrier look and insisted that she wear French designs in the remaining 13 episodes. Furthermore, they wanted

2.86 Rank's return to film financing was heralded by ... Wombling Free!

more violence – a controversial point that didn't go down well with either the producers or the fans.

The especially disappointing news for Pinewood, however, was that the French insisted several episodes be filmed in France, and another four in Canada. To help get the series off the ground, Pinewood had done a deal whereby they offered stage space in return for a percentage of the profits, so this new situation was unsatisfactory in the extreme. The changes were implemented nevertheless, but the second series lost out in the ratings, owing to scheduling problems but also to the unpopularity of the new 'look'.

Along with *The New Avengers*, Gerry and Sylvia Anderson's *Space: 1999* helped keep the studio ticking over towards the end of its 40th year, which was not only one of the leanest ever but also the year of managing director Kip Herren's untimely death. The previous year had seen the studio lose some £450,000 and the industry didn't show any signs of picking up, particularly with the double taxation convention with the USA looming large. Taxation had already made life difficult when Equus was lost to Canada, after the film had been prepared at Pinewood. Redundancies were unavoidable. Pinewood's labour force was cut from 1,483 to just 700, and rumours were rife that the Rank Organisation was intent on selling off the studio.

New regime

When Kip Herren suddenly died, Cyril Howard stepped in as acting managing director at what must have been a very difficult time both on a personal and business level. Soon afterwards he took on the role permanently, having progressed, as he puts it, from general gopher to managing director in 'just 30 years!'

Given the volatile production environment at the time, Howard was horrified when called into the boardroom to see Rank's new chairman Ed Chilton. ' "Cyril", he said, "I've decided that we're going back into film financing, and the first project will be *Wombling Free*." I just stood there and thought "You're bloody mad." I honestly couldn't believe what I was hearing.'

More of Rank's return to production is in the chapter 'Rank Film Distributors: the last 20 years'.

Ed Chilton used to visit the studio every Friday and on one occasion he blithely asked Cyril Howard to introduce a studio tour. ('That's how he was,' says Howard. 'He was a lovely man, but he'd just think of something and as far as he was concerned that was it.') Plans were set in motion for the tour, which took place over a weekend in July 1977. Howard contacted the

2.87 Part of the Statue of Liberty, left over from the filming of Superman

local press about the event and took the opportunity of picking their brains as to the sort of turnout the studio could expect.

'They said that similar events usually drew about 5,000 people. In fact, 40,000 turned up! A frightening experience. All we charged was £1 a car. As the day wore on, we realised just how overwhelmed we had become. Farmers' fields in the area were opened and duly filled with cars, and the local roads were blocked with parked cars, in fact even the main motor-ways in the area suffered heavy jams. Many of the special guests, including Roger Moore, couldn't get near the studio and just ended up turning round and going home. It was chaotic to say the least. Eventually, the police turned up and asked what we were going to do about all the crowds. I was full of abject apologies and informed them that it was our first attempt at this sort of thing – and it was for charity. That sort of swayed them and they left saying "Well, don't do it again!"'

They did do it again, however, in August 1982. Only this time, as Cyril Howard explained, a higher admission price was imposed. 'We charged £25 per car, limiting it to 600 cars and everyone received a lunch box in the price. It was glorious weather, and we were very fortunate in that respect, because people could wander around and then stroll into the gardens with their picnic lunches and so on. It was certainly better planned and handled than the first time around, but I wouldn't advise any potential managing director keen to make his name to introduce studio tours!'

Rank reported encouraging news that profits were improving in 1977, led by increasing cinema audiences and – for the first time since 1972 – the hotels division not making a loss. A large percentage of the financial improvements came from the five London hotels now owned by Rank and the sale of The Merrion Hotel in Leeds.

Return to Pinewood

Kevin Connor and John Dark returned to Pinewood with two productions in 1977, *The People That Time Forgot and Warlords of Atlantis*. Meanwhile *The New Avengers* kept the studio ticking over. Times were tough, but Pinewood's fortunes then took a dramatic change for the better when the phone rang and in flew *Superman*.

The last film to lens in 1977 came from Bryan Forbes and was a belated sequel to the 1944 classic *National Velvet*. *International Velvet* was the story of how a hostile orphan becomes an accomplished international horsewoman. Tatum O'Neal played the orphan, while Anthony Hopkins, Nanette Newman, Christopher Plummer and Dinsdale Landen took on the adult roles. O'Neal had been unfairly dubbed 'Tantrum O'Neal' but turned out to be a consummate professional, always on time, knowing all her lines and bursting with enthusiasm. She even performed most of the film's cross-country riding.

For a sequence involving the transportation of five horses by plane, a replica of a cargo jet was built at the studio. Four of the horses were housed in rigid stalls but the fifth was not, for this horse was required to literally kick up a fuss. His stall was made of less rigid material so that it would come apart without hurting him. A jet of compressed air was fired at the stallion's testicles by John Oram, who was concealed in the stall. It did the trick but once the horse had a taste for demolishing his stall, he continued on the rest of the set. Anthony Hopkins, who was on set at the time, jumped to safety and vowed never to return. The horse took some 15 minutes to calm down and, not surprisingly, no second take was called for.

Trains

Sean Connery's next picture at Pinewood nearly wasn't. *The First Great Train Robbery* was put to Connery after he completed *A Bridge Too Far*, but he turned it down. The film's director and screenwriter, Michael Crichton, then rewrote the script to Connery's satisfaction, but when it was announced that filming was to take place at Pinewood, Connery had to withdraw from the project. The tax laws were such that had he worked in the UK for more than a token number of days he would effectively have been making the film for nothing.

After extensive recces, the production team decided that they couldn't recreate the film's Victorian period in English locations. The answer was found over the Irish Sea and period trains were donated and manned by the Railway Preservation Society. Upon hearing of the move, Connery re-joined the project. Eight weeks in Ireland were followed by carefully scheduled interiors at Pinewood, along with use of the gardens and mansion.

The unfavourable tax laws also saw one of Pinewood's most faithful customers move out. Cubby Broccoli announced that he was relocating to Paris, and along with him he was taking the next Bond film, *Moonraker*. A farewell party was thrown at the studio and emotions were running very high. In the event, Derek Meddings' model department on *Moonraker* utilised the studio considerably.

Superman II was underway at the start of 1979 under the direction of Richard Lester while *Clash of the Titans* was the latest fantasy epic from stop-motion master Ray Harryhausen. Harry Hamblin, now best known for his role in the TV series *LA Law*, was cast as Perseus in this ambitious retelling of the Greek legend. Speaking to Film Review magazine, he particularly remembered the lunches at the studio. 'The lunches were daunting. There would be six or seven of us sitting around a table, with Maggie Smith dominating the conversation. She is so fast and witty, and so cutting as well. So, with Laurence Olivier also there, I felt very understaffed in the brainwave department!'

The scenes featuring the Gods – Olivier as Zeus, Ursula Andress as Aphrodite, Maggie Smith as Thetis, and Jack Gwillim as Poseidon – were filmed at Pinewood in about a week. No such luxury for Harryhausen and

2.88 Roger Moore on set for North Sea Hijack with director Andrew V. McLaglen

his special effects team, whose patient and painstaking work meant that they were still at the studio in early 1981. Though critically mauled, the film was a box-office success, collecting around $100 million. A sequel, called *Force of the Trojans*, was planned and a production team occupied offices at Pinewood, but a change in management at Columbia-TriStar saw the project scrapped.

Hijacking

British-born Andrew V McLaglen's first film in London had been Euan Lloyd's production, *The Wild Geese* in 1978, based at Twickenham Film Studios. His next project, again with Roger Moore, was *North Sea Hijack*, a thriller co-starring Anthony Perkins and James Mason.

'The locations were completed around Galway,' recalled McLaglen, 'and we then pulled back to Pinewood for interiors. The boat which Tony Perkins hijacks, Ruth, was supposed to be swishing and swaying around the North Sea, and so to film interiors we set the boat on rockers on one of the stages. It was very effective. All the long and approach shots of the boat and oil rigs were actually achieved with miniatures, as was the helicopter landing on the rig, out on the paddock tank. John Richardson headed the special effects team and I challenge anyone to notice that the rigs were models!' (Keen-eyed viewers will also notice that the Prime Minister's office is actually the Green Room.) 'It was a very enjoyable shoot, and I particularly remember Roger feeling very much at home. But then, with all those baronial lunches in the restaurant, we all felt at home! Regrettably, I only returned to the studio with one more picture, and that was for post-production work on *Return to the River Kwai*.'

After dissolving his partnership with Cubby Broccoli, Harry Saltzman made a film which couldn't have been more different from those with which he had been previously associated. Starring Alan Bates and Alan Badel among others, *Nijinsky* was a study of the dancer's complex relationship with his mentor Diaghilev. Saltzman made only one further film, the little seen *Dom Za Vesanje* (1989), before his death in 1994.

1979, a year in which the studio hosted Rank's last feature also saw the end of its 27-year-old association with Walt Disney. Disney's last Pinewood film (until *Star Wars* returned three decades later) was *The Watcher in the Woods*. It was also Bette Davis's last feature at the studio, and one on which she held an unprecedented press conference for all the local papers, whose representatives couldn't believe their luck at being invited to the Green Room to meet the Hollywood superstar. Directed by John Hough, the picture was an unusual departure for Disney in that they tried to combine the family cuteness of earlier films with Hammer-style horror. In an attempt to appeal to a wider audience, they alienated their most loyal. The balance wasn't successfully struck, and the film received only a limited release. Two years later, having had additional sequences shot by Vincent McEveety and after some heavy re-editing, the film was re-released (some 15 minutes shorter) but fared just as poorly.

Rank Film Laboratories meanwhile delivered record results with over 313 million feet of film processed; and Pinewood ended its fifth decade in a reasonably healthy but somewhat precarious state. One thing was certain, however – the road ahead would not be smooth for either the studio or its parent.

Part 3

The Downfall of the Empire

~ 1 ~

The 1980s

1980 kicked off with one of the most disastrous films ever made. An epic 'cattlemen vs immigrants' Western, *Heaven's Gate* was written, produced and directed by Michael Cimino, fresh from the tremendous success of *The Deer Hunter*. He was virtually given a blank cheque to make the film, plus a cast to die for (Kris Kristofferson, Christopher Walken, John Hurt, Sam Waterstone, Joseph Cotten and Jeff Bridges), and the bloated result brought United Artists to its knees.

It wouldn't have been so bad had it been half the success of Cimino's first feature, but the picture was savagely lampooned by the critics and failed miserably. It cost $36m – three times its original budget – after having been re-edited in the wake of a disastrous première. 'The trade must marvel that directors now have such power that no one, in the endless months since work on the picture began, was able to impose some structure and sense,' opined Variety. While, according to the New York Times, 'It fails so completely that you might suspect Mr Cimino sold his soul to the Devil to obtain the success of *The Deer Hunter*, and the Devil has just come around to collect.'

It is said that *Heaven's Gate* is probably the most talked about and least seen film ever made. Several sequences were shot at Pinewood and, despite the swift burial given the film itself, its effects were still being felt some time later, as Teddy Joseph, then head of UA's production interests in London, testified. 'I thought it was much better to move the production arm of UA out to Pinewood, rather than being based at Mortimer Street with the distribution people, like Warner Bros were. So, in the mid seventies we

221

3.1 Heaven's Gate the film that brought down United Artists

moved into the old house, next door to Peter Rogers. I thought I was going to retire there! It was absolutely marvellous. However, one day after the *Heaven's Gate* fiasco, I received a phone call from MGM – we'd been told that they were going to take us over – and the head of production told me to clear my desk by Friday. I argued that I had six months to run on my contract, but he didn't care and said MGM were taking over UA and all production was being closed down. And that was that.'

Peter Hyams' *Outland*, one of the next pictures to roll at the studio, starred Sean Connery and was dubbed 'High Noon in Space', much to the displeasure of *High Noon's* director Fred Zinnemann. Pinewood played host to the entire film, and a spectacular model of Jupiter's moon Io was built by Martin Bower, Bill Pearson and John Stears. Eighteen feet wide, it contained more than four miles of fibre optics. Other sets included a gigantic greenhouse and the exterior of a mine camp, which towered above the planet's sands.

Lean times

The last feature to turn-over at Pinewood in the lean production year of 1980 was the new Bond adventure, *For Your Eyes Only*, which saw Roger Moore return to a more down-to-earth plotline after *Moonraker's* sojourn in outer space. A new director, in the shape of former editor and second unit director John Glen, took the reins and made extensive use of the pad-dock tank (for the St George's sinking sequence) and, just a few miles from the studio, Stoke Poges churchyard (for the grave of Bond's wife Tracy in the pre-credit sequence).

On December 28, 1980, the Independent Broadcasting Authority (IBA) announced Southern Television would not have its broadcasting franchise renewed. It took Rank, and much of the country, by surprise. But Television South (TVS) simply offered more money in the franchise bidding process.

In 1981 Rank reported profits were 15 per-cent lower in, what they called, 'tough trading conditions'.

The conditions were certainly reflected at Pinewood with only four pro-ductions, two of them for TV. First up was Blake Edwards' *Victor/Victoria*, a remake of the 1933 German film *Viktor und Viktoria* by Rheinhold Schünzel and Hans Homburg. Described as 'a musical boudoir farce', Edwards' wife Julie Andrews played a British singer in Paris whose gay friend (Robert Preston) persuades her to take to the stage as a female impersonator, much to the confusion of James Garner's Chicago gangster. The film's production designer, Roger Maus, created some wonderfully colourful sets; particularly impressive was the Parisian street contained on E Stage.

Douglas Camfield's version of *Ivanhoe* with James Mason and Anthony Andrews was the first TV movie of the year, swiftly followed by Michael Tuchner's *The Hunchback of Notre Dame* with Anthony Hopkins, Lesley Anne Down and John Gielgud. 'We had a wonderful cast – and I was quite mesmerised by Lesley Anne Down. She was so beautiful!' said Tuchner. 'We recreated part of Notre Dame cathedral on the backlot, but only to about a third of the way up; the rest was completed with some brilliant matte work. We built the town square there, too, and shot some very moving scenes there with Tony. It was a marvellous experience.'

The other theatrical feature shot at Pinewood in 1981 saw the return of Alan Parker with *Pink Floyd: The Wall,* it was a disturbing and blood-spattered musical that starred Bob Geldof, Christine Hargreaves, Bob Hoskins and, of course, the powerful music of Pink Floyd.

Daring to win

'1982 saw the infamous terrorist attack on London's Iranian Embassy hit the headlines all over the world,' observed producer Euan Lloyd. 'I elected to make *Who Dares Wins* to mark the success of Britain's Special Forces in relieving the siege. Reginald Rose's screenplay pictured a terrorist take-over of the American Ambassador's residence, holding 50 or so dinner guests as hostages. In her first film role outside her native Australia, Judy Davis was cast as the terrorist leader. Her motives were eloquently expounded to her captive Ambassador, played by Richard Widmark. That scene called for a sumptuous set. Equally, the exterior of the Embassy, violently attacked after the Davis-Widmark confrontation, had many critical requirements. After scouring Hertfordshire and the southern counties, production designer Syd Cain came to me with a lifesaver, "We don't have to build either set, they exist at Pinewood."

3.2 Victor Victoria filming on Pinewood's E-stage

'The façade of the old mansion and the studio's main restaurant were dressed to meet director Ian Sharp's needs. The sound of helicopter gunships, the smell of cordite, the fire and smoke did not exactly endear me to other producers at the studio, or the staff who were forced to endure the attack over a week or more. But it was a highlight of the film. In one of his rare letters, Stanley Kubrick complimented me on the realism achieved by the use of Pinewood's major set-pieces, also for the casting of Judy Davis which he described as inspirational. The picture gallery, the backlot and the construction stages all made me thankful for Syd Cain's foresight and to Mr Charles Boot for building my sets back in the 1930s!'

Lloyd also registered seven potential titles for the film, to deter any other producers from tackling the same subject.

Lewis Collins, Ingrid Pitt, Edward Woodward and Kenneth Griffith starred in the film and it went on to make a small fortune, according to former Rank Film Distributors MD, Fred Turner. 'Lewis Collins was very big on TV with *The Professionals* at the time, and was massively popular with the ladies, who flocked into the cinemas. We made our money back in just a few weeks!' Blake Edwards returned to shoot two of his Pink Panther pictures

3.3 Star Lewis Collins, producer Euan Lloyd and director Ian Sharp

3.4 Who Dares Wins

back-to-back. Sadly, Peter Sellers had died two years earlier, but Edwards decided to make the first film, *The Trail of the Pink Panther*, from previously unseen Sellers footage, with Clouseau 'disappearing' halfway through the film in a plane crash and TV reporter Joanna Lumley piecing together the mystery in his absence. Series regulars Herbert Lom and Burt Kwouk resumed their roles as Inspector Dreyfuss and Cato respectively, while further support came from David Niven and Leonard Rossiter. The second film, *The Curse of the Pink Panther*, saw Dreyfuss select the world's worst detective (Ted Wass) to replace Clouseau. Lumley, Lom, Niven and Kwouk returned along with Robert Wagner. David Niven was very ill and couldn't speak; his voice was dubbed. He died shortly after filming was completed.

Roger Moore made an uncredited appearance in *Curse* as a post-plastic surgery Clouseau. It's almost worth watching the film just to see Moore's mad five minutes.

'Blake said they could film at Pinewood, at the tail end of *Octopussy*, recalled Moore. 'I figured it would be five-days of filming and as they were offering $100,000 a day, it seemed pretty attractive. However they worked me from early morning until late at night, and got it all in just one day!'

Burt Kwouk, who got his first taste of acting in *Windom's Way* at Pinewood back in 1957 when he was thrust from being an extra into an artist with one (Malaysian) line, will forever be remembered as Clouseau's manservant Cato. 'That's on the gravestone!' confirmed Kwouk. 'The Panthers were quite possibly more fun to make than to watch. I'm always asked if I was ever hurt in those sequences where I leapt out of fridges or cupboards and attacked Peter. I never was, not even a scratch! Peter was great fun. He was a very volatile character, but I always remember the light side of him – the entertaining, amusing, funny guy. He loved dressing up in disguises and putting on different voices and faces and that was always wonderful to see.'

Picking up

1983 saw a sudden upturn in big television productions, including *The Last Days of Pompeii*, directed by Peter H Hunt and starring Ned Beatty, Ernest Borgnine and Lesley Anne Down with the doomed city recreated on the paddock tank; *The First Modern Olympics – Athens 1896* with David Ogden Steirs, Angela Lansbury and Honor Blackman; and Kevin Connor's *Master of the Game*. 'The show was based on Sidney Sheldon's book,' said Connor, 'and I directed the first half of the mini-series – Harvey Hart did the second – with Donald Pleasence and Dyan Cannon. It was my first major TV show at the studio.'

Business started to pick up again in 1984, with several large-scale features shooting. However, it was in many ways 'too little too late'. The industry's last fully serviced studio was struggling to keep its head above water and maintain a full staff on the payroll: echoes of the late 1930s when Richard Norton set-up Pinebrook Films. A further nail in the coffin was the Conservative administration's abolition of the Eady Levy. Many foreign producers who had previously chosen to base themselves in Britain looked elsewhere, and along with them went their films. 'I often wonder which group of "experts" Maggie Thatcher talked to when she decided to scrap the Eady Plan – a plan that had worked well in the past,' growled Bond director John Glen.

Of the 13 features to shoot at Pinewood in the three-year period ending in 1986 there were some notable titles including Joseph Losey's *Steaming*, Ridley Scott's fairy-tale sword and sorcery extravaganza *Legend*, another Bond adventure *A View To A Kill, Santa Claus the Movie, Little Shop of Horrors* and Stanley Kubrick's penultimate film, the Vietnam drama *Full Metal Jacket*. The studio had been banking on the fourth Superman film, however, when the franchise was taken over by Menahem Golan and Yoram Globus (who had recently acquired Elstree Studios), Pinewood was plunged into panic.

Golden Anniversary

Putting on a brave face, in September 1986, the studio celebrated 50 glorious years and to mark the occasion a special luncheon was held in the grand restaurant with friends, new and old, popping in to pay tribute to the great studio. But with a mere handful of features and a few TV films pencilled in the diary a further, and somewhat fatal, blow came when the planned production of *A Fish Called Wanda* moved elsewhere.

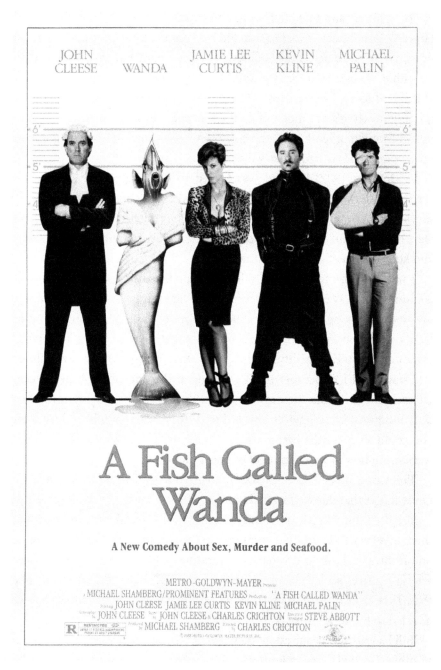

3.5 *A Fish Called Wanda was, and then wasn't, destined for Pinewood*

'The phone rang one afternoon, and it was John Cleese,' recalled Cyril Howard. 'And he said "Sorry, Cyril old boy, but I'm afraid I've got some bad news. We've had a better deal offered at Twickenham and so we're having to go with it." I suggested that we could try and match it, but he was adamant that it had to be Twickenham. "Don't worry though," he said. "You're not missing much, it's not much of a film really." So, despite needing the business, I thought at least I had the consolation of knowing it wasn't going to be very good. How wrong we were!'

In October 1987, Howard was forced to bite the bullet. Despite his earlier insistence that the only way Pinewood could continue was as a fully serviced studio, he realised he was wrong. The returns into Rank's coffers were minimal and the studio badly needed money spending to refurbish it and keep on top of general maintenance.

'I was fooling myself really,' said Howard, 'because deep down knew it couldn't go on. We were losing money; we had a huge staff and there was no product. So, one morning I called everyone onto a stage and stood in front of them on a rostrum. I broke the news that we were going "four-wall" [becoming a studio facility, where filmmakers bring in their own labour and staff] and I remember them clapping at the end of my little speech. Of course, then came the negotiations with the unions, but we came to a deal and the staff, or payroll, was reduced from nearly 500 to 145. At least you could sleep a little better and not wake up in the middle of the night wondering how you would meet the next payroll.

'Pinewood was the last film studio to go four-walled,' he added, 'and I'll never forget that day as long as I live.'

Despite reducing his payroll, Howard was still faced with the fact that there was very little product coming into the studio. 'If things go wrong on one front, you have to diversify,' he continues. 'It's easy to say "OK, there are no features so let's bring in some more TV," but it doesn't work like that. They're not queuing up to come; they have their own venues. So, we decided to hit another market.

'Bill Harrison was our estate manager as well as being a very good friend of mine. I called him up and said "Bill, we're having to get rid of all the heads of department, but I've decided to keep you. I want you to start putting the idea around that we're now looking at housing commercials as well as feature films, and you'll be in charge of them." Well, he couldn't get out of the office quick enough. Talk about a dog with two tails! He did an absolutely marvellous job. He had a personality a mile wide and everybody loved him. Commercials and pop promos became very big business and Bill brought in over a hundred per year. Granted, we couldn't survive on them alone, but with those and a few big features every year, we had our bread and butter.'

Compilations

A year after Pinewood, Rank Film Distributors celebrated its golden anniversary in 1987. Mindful of the success the half-hour *Carry On* film compilation shows had recently enjoyed on the BBC; Robert Sidaway, Ashley Sidaway, Maurice Sellar and Lou Jones created a similar format (again for the BBC) called *Best Of British*. Running between 1987 and 1994 the clips came from films in the RFD archive. The 25-minute compilation shows were broken down into themed episodes such as *Heroes, Classic Tales, Action Men,* and *Going Places* and narrated by John Mills and Anthony Quayle.

RFD obviously hoped viewer's appetites would be whetted and a surge in video sales might follow – thus deriving further value from the library.

The Big Bat

1988 was, thankfully, somewhat busier for Rank-owned Pinewood and another comic book hero arrived – the 'dark knight' himself, Batman.

He came at a time when the Bond producers had already decided to move out of the studio because of the UK's unfavourable exchange rate, and cheaper studio space elsewhere – namely, Mexico.

Director Tim Burton's *Batman* film heralded the arrival of a new kind of blockbuster. Pinewood had participated in the birth of the 'event' movie. It was hoped that a sequel would return to the complex – to that end, Gotham City remained in place at the studio long after production ceased – but it wasn't to be. A further blow came when Jack Nicholson tore into the British taxation regime, vowing never again to work in Britain after a large chunk of his salary had been withheld by the Exchequer for months on end.

Jack the Ripper, the first of two Michael Caine vehicles, was also shot at the studio in 1988. 'We filmed the whole thing at the studio and had great fun in building those wonderful Victorian sets across, I think, about three stages,' said director David Wickes. 'It was quite something for us, because it was Michael Caine's first TV mini-series and the first British TV show to air prime-time on CBS over two nights. It was a tremendous ratings winner, both in America and the UK where it knocked Coronation Street off the top spot!'

Meanwhile, Wickes was devising another fascinating Pinewood project – no less than the purchase of the studio itself. 'It was at a time when the studio was struggling a bit, and rumours were rife the Rank Organisation were preparing to sell it off, or something awful like that. I, like many of my colleagues, was horrified and set about wondering what we could do to save the studio. At that time, we had a hotel group called Queen's Moat House and one of my friends happened to know the chairman of the group. There was no hotel of a really high standard between London and Heathrow back then, and it was suggested that if they could get permission to build one beyond the big house in a corner of the gardens – taking a couple of acres out of Pinewood's one hundred – the amount of money they would plough into the deal would keep the studio going for a long time. We might have been able to underwrite its losses for five years or more.

'We took the idea to the then chairman of Rank, who was quite interested, and several negotiations followed in South Street with the top brass of the Organisation. Because of the hotel offer, and on the basis of Pinewood's future financial viability, we were able to borrow money from a bank to buy the complex. Obviously, there was a limit as to how high the bank would go, and to our minds it was an extremely fair amount: an awful lot of millions. We went in with our offer and honestly thought it was an offer Rank couldn't refuse. However, we were wrong. They asked for a lot more than we were able to offer. So, we had to walk away. It was a very sad day for me, and I was very surprised they turned the offer down. But Pinewood survived. Michael Grade attempted a similar take-over several years later, but on that occasion he was unsuccessful.'

⤜ 2 ⤚

The Michael B Gifford Years
(CEO, 1983 to 1996)

Although it had given up on the risky business of film production, save for buying international rights through Rank Film Distributors, and the British film industry was certainly going through one of its regular slumps in the early 1980s and The Rank Organisation portfolio had expanded in many and all directions over the years.

In 1983 it owned motorway service stations, holiday companies, radio and television manufacturers, a precision engineering company, a significant stake in Rank-Xero photocopying, pubs, Strand lighting, bingo, nightclubs, fruit machines ... and more.

The City of London felt it a sprawling giant, with a leviathan structure that lacked focus and direction.

But which direction did Rank's future lie?

The writing on the wall

Two Chief Executives through the 1980s and 1990s decided it would not and should not be film, but firmly in other areas of the Leisure and Entertainment area.

In July 1983, after a four-month search, the Rank Organisation, appointed Michael B. Gifford as group chief executive, effective September 1. Gifford, then aged 47, was previously finance director for Cadbury

Schweppes, the confectionary, soft drinks and food company which had recorded international sales in the year prior of $2.47 billion – a flourishing company if ever there was one.

Rank had been seeking a new chief executive since March that year, when nine institutional shareholders who controlled 30 per-cent of the company between them, ordered a management shake-up after four years of sagging profits, and City of London criticism of making 'incorrect strategy decisions'.

One city analyst, David Nolder, greeted the news positively at the time in a statement to The Times newspaper.

'I have every confidence that Mr. Gifford will do a good job. He has brought a sharpness to the controls at Cadbury Schweppes. He's very down-to-earth, answers questions in a straightforward manner, and I think he will contribute a lot to the planning and budgeting process at Rank.'

Gifford, a graduate of the London School of Economics, had pitched to win promotion to the post of chief executive at Cadbury Schweppes earlier in 1983, but failed, and that was seen as prompting his decision to leave and join Rank. In turn, Rank saw Gifford and his previous overseas experience as chief Cadbury Schweppes Australia Ltd. for three years – until he moved in 1978 to London to become finance director – as being potentially invaluable in helping shake up their Australian operations, which had been seen as a steady drag on the organisation.

'He has a proven track record of running big companies himself,' said Rodney Rycroft, Rank's chief press officer. Asked if Mr. Gifford's lack of direct experience in the hotel, copier or entertainment industries, in which Rank concentrated, might be a drawback to his performance, Mr. Rycroft replied, 'He's an expert manager of businesses, and that's what Rank's looking for.'

Rank did seem to rebound under the management of its new CEO, and by 1988 all but one of its divisions reported a healthy increase in profits, and the balance of earnings between Rank and Rank-Xerox was close to a 50-50 split. Within those five years of Gifford taking the helm the organisation's holidays and recreation division had become the company's largest, and its collection of resorts and travel interests netted £58 million on sales of £276 million.

3.6 Rank CEO Michael Gifford and Chairman Sir Leslie Fletcher (1992–1995)

Investments

Under Gifford's direction, the organisation made two major additional investments.

In 1988, they entered into a partnership with MCA to build the $600 million Universal Studios Florida theme park in Orlando. Rank invested £115 million for a 50 percent interest in the project, which opened in 1990, and by 1994 was attracting seven million visitors a year and generating £11.4 million in profits for Rank. In 1995, MCA and Rank began work on a $2 billion expansion that would include a second theme park called Islands of Adventure, scheduled to open in 1999.

The other major investment was made in 1990, when Rank acquired Mecca Leisure Group. Mecca's holdings – hotels, theme parks, 85 bingo parlours, and 11 Hard Rock Cafes – actually all fitted in rather well with Rank's operations.

Mecca had been founded in 1933 and primarily operated dance halls. Most notably they introduced 'the revolving bandstand', the first being at Mecca's flagship hall, the Locarno in Streatham, south London, in 1931, thus allowing non-stop music when a change of band was required, while the first was still performing, and also added a theatrical air to the evening's proceedings.

It was Eric Morley, the British TV host and founder of the Miss World pageant who in 1952 was Mecca's general manager of dancing, it is said popularised bingo at their venues throughout the United Kingdom, filling them during the day and some evenings when not in use for dancing. In 1990, the Rank Organisation made an offer of £512 million to acquire Mecca Leisure Group, which was initially rejected, then – having had a rethink – was accepted two months later.

Under Rank, some of Mecca's operations were expanded, such as the Hard Rock Cafes – that chain grew to 15 units by 1995 – while others were closed or sold off such as some of the underperforming hotels in London(Grand Plaza Hotel), Saltdean, and Torremolinos. Butlins locations at Clacton and Filey were closed in 1983, whilst the camp at Barry was sold in 1986. The remaining camps, which had a major image problem of still being seen as providing regimented holidays á la 1960s, caused Rank to all but abandon the Butlins name at its remaining resorts rebranding them as Funcoast World, Starcoast World, Southcoast World etc.

Rank next sold its motorway service stations portfolio to Michael Guthrie the former CEO of Mecca, for £95 million, and all were rebranded Pavilion a few months later. Rank had also sold him Pizzaland and Prima Pasta.

With Mecca under its control, Rank's revenue surged from £1.33 billion in 1990 to £2.11 billion in 1991.

Over the next few years, Gifford disposed of what he regarded as unwanted baggage, including joint ventures in Australia and New Zealand, yacht marinas, a military thermal imaging business and an investment in US telephone systems totalling some £450 million. Revenue for the company increased slightly to £2.2 billion in 1994.

Curiously, Gifford had meanwhile been appointed a director of English China Clays Plc (ECC) on May 12, 1992, in addition to his role as Rank CEO. ECC was a mining company involved in the extraction of china clay, based in St Austell, Cornwall, and not seen as a competitor to any of Rank's divisions. Its importance lies in Gifford's successor which we will come to shortly.

Gifford had focused very heavily on leisure and recreation during his reign at Rank but profits generated by Rank-Xerox (R-X) still formed 50

3.7 Rank Chairman Sir Denys Henderson (1995–2001) opening a new Odeon cinema complex in Hemel Hempstead

percent of the organisations overall income by the mid-1990s – admittedly much less than in previous decades – but still seemed to be tilting the company in a direction the CEO didn't see as the organisation's 'core activity' going forward.

Gifford made a move to lessen the role of R-X in the company's future and in January 1995 sold 40 per-cent of its interest in R-X for £620 million – to its partner, Xerox. Gifford said it intended to use the funds to 'invest in leisure and recreation businesses'.

Profits

Under Gifford pre-tax profit at Rank grew from £69 million to £650 million, though most of that was due to a one-off gain from the disposal of the Rank-Xerox stake. Removing that from the equation, operating profits rose by a steadier 6 per cent to £253 million.

Gifford had secured Rank some significant buying power but at the same time reduced the organisation's stake in its most important and profitable holding outside his perceived core activities – was it to be his biggest mistake?

On February 6, 1995, The Rank Organisation came under pressure to clarify the position of its chief executive, Michael Gifford, after speculation he was to leave the company within months.

The press reported, 'A Rank spokeswoman refused to confirm or deny suggestions that Mr Gifford had planned to announce his resignation at the company's annual meeting later this month.' Nor would she comment on rumours of increasing tension between Gifford and Sir Denys Henderson, the former ICI executive who was due to take over as chairman on March 1.

Henderson was rumoured to be unsure about recent decisions made by Gifford; his disposal of 40 per-cent in Rank Xerox for £620 million had disappointed investors who felt the shareholding was worth more.

Whatever was on the cards with Henderson, Gifford was not going to stay around to find out, as a short time later he announced that he would be retiring the following year.

Gifford, then aged 59, was praised for his bluntness and autocratic style and was said to have negotiated a very handsome £1 million pay-off.

Just ahead of Gifford's departure from Rank, he made one important change.

'There were always potentially large tax implications in selling off parts of the organisation (namely its share in Xerox),' RFD's last managing director George Helyer revealed, 'and Gifford had consulted with tax accountants to the point where in February 1996, the Rank name and some of the remaining assets were absorbed into the newly structured The Rank Group Plc.'

The 'Rank Organisation' itself became a wholly owned subsidiary of Xerox on June 30, 1997, and was renamed XRO Limited.

It was clear further disposals were on the cards.

～ 3 ～

Pinewood Continued – Into the 1990s

The 1990s started just as the 1980s had ended: with a modest mixture of TV and features.

A tasteless sitcom starring Sam Kelly as Adolf Hitler, called *Heil Honey I'm Home*, that didn't get beyond pilot stage, was followed by a Fraser Heston project, *The Crucifer of Blood*, in which his father Charlton played Sherlock Holmes to Richard Johnson's Dr Watson. 'Pinewood lent itself so well to the production,' recalled Charlton Heston, 'as many of the house's rooms fitted in so well with the period. I remember we used the ballroom to great effect in several sequences. The gardens were also used extensively. Fraser came in for some criticism when he said he was going to film a scene which was supposed to represent the Red Fort of Agra in India, "the only structure in the world with a hundred gates," as Holmes describes it. Fray [Fraser] looked at the set and said, "All I need to bring it alive is a troop of British lancers riding up the street in the opening shot." Nobody thought it would work – it would cost too much; the set wouldn't stand it – but I'm here to tell you it did. Fray argued for 40 horsemen and got them: plus one elephant! I will always have a tremendous soft spot for Pinewood, as it's been very kind to me in my career.'

The second *Alien* sequel, *Alien 3*, kicked off production in 1991 and made extensive, and impressive, use of the 007 Stage and Pinewood's effects and 'creatures' companies, receiving an Oscar nomination for Best Visual Effects.

Patriot Games was Philip Noyce's follow-up to *The Hunt for Red October*, with Harrison Ford taking on Alec Baldwin's role as CIA man Jack Ryan. The film left its mark on Pinewood when the boardroom was split in two to represent James Fox's office and ante-room. Such was the skill with which it was done, it remains so to this day, providing Pinewood with a small as well as a large boardroom.

Revivals

1992 began with the somewhat embarrassing revival of two old series – *Carry On Columbus* and *Son of the Pink Panther*, (the latter went straight-to-video in the UK). Kevin Connor returned to direct the TV mini-series of Andrew Morton's best-seller *Diana: Her True Story*, with Serena Scott Thomas in the title role. And Agnieszka Holland's wonderfully crafted version of the children's classic *The Secret Garden* made full use of Pinewood's gardens, even boarding over part of the Pinewood pond.

A little bit of history was made that year with Pinewood's first live TV broadcast. The BBC's Saturday morning children's magazine show, *Parallel 9* – set in a distant galaxy – made wonderful use of E Stage in recreating space settings, while out on the backlot sat a little caravan where visiting guest stars needed to stop off in order to be 'transported' to Parallel 9. Thankfully, Saturday mornings were reasonably quiet at the studio and broadcasting live from the backlot wasn't a problem. In fact, so happy were the programme makers that they returned for the '93 and '94 seasons, which guaranteed several months' bookings each time.

In October 1992, cameras were due to start rolling on *Shakespeare In Love*, which was set to star Julia Roberts. Days before principal photography was to start, however, the film was abandoned, along with it 200 crew members and several months of stage space at the studio. Roberts was insistent on Daniel Day-Lewis playing the Bard and, when he declined, she left the production. 'That was a great blow,' said Cyril Howard, who was then in his retirement year, 'as we were depending on that work to keep us going. But seven years later, the film's been made [at Shepperton, with Gwyneth Paltrow and Joseph Fiennes] and it's done so well!'

3.8 Pinewood Managing Director Steve Jaggs (1993–2005)

Under New Management

1993 ushered in several new productions, as well as a new managing director in Steve Jaggs. Formerly manager of Agfa's motion picture division.

'When I joined the studio, actually on November 2, 1992, for an eight-week hand-over period,' said Jaggs, 'we didn't have very much on at all, which gave me the opportunity to look at the business and at the buildings themselves. I have to tell you; it was a shock – but that's not a criticism of the previous management. There just weren't the monies available. Fortunately, since that time, the Rank Group [the new name for the Rank Organisation] have been very supportive of what we've wanted to do, and a lot of work has been undertaken in picking up many years of neglect. We started looking at the studio from the roof down. It used to leak like a sieve, but it doesn't now!

'We had to bring things up to a standard which would not only be acceptable to ourselves, but to our clients; and doing things for longevity, not just saying "That'll do for now." Then, as business picked up, and the various stages of improvements were completed, we were able to think about expanding.'

May 1993 brought news of the death of Sir John Davis, former Chairman of the Rank Organisation. 'I remember that day very well,' said Dinah Sheridan with a wry smile. 'Particularly when my son Jeremy came to the telephone singing "Oh what a beautiful morning"!' 'The British film industry needs someone like John Davis,' countered Daniel Angel, producer of *Carve Her Name With Pride* and *Reach For the Sky*, 'as at least he could make a decision and green-light a picture. No one person can do that nowadays. He may have had his dark side, but at least he made films!'

Vampires, Monsters and Fish

Production continued apace with films such as *Interview With the Vampire*, starring Tom Cruise and Brad Pitt; *Mary Reilly*, another rendition of Jekyll and Hyde, only this time told through the eyes of Jekyll's maid played by Julia Roberts; Iain Softley's *Hackers*, a fast-moving thriller set in the world of

3.9 The sequel to Wanda, Fierce Creatures was this time destined for Pinewood

computers and featuring an attractive mix of newcomers including Jonny Lee Miller and Angelina Jolie; and, the most expensive science fiction project ever to shoot in the UK, Gerry Anderson's *Space Precinct* had a huge unit, spread across both Pinewood (for live action) and Shepperton (for special effects).

Animatronic creatures were also around the studio for *Loch Ness*, the story of 'Nessie', the legendary monster of the Scottish loch (last seen at Pinewood in *The Private Life of Sherlock Holmes*); *First Knight*, yet another screen adaptation of the King Arthur legend – this time with a modern living legend in the shape of Sean Connery and Hollywood heart throb Richard Gere as Sir Lancelot.

Then, came 1995 – phenomenally busy for the studio – kicking off the year was the long awaited follow-up to *A Fish Called Wanda*. Originally called *Death Fish 2*, the story was set to reunite *Wanda* stars John Cleese, Jamie Lee Curtis, Kevin Kline and Michael Palin in a zoo-set comedy. *Fierce Creatures*, as the film was eventually retitled, witnessed the construction of one of Pinewood's most delightful and ambitious exterior sets ever – a complete zoo, along with live animal residents. But what of the old adage, never work with children or animals?

'Generally, the animals were brilliant, thanks to our trainer Rona Brown,' said Cleese, 'but we did discover that the ostrich chick was quite alarmed by the kowati because its main diet is eggs and chicks. So, in any scene that seems to feature a kowati and ostrich together, the answer is that the kowati was animatronic.'

The smaller animals were not always required on set and resided in their own 'mini-zoo' on the lot, which attracted Tom Cruise and his children as well as the Princess of Wales and the Duchess of York. Once shooting was completed, the sets were destroyed in a matter of days, but a year later most of them had to be rebuilt for further shooting, with a new director, Fred Schepisi, taking over from Robert Young.

'We'd made a couple of mistakes in the script,' explained Cleese. 'I wrote an ending that was a bit crazy, particularly as it involved Kevin Kline's character being killed off early. The other thing was, I tried to create a little Ealing comedy ensemble with the zoo-keepers but, to my surprise, English audiences just weren't interested in them, only in the main characters. Michael Palin was off around the world and wasn't available for a year, and when we did reunite in 1996, we found the re-shoots were very expensive.

3.10 One of the backlot sets

With everyone demanding big fees, the budget shot up from the low $20 millions to the very high $20 millions.'

Tom's return

The second big feature to shoot in 1995 came in the shape of an updated 1960s TV series when Tom Cruise, a regular visitor to Pinewood, brought his first movie as producer to the studio. *Mission: Impossible* came with a solid supporting cast (Vanessa Redgrave, Jon Voight, Ving Rhames etc), a $64 million budget and director Brian DePalma, whose previous hits ranged from *Carrie* to *The Untouchables*. To the discomfiture of both stuntmen and insurance people, Cruise did many of his own stunts, including one on the 007 Stage when he was sent flying by an exploding carriage. As he told Film Review magazine, 'I was flying across the James Bond Stage at Pinewood Studios and I hit a train. It really hurt and I didn't have to act at all.' The film was a summer box-office smash on both sides of the Atlantic and a sequel was guaranteed, ensuring that Pinewood maintained its global reputation for housing successful blockbusters.

Television continued to play a vital part in the studio's output. Playwright Dennis Potter's final two shows, *Karaoke* and *Cold Lazarus*, made broadcasting history when the BBC and Channel 4 joined forces to fund and produce the dramas, which aired on both channels later in the year. *Last of the Summer Wine* also made itself comfortable after locations in Yorkshire and other TV shows followed suit – *Little Orphan Annie*, the revived version of *Poldark*, *Deadly Voyage*, *Potamus Park* and, defecting from Shepperton, the lavish game show *You Bet!*

Sir Anthony Hopkins returned to his 'favourite studio' sporting a shaven head and bronze sun-tan with Merchant-Ivory's production of *Surviving Picasso*, which was shooting on C Stage when pop group Simply Red took up residence on the adjoining B Stage to rehearse for an upcoming tour. Disrupting the period feel of the Picasso biopic, the group was rapidly transferred to A Stage. Shortly afterwards, more music emanated from Pinewood's stages when Alan Parker brought Madonna over to record tracks for *Evita*, his biopic of Eva Peron.

New additions

Meanwhile, two further stages were added to Pinewood's already significant facilities. Dubbed N & P Stages, they replaced the former paint shop and electrical maintenance department, adjacent to F Stage. Uniquely among Pinewood's stages, N & P are inter-connected and can be used singly, or if desired, opened up to form one large stage.

1996 was just as busy for Pinewood, with Bruce Willis making two big features: *The Fifth Element* and *The Jackal*.

Next was Paramount's thriller *The Saint*, starring Val Kilmer and directed by Phillip Noyce; whilst 1997 got underway with a high-budget space thriller, *Event Horizon*, from the young director-producer team of Paul Anderson and Jeremy Bolt.

Stanley's Farewell

Stanley Kubrick returned to Pinewood in 1997. He hadn't made a film since *Full Metal Jacket* in 1986, but sometime in the winter of 1995 Tom

3.11 Stanley Kubrick made his last film at Pinewood. Eyes Wide Shut was released in 1999

Cruise and Nicole Kidman flew in by helicopter to the reclusive director's Hertfordshire home to discuss a project called *Eyes Wide Shut*. The film was brought into Pinewood with an estimated six to eight month shoot but with very little else known about it. Such was the secrecy that would surround the film for its entire stay.

The story, it was said in a Warner Bros press release, was to be based on a novella by Arthur Schnitzler which Kubrick had purchased the rights to sometime in the 1960s. Production began in 1997 and, lasting two years, saw changes of cast mid-shoot. The stars had to reschedule other projects and Cruise developed an ulcer.

Like all his later films, *Eyes Wide Shut* was shot entirely in the UK. Kubrick's fear of flying meant that he wouldn't travel to the USA for the New York street scenes, preferring instead to build New York on the back-lot – or at least a few blocks of it. And so a little bit of Manhattan could be found in downtown Iver Heath and it really came to life for the night

3.12 *The big screen outing for The Avengers*

shoots with a haze of sodium street lighting hovering over the studio. You could even hail one of the many yellow cabs that drove around the set to give the impression of a constant traffic flow.

Needless to say, with one of the world's legendary directors helming a much-anticipated film starring two of the business's top names, press interest was immense. And so began the rumours. One suggested that it was a high-budget porno film, another that it involved necrophilia, still another that in it Tom Cruise wore a dress. Repeated takes were called for, it was reported, sometimes as many as 80, which allegedly drove Tom Cruise to despair. All these rumours proved less than accurate.

In February 1998, 18 months after Cruise and Kidman had started work on the project, they returned home to LA. However, less than two months later, they were recalled as the director wasn't happy with location scenes he'd shot with Jennifer Jason Leigh. Indeed, Leigh had to be recast owing to other filming commitments, and several months of re-shoots ensued. In March 1999, the film was finally completed, and a private screening arranged for the stars and studio executives in LA, on March 2. Five days later, Kubrick died in his sleep, aged 70.

Avenging again

For almost ten years it was mooted that a feature version of the 1960s series *The Avengers* was on the cards. Rumours persisted and, on June 2, 1997, the cameras finally started rolling. Ralph Fiennes was cast as the debonair John Steed and Uma Thurman as Emma Peel, while Sean Connery portrayed the villain Sir August DeWynter. Patrick Macnee – the original Steed – had a cameo part in the film as 'Invisible Jones'. The picture was filmed entirely in England, utilising Shepperton as well as Pinewood.

Three-time Academy Award winner Stuart Craig was the production designer charged with creating 'Avengerland'. 'One of the economies we made was with the London street, which we built on the backlot at Pinewood,' he said. 'We used false perspective to very good effect. We can make a five-yard street look like a 500-yard street – only the first part is full size, with the second in false perspective and the last little bit two dimensional only.'

As well as using the backlot to great effect, the 'snow' sequences were created and filmed in Pinewood's gardens, with gigantic wind machines for the blizzards: a rather strange sight at the height of summer. The production had its share of problems, however, most notably on May 13. An electrical fault sparked a roof fire on E Stage and, although swiftly brought under control – thanks to dozens of local fire brigades and Pinewood's own fire department – the damage was significant. The stage, which was shortly due to be renovated in any case, was closed but the film's sets were accommodated on other stages and the production lost very little time as a result. Even so, the movie flopped badly following some of the most savage reviews ever written.

Laughs

For the big screen début of Rowan Atkinson's Chaplinesque Mr Bean, writer Richard Curtis and actor-turned-director Mel Smith decided to take the disaster-prone Bean to America. However, early scenes in *Bean: The Ultimate Disaster Movie* were London-based, with several shot at Pinewood. The studio's oak-panelled boardroom was actually used as a boardroom for once and the 'board of directors' was chaired by none other than Sir John Mills. 'It's quite fantastic,' he pointed out, 'to think that there I was sitting in the room where 50 years earlier I had sat with J Arthur Rank to sign my contract. He was heading the table then, but in *Bean* it was my turn!'

1998 had kicked off with Dick Clement and Ian La Frenais' *Still Crazy*, a comedy about Strange Fruit, a group of washed-up rockers played by Stephen Rea, Billy Connolly, Timothy Spall, Jimmy Nail and Bill Nighy. One of the early sequences features a wedding party in the Pinewood restaurant and later the garden and admin block are used to great effect as a mental institution. The most interesting set, however, was a gigantic concert hall built on the 007 Stage.

Sean Connery returned with Catherine Zeta Jones and his own production of the slick crime caper *Entrapment*. One of the most breath-taking sets ever constructed at Pinewood was on E Stage: the heavily guarded 'mask' room. The room, which had a full ceiling for shots looking up from below ground level, was built from marble, but thanks to the talented and cost-conscious people in the construction department not a stone of real marble was used.

Late in 1998, work commenced on Pinewood's two new large stages, along with the adjoining office accommodation dubbed The Stanley Kubrick Building, and in the summer of 1999 they opened for business.

Production remained buoyant with Eon's 19th Bond adventure kick-starting the year. *The World Is Not Enough* marked the return 'proper' to Pinewood of Eon Productions after over ten years' absence. *The Tenth Kingdom* was a collaboration between Sky and Hallmark Productions and saw several stages transformed into a fairy-tale land, complete with trolls, goblins and giants. And Ridley Scott's *RKO 281* detailed the making of Citizen Kane, rather cheekily transforming Pinewood into RKO studios, complete with a giant sign on the side of E Stage.

It was also the year in which The Really Useful Group brought two of their most successful stage productions to Pinewood to produce full-length videos of them. *Joseph and His Amazing Technicolor Dreamcoat*, starring Donny Osmond, Richard Attenborough and Joan Collins, was first into the studio, closely followed by *Jesus Christ Superstar*. Michael Tuchner's *Return to the Secret Garden* was mainly filmed in Berlin but made a brief hop over to the Pinewood gardens for some exterior scenes. The BBC chose Pinewood for its *Comic Relief* skit *Doctor Who – The Curse of the Fatal Death*, the second series of *Heartburn Hotel* and the children's drama *Natureboy*. Meanwhile, on August 5, the big-budget period drama *Quills* started shooting under Philip Kaufman's direction and witnessed the return of Michael Caine to his old stamping ground, alongside co-stars Kate Winslet, Geoffrey Rush and Joaquin Phoenix.

The film chronicles the last days of the Marquis de Sade (a character last seen at Pinewood in *Marat/Sade* in 1966) and brought with it a kaleidoscope of technical talent, including Oscar-winning production designer Martin Childs. 'This is actually my first time at Pinewood, as I've worked mainly at Shepperton, Ealing and on location. I started on *Quills* at the beginning of April and by the time we finish it'll have been about 30 weeks. We took two stages, A and F, and also used B Stage very briefly. A Stage was completely taken over by dungeons, cellars and underground rooms. It's proven to be quite a challenge as it's mostly French architecture, which I've never done before, but fortunately for us the wealthy folk of nineteenth-century England built in the style of eighteenth-century Paris. At Luton Hoo, for instance, we added extra roofs and did various things to the inside, and then we moved to Oxford, which we used as Paris.'

It had been a busy time for the studio, with lots of bookings in the diary for the year ahead … but change was about to come.

≈ 4 ≈

The Andrew Teare Years –
Part 1 (CEO, 1996–1998)

Whilst Pinewood strode buoyantly through the 1990s, its fate was about to be sealed mid-way through the decade when Andrew Teare was head-hunted by Rank chairman Sir Denys Henderson.

He seemed an odd choice for a leisure and entertainment conglomerate as, after all, he had spent most of his working life in the building and industrial materials trade, latterly at English China Clays.

When Teare stood up at the Rank annual general meeting in April to be introduced as the company's new chief executive, the shareholders were understandably nervous.

Michael Gifford, the outgoing chief executive, was a known quantity who had guided them through 12 years in leisure and film. Mind you, the chairman, Sir Denys Henderson's background did not lie in leisure either, as he had spent 35-years at ICI.

Teare was a burly fellow from the West Country who had just spent six years restructuring a supplier of raw materials to the paper industry. What on earth was Rank doing?

In the event the shareholders' fears were assuaged when Teare revealed himself the sort of person who would not shrink in the face of a challenge.

An acid question from one shareholder followed-up: what film had Teare seen most recently at the cinema?

'*Sense and Sensibility*,' he responded with a smile. 'In a Rank cinema.'

3.13 New Rank CEO Andrew Teare, seen here in the Noddy car with Jerry Fowden (Director of Rank Hotels) as he banked on a major investment in Butlin's turning the division around.

It gave the film division a little glimmer of hope that it would remain central to the new CEO's plans, but in recruiting Teare, Rank had a strategist, a deep thinker, and a man with a reputation of cost-cutting and restructuring.

Sell, Sell, Sell!

Within weeks of him taking charge, a clearer view of his plan emerged. He was to announce another disposal programme, which was said was going to raise in excess of £300 million. It included the sale of Rank Precision Industries, which made equipment for the entertainment industry; and Rank's 29 per-cent stake in Rank-Xerox was manoeuvred to an arm's length position to better avoid capital gains on its upcoming sale. It still accounted for 40 per-cent of the company's products, with an estimated value of £1bn.

Also, on the list was Shearings Holidays, the coach holiday company and rumours were rife of a demerger or sale of film and television interests.

It became clear he was brought in to dissect Rank and to convince the City that the shares were an exciting prospect once again. The Rank Organisation/Group Teare inherited was a leisure conglomerate that had many assets but less direction, but was he the man to give it the direction it needed?

Under Michael Gifford, the company realised £400 million from disposals and spent £1.3bn, including the purchase of Mecca.

Xerox

Teare would have undoubtedly realised it is a brave man who disposed of a steady and historically successful income, such as that of (Rank-Xerox) R-X, in favour of the development of a holiday sector that is subject to the uncertainties of consumer spending. Or did he?

George Helyer, the last Managing Director of Rank Film Distributors suggested, 'The new CEO – much like management before him – wanted to stand up and tell the shareholders "I'm doing a great job here, and taking the company in the right direction" but for him to acknowledge more than half the company's income continued to come in from a source that they'd invested in decades earlier, and had no day to day management involvement with, well it kind of undermined his own plan. Teare had to prove himself and prove he could manage Rank's assets better, and his plan was to dispose of the old (regardless of its success) and acquire new businesses that he felt would have the Midas touch.'

Teare's first spending spree was in buying the remaining shares that it did not already own in Hard Rock Cafe, for £270 million which was widely applauded.

But then came worrying news; not long after Teare got his feet under the table at Rank's head office, the bottom fell out of the English China Clays (ECC) share price. Teare had been lauded for restructuring, but ECC was now showing the results of what turned into an ill-advised purchase of Calgon in 1993, overseen by Teare just before joined Rank. Had Teare been the right choice after all?

When Teare then announced that Rank would only see profit growth in the first half of the year from a one-off gain in its Strand lighting division, the profits warning immediately knocked 6 per-cent off the share price.

It spurred Teare into disposing of other 'non-core' companies within the organisation, in order to give him extra buying power. He set about a two-year, selling spree.

Sell, Sell, Sell – again!

Rank Precision Industries was sold for £72 million and Shearings holiday coach firm was sold for £75 million, in a management buyout, to pay for the acquisition of the independent UK pub restaurant chain Tom Cobleigh for £123 million – which Teare planned to incorporate into Odeon sites to offer restaurant and bar facilities for customers. However, many Odeon's were in old buildings, in city centres, with limited space to expand.

Then American holiday company Kingston Plantation was sold for £30 million; various amusement arcades were sold for £25 million; and its remaining interest in Rank-Xerox was disposed of for £930 million.

This was not so much a selling spree as a total clear-out. Teare had seemingly set his sights on Mecca Bingo and on the Casino businesses as being the most profitable and future proof aspects of the organisation's portfolio.

In early 1997 the rumour mill had reported an impending breakup and sale of Rank's film interests.

⊶ 5 ⊷

Rank Film Distributors:
The Last Twenty Years

R FD's last ever managing director, George Helyer, shuddered when he
heard the name 'Ed Chilton' mentioned during an interview with this
author. He firmly pinned 'when the rot set in' Rank's film division at the
feet of Chilton who headed the Rank Leisure division from 1976. Company Chairman John Davis, who had effectively ruled the Organisation
since becoming managing director in 1948, and chairman from 1962, with
a very cautious and largely successful approach stepped down in the same
year and keen to put his own stamp on the organisation, Chilton immediately began looking for new opportunities to help make his name as the
new head of the division, and as an executive seen to be breathing fresh life
into the company and its shares.

Film return

He was mindful of the success *Bugsy Malone* had enjoyed at the box office,
which Rank Film Distributors had 50 per-cent financed against international distribution rights (with Paramount taking US rights for the other
50 per-cent) in 1976.

Director Alan Parker explained, 'I had tried to get the film set up for
some time, visiting the offices of would-be financiers – the few that there
were at the time. I was very successful in TV commercials but had no track

3.14 Bugsy Malone's success made Ed Chilton think Rank should get back into film finance

record of anything longer than 30 seconds, so they were very suspicious of me. I explained that it was a gangster movie pastiche that would be done in a contemporary way but as a homage to old Hollywood ... er ... er ... oh, and, by the way, it has an entire cast of children. The moment they heard the last bit they used to cough and say politely "Not today thank you". Fortunately, Frank Poole (MD) at Rank Film Distributors went with it – 50 per-cent anyway – with a little bit of arm twisting of the then Rank Leisure chairman Ed Chilton by Evelyn de Rothschild, all orchestrated in his inimitable way by David Puttnam, who was executive producer on the film.'

Given the volatile production environment at the time, where many of Pinewood's stages lay empty and even the ever-dependable James Bond was decamping to Paris for the next adventure, *Moonraker*, Pinewood MD Cyril Howard was understandably horrified when called into the board-room to see Ed Chilton.

Tony Williams was seconded to RFD from Rank Leisure Services in 1977, by Chilton, to restart in-house production based at Pinewood Studios. Between 1971 and 1976 Rank had only invested around £1.5 million a year in film production, and consequently its returns were just as modest. According to Tony Williams 'the two main income streams were down to was *Carry On* pictures and horror films made by Kevin Francis'.

Chilton wanted to know why RFD and its 600+ library wasn't more profitable, as surely *Bugsy* demonstrated it had the potential to be?

'The problem with library material is it has to be renewed,' said Tony Williams. 'And unless you keep feeding in more and more new titles, the library becomes very stale and it is difficult to sell the old titles, or certainly the old titles at the right price – at a good price.

'Rank was faced with a choice of either getting out of film completely, shut the whole thing down or become more serious about it again. They made the decision to increase their investment considerably and I was appointed Head of Production or Head of Production Worldwide Theatrical Films.'

The immediate problem Williams faced was that the cost of production had spiralled in the years since John Davis had ordered all Rank films would be budgeted at £150,000 or under; those modest budget films were able to pretty much cover their production costs in the UK cinemas alone, or with some Commonwealth income, but by 1977 they weren't. The income from its UK distribution and cinema arms was dropping because cinemas were closing, and bingo halls were opening in their place. Rank Film Productions was set up as a limited company and Williams ran that business, reporting directly to Ed Chilton.

There was a big publicity launch detailing how the Organisation was embarking upon a new and exciting production programme. Lionel Jeffries was brought into helm *Wombling Free*, based on the children's TV series about cuddly rubbish collector's resident in warrens beneath Wimbledon Common.

'Don't talk to me about that film!' he exclaimed. 'It ought to have been flushed down the lavatory. It was a horrible experience, and the producer was on the floor every day criticising the set-ups whenever I was not looking. It wasn't a happy experience, and it was a terrible flop.' Indeed, the film failed to receive a general release.

3.15 Silver Dream Racer was one of the Rank-produced films, which failed to perform

3.16 Star of Rank's The 39 Steps, Robert Powell, at a lunch in Cannes publicising the production. (Photo: Richard Blanshard)

Losses

Over two years Rank made eight films costing £10 million, which also included *Eagle's Wing, The Shout, The Thirty-Nine Steps, The Lady Vanishes, Riddle of the Sands, Tarka The Otter, Bad Timing* and *Silver Dream Racer* – the latter, a story following a garage mechanic (David Essex) who dreams of becoming a motorcycle racer only to be killed at the peak of his career was, like the others before it, less than successful and Rank paused their new film financing initiative. The films lost £1.6 million overall.

Many of the films in the 1977–1979 programme were purposely set in the past, as explained by Tony Williams who felt that was part of the

3.17 The Lady Vanishes was a Rank-financed Hammer-produced remake that performed poorly and in fact became the last film Hammer produced until 2008

problem. 'They decided to go back in time to tell stories that didn't have to face what were regarded as "seventies problems". What people are nostalgic for isn't necessarily any particular period, but the happier values that Rank perceived as being missing.'

Film critic Alexander Walker commentated, 'Tony Williams's enthusiasm was boundless; his knowledge of boardroom politics and organisation rivalries was narrower but like Bryan Forbes at EMI, he found his own company's distribution outfit was not always the most eager taker for many of the pictures he put into production'.

Another return?

Perhaps without taking the mood of shareholders first, at the Cannes Film Festival in 1980 Ed Chilton announced a £12 million slate of new projects. 'The decision was made to plunge on in and then it was pulled back', said Williams.

Films announced included an adaptation of *HMS Ulysses, The Rocking Horse Winner,* and a feature version of BBC comedy *To The Manor Born* – all were cancelled just a month later and The Rank Organisation withdrew from film production.

'It now takes too long to recoup money on films,' said a spokesman for Rank, as being the reason. Though in truth, it's highly likely Chilton acted to score a PR success at the looming festival without the board having full knowledge of his plan. This was underlined by *To The Manor Born* writer Peter Spence who said, 'It is news to me. Yes, the film rights were optioned 40 or so years back [in 1979/1980] but not by Rank so how we got from there to Rank announcing it as a project in Cannes is anybody's guess. But certainly, no film was ever made.'

Management team

George Helyer was Business Affairs Director and Deputy MD to Managing Director Fred Turner at Rank Film Distributors from January 1984.

'When Fred Turner took over as MD in the early 1980s, not long after Rank's misguided return to film production had been abandoned, the distribution arm was at a low ebb and there were voices within Rank arguing that it should be closed down,' said Helyer. Although TV had impacted negatively on cinema income, the advent of home video gave films a second life and there was an increased demand for library material.

'After a time, RFD was in trouble,' suggested Tony Williams, 'because they hadn't got any new product.' In striking deals with video labels, Fred Turner stabilized RFDs finances and started to deliver profits. As a result, he was asked to deliver a business plan to develop new product.

'Mike Gifford had looked at RFD and asked, "Are we in the business of film production or film investment?" revealed George Helyer. 'To Rank's investors, "film production" was a dirty word … or couple of words.

"If we are in investment, and you want to keep RFD going, what is your strategy, what will you invest and what will the return be?" he asked Fred.

'Fred agreed Rank should not produce films', added Helyer, 'but would look for projects with potential to be successful internationally that already had a North America release, to give it presence, and we'd take the rest of the world distribution rights in exchange for our investment – usually, and typically, 30–40per-cent of the budget.'

'Rank would not directly make them, they just bought into pictures. They did an output deal with Orion and that carried on until they sold the shooting match,' concluded Tony Williams.

Deals were set-up with individual producers too, who were in a position to deliver a film with a North American release and international stars, and that was the main thrust of Turner's plan, to which Gifford gave the go-ahead. As an addendum it was agreed if the film was made in the UK, every effort would be taken to shoot at Pinewood, print at Rank Film Laboratories and distribute through Odeon cinemas – they weren't deal breaking conditions, but it made sense to use every part of Rank's film combine.

Funding

As a result, RFD was given the greenlight to create a revolving $100 million production fund. Though they never came close to fully investing the full amount because 'there were not enough projects that met our investment criteria', said CEO Michael Gifford.

'The fund had been substantially underused not because of unwillingness to invest … but because the opportunities to invest were not there,' added the film division head Jim Daly.

'The RFD film library was returning £3 million – £4 million a year in profit, and with pre-sales of new film projects internationally, the company never really called on Rank's financial coffers as it was pretty much self-financing,' Helyer explained.

'Fred and I dealt directly with producers such as Martin Ransohoff (who'd just produced *Jagged Edge*), and Brad Krevoy who knew how to make a commercial film for a price, due to his early start working for Roger Corman. We agreed multi-film projects that were all cross-collateralised and we had approval of each script, and input on casting. We looked to form partnerships and relationships based on mutual respect.

3.18 Joan Collins attends a Rank Film Distributors reception at the Cannes Film Festival (Photo: Richard Blanshard)

'Then came producer David Begelman, the former head of Columbia Studios, who greenlit films such as *Close Encounters, Annie, Shampoo, Funny Lady*, etc in the mid 1970s and was generally highly successful,' recalled Helyer.

'In a bizarre true life story he had actually been convicted of fraud when he forged a cheque supposedly meant for actor Cliff Robertson – it was a well-publicised scandal in 1977 – but roll on to 1993 and through our representative in LA we were introduced to David who, at that point had a deal with MGM and Live Entertainment (which owned Vestron Home Video) for US rights to his movies. He had recently produced such films as *Mannequin, Weekend at Bernie's, The Fabulous Baker Boys, Short Time* and *Mannequin Two: On the Move* and overall made decent financial returns [some to RFD]. It sounded the ideal scenario for Rank Film Distributors, and we agreed in principle to a 10-film and $150-million production plan – committing to 33per-cent of the budgets for all international rights in perpetuity.

'The deal was subject to main board approval,' added Helyer. 'Our film and TV division chief Jim Daly said he'd discuss it all with Gifford. We were perfectly honest and said this man had been convicted for fraud in the past, but his recent business all seemed above board and we felt confident.'

Gifford allegedly said something along the lines of 'Producers are crooks by nature anyway,' when Daly told him of Begelman's past and reported back to Helyer that it was up to him and Fred Turner to ensure the deal was watertight.

Flack

'We announced it all in Cannes that year, where we got tremendous flack from the UK press for investing in American films rather than the British industry,' Helyer revealed.

'But Begelman had scripts and talent that we felt confident in. Nothing like that was coming to us from within the British film industry. A case in point was when we were offered [the last] *Carry On* film – *Columbus* – by John Goldsmith and Gerald Thomas. It was a very questionable script with a £3 million budget. It is one thing to come along with a little comedy film costing £300,000 that might stand a chance of recouping its money at the UK box office, but £3 million? Please!'

The Begelman deal actually returned RFD a significant profit, and whilst company policy was 'never to comment', Helyer drafted a letter to trade magazine Screen International in answer to criticism from the UK industry, saying, 'We were under strict instructions to deliver profits, and at the time the British production sector was awash with red ink. Whilst it was customary for British producers sporting mediocre scripts to run down Rank, could any of them offer us a slate of films with US distribution and international cast attached?' By ensuring RFD made an annual profit, Fred Turner and George Helyer had the confidence and backing of the Rank Board, and in particular Michael Gifford.

'Fred and I had to deliver our yearly strategic plans to Rank head office in Connaught Place to be approved by Gifford, and I remember for one such meeting Fred was overseas and I went along with my chief accountant. Gifford invited us straight in.

"George, do you want a short meeting or a long meeting?" he asked me.

"That's for you to decide Mr Gifford. I'm here to assure you of our plan and if it takes all day for me to do that, then I'll be here all day," I countered. Gifford smiled. I later discovered the person who had previously held my post had been asked the same question and when he replied "short", Gifford showed him the door and fired him.

'I liked Gifford. He was straight talking and to the point. He was also very loyal and if you work hard for him, he recognised that.'

British Films

RFD did get involved in some British movies, such as *Defence of the Realm*, *The Fourth Protocol*, *Under Suspicion* and *Wilt*.

'We had a policy if investing in at least one British film a year – more if we could – but we had to believe in them' revealed Helyer. 'But I was mindful had I delivered even one big failure, then I was out'.

'To be frank, we received endless crap scripts. They poured

3.19 Disgraced executive David Begelman had a colourful past, but gained Rank's confidence in being able to mount a production slate

in. Every now and again we might be approached by someone like Tim Bevan of Working Title, with an appealing project which had a good script, a realistic budget and what I'd see as a reasonably low risk – that's how *Four*

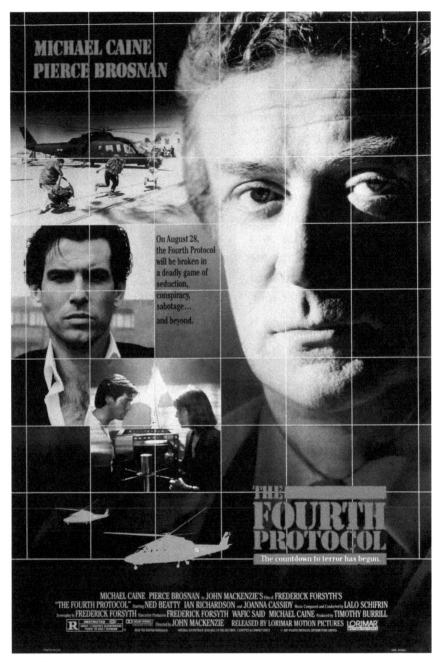

3.20 The Fourth Protocol was a Rank Film Distributors project which turned a healthy profit

3.21 RFD was offered Carry On Columbus but 'did not have sufficient confidence' in the project

Weddings And A Funeral came about, and similarly London Weekend Television brought us a script called *Wilt*, David Puttnam brought us *Defence Of The Realm,* and a comedy called *Just Like A Woman* from Zenith (Central TV). They were all pretty good scripts, good investment propositions and stood a chance of a fairly decent return.

'Rank was under massive pressure to support the British film industry from the vociferous UK press, and Fred and I were under great pressure, in turn, from the board. But any investment needed to be balanced with business judgement – and good scripts. We also bought finished films.'

Giving an example of how completed film acquisitions worked, Helyer explained.

'I saw *Strictly Ballroom* at an early screening at the Cannes Film Festival. I thought it a terrific movie and wanted to make them an offer for international distribution. I ran to the sales agent's office saying I was going on to see Fred to formulate an offer, but we definitely wanted it and we would premiere it in Leicester Square. We agreed to meet the next morning to sign it all off.

3.22 Just Like a Woman was a Zenith / RFD co-production

It had opened big in Australia and Fred shared my enthusiasm. We opened on offering (US)$250,000 and £400,000 in prints and advertising minimum. I knew we could sell video rights to VCI, and TV rights to Sky (with whom we had just done an output deal). Anyhow, we got up to (US)$800,000 and Fred started looking a bit concerned, but they agreed – providing we took a Kylie Minogue picture for (US)$200,000.

We shook hands.

'I rang my friend at VCI and enthused about our purchase of the best film at Cannes, and told him we wanted (US)$750,000 for video rights and a 33per-cent royalty – I think that was adjusted (downwards a bit), but even then I knew with my Sky deal I had pretty much covered off the purchase price, and on release we made a fortune at the box office – about £20 million.' In a similar vein, Fred Turner recounted how one of his favourite films came about in 1995, 'Frank Price of Savoy Pictures called. He had set up an Irish romantic comedy called *Circle of Friends* with Sony Pictures but did not have an international distribution deal. I read the script, liked it, and asked about casting as I felt that was key. Frank said Minnie Driver (who was relatively unknown then) as the female lead and they were in talks with Chris O'Donnell. I'd just seen him in *Scent of a Woman* and said, "if you can get him, you have a deal". In 1991 gross revenues for The Rank Organisation were reported to be £2.3 billion. Since Gifford took over in 1983, revenues had more than tripled, earnings per share quadrupled and trading profits multiplied sixfold. RFD enjoyed great success under Turner's strategic plan and distributed films such as *The Fabulous Baker Boys, Fried Green Tomatoes, Silence of the Lambs, Educating Rita* and *Hannah and Her Sisters*.

But along with the success stories was the long list of opportunities Rank did not buy into were notable.

Partnerships

The company turned away US film companies keen to be bought-out that were rumoured to include MGM, Orion and Carolco, and Rank opted out of the race to become a commercial TV operator in the UK when the licence to run a Channel 3 franchise (now ITV) was offered to tender, and likewise early approaches from satellite tv consortium BSB were spurned. However, the Organisation did bid for Granada, which owned the commercial TV franchise for the northwest of England, which led to speculation that Rank was interested in moving into television production. But the bid was aimed, said Gifford, 'at Granada's non-tv businesses, which include bingo halls and roadside service stations'.

3.23 The Irish romantic comedy won the backing of RFD when Chris O'Donnell signed-on to star

3.24 Won over by Strictly Ballroom in Cannes, RFD bid high to acquire it

Jim Daly, managing director of Rank's film and TV services division stated categorically, 'We are not filmmakers. We don't believe we have creative talent,' a sentiment extended to television too.

But by the mid '90s, underlining their commitment to the UK industry, Rank Film Distributors formed a partnership with Granada Film (the feature department of Granada TV) to produce comedy films with budgets in the region of £1 million – £2 million. Granada/Rank Film Distributors productions announced *Up On The Roof* as being the first collaboration – their one and only as it turned out.

Based on a play written by Simon Moore and Jane Prowse, it was produced by Brian Eastman.

'After we produced the play, I commissioned Jane and Simon to write a movie adaptation,' revealed Eastman. 'I was already working with Granada and drew it to their attention. Pippa Cross at Granada liked the script, so she took it to Rank'.

'I can't remember the exact budget, but I am sure it was under £2 million. The film was made by Granada and all our artistic and script decisions were made with Pippa. I do not know if she double-checked any of these with Fred and George at Rank? In the previous two films I had made with Rank, once we had agreed a budget and the main casting, Fred and George were very happy to leave us alone. So, imagine that was true of Pippa's relationship with them too.'

'Rank discussed their release/P&A strategy with us. That was just before the Carlton deal was announced so we thought it was business as usual. We looked at the proposed poster and advertising campaign, which we did not like. So, we commissioned an alternative and took it into Rank, and they were happy to go with it.' But change was on the horizon.

'When Andrew Teare took over as CEO, he told us RFD was going to continue as a core business within Rank but asked us for a valuation. There was nothing unusual in his request, but nobody really knew what the film library was worth; we all had ideas, and with it making £4 million a year plus regular pre-sales coming in, plus new media emerging like DVD, it continually gave the library a new lease of life, as did expanding TV opportunities. 'I was conscious if we valued it too high, we'd be accused of having a poor return on capital; had it been too low we'd be accused of not doing enough!'

3.25 The last film made by The Rank Group – Lawn Dogs

Fully-financing

Teare chatted with Turner and Helyer about how they might take RFD forward. Turner revealed it was becoming more and more difficult to find studio scripts with US distribution deals that had not been sown up internationally – or ones that were not asking silly money for the international rights.

Then came *Lawn Dogs*.

'It was a beautiful script from producer Duncan Kenworthy. We were keen to develop more producer relationships, and who better than Britain's most successful who – a few years earlier – delivered *Four Weddings and a Funeral*? Fred and I loved the script. It did not have any US distribution at this point, and that's where we saw an opportunity.

'The budget was around $7 million – not enormous. We went to Andrew Teare and said if we could 100per-cent finance *Lawn Dogs*, we could sell the US rights ourselves to a distributor, and into the bargain develop that all-important relationship with a UK producer – and this would be the first of many collaborations! It'd give us more buying power and began a new

3.26 A dubious mix of films ended Rank's last American co-production programme, this being one

era of RFD.' Teare gave the go ahead and at the 1996 Cannes Film Festival Rank's return to 100per-cent financing of movies – albeit by acquiring rights rather than direct investment as a producer – was heralded.

Over in LA, Helyer was dispatched to tie-up a deal with their old friend Brad Krevoy.

'Brad was now co-president of Orion Pictures, with a six-picture producing deal, and so we finalised a deal with them for films including *8 Heads in A Duffel Bag* and *Best Men*. I thought it was a poor deal (for RFD). They were pictures of questionable quality, if I'm honest' added Helyer, 'but RFD needed product.'

Then came what Helyer described as a 'sense of uncertainty from Teare'.

'I felt there were some holes in the Rank corporate balance sheet that he needed to fill, and he clearly thought RFD was more valuable than it turned out to be.'

Debts

Teare had made some hefty acquisitions and pledged significant investment to the holiday sector – namely Butlins – and company debt was increasing. He needed to raise some money to redress the balance, and the obvious answer was to sell-off some divisions within the company. Teare felt Rank's fortunes lay in their holiday companies, Hard Rock, and bingo – and not in film.

In January 1997, the trade press newspaper Variety reported, 'Carlton Communications is believed to be considering a bid for Rank Film Distributors, after both Polygram and Pearson dropped out of the running to buy the famous British company in recent weeks. Rank Group is refusing to confirm reports that RFD is up for sale, but industry sources say that Rank chief executive Andrew Teare has been quietly entertaining suitors for the past couple of months. Rank is understood to be inviting offers for RFD at between £100 million and £150 million ($162 million and $240 million). Polygram looked two months ago, and Pearson recently followed, but both decided the asking price was too rich.'

Whilst the main value of RFD lay in its big library, it consisted primarily of classic British movies, topped up with foreign rights to some more recent American fare, but it was dominated by British black-and-white movies of limited value outside English-speaking territories. Plus, it emerged the library has been very heavily pre-sold for some time to come, leaving little scope for a buyer to do much with it.

US rights were tied up with Goldwyn under a 10-year deal, and Goldwyn had an option to renew for another 10 years.

On April 2, 1997, the deal was confirmed in the trade newspapers – Carlton had bought RFD for £65 million. It immediately rebranded Carlton/RFD Ltd and Fred Turner took early retirement, whilst George Helyer was promoted to MD.

The big question was, would Carlton keep the company in distribution?

Stripping out the library

Producer Brian Eastman explained, 'Just before the release of *Up on The Roof*, the Carlton takeover was announced, although of course Fred and George must have known it was on the way. I wrote to Michael Green at Carlton asking for re-assurance that the film would still be widely distributed which he assured me it would. But that was not the case! They were only buying the library was widely felt to be true at the time – so it wasn't really a surprise we were 'dumped'.'

'We only had a release of about a week in cinemas because companies backing the film were changing and we got caught in the handover,' added screenwriter Jane Prowse.

'I fronted negotiations with Michael Green,' revealed Helyer. 'It was clear in my mind that was the end for us in distribution. Everything I suggested, put forward etc, was rejected.'

Fred Turner added, 'I felt sorry for George. They stripped the library and thus the company's income stream out, they didn't allow him to make any acquisitions, they didn't give him any budget and yet maintained the façade of being in business.'

In May 1997, Carlton Film Distributors made one-third of its staff redundant, which signalled the company's obvious intentions.

A few months later, on September 22, 1997, Carlton announced it was shutting down the international operations of its distribution arm, the rebadged Carlton Film Distributors, and would end its UK distribution by the end of the year. Sales, distribution, and marketing for the slate it inherited was to be assumed by Village Intermedia Pictures. As Rank's releasing venture with Castle Rock/Turner was to expire on December 31, it seemed timely to shut everything down then.

A Carlton spokesman said, '... the company is in discussions with other British distributors that may be interested in acquiring its distribution infrastructure, and that distribution had only been a small part of the Rank acquisition.'

He added that Carlton, 'is talking to the Film Consortium — one of the three lottery franchise winners, which had a distribution deal through RFD — about how the changes will affect them.' In effect, they pulled out. George Helyer reflected, 'I got a great pay off in the end, so can't be bitter, but it did sadden me all the same that this was the end of an extraordinary era.' Fred Turner died June 25, 2004 at the age of 71. His death was caused by sudden complications from myelodysplasia, which he had lived with for several years. He had been with Rank for 51 years, joining as an office boy in 1946.

Rank was the only company he ever worked for.

6

The Andrew Teare Years – Part 2

Following the sale of RFD a noticeable change occurred at the main entrance to Pinewood Studios; in the early summer of 1998 the 'Man With the Gong' logo was replaced by a large red dot and the brand name 'Deluxe'.

In fact, 'Deluxe Entertainment Services' was born a couple of months earlier in May 1998, at the Cannes Film Festival, to encompass Rank Film Laboratories, Rank Video Services and Pinewood Studios under a new 'umbrella'.

'Rank bought Deluxe some years ago,' former Pinewood MD Steve Jaggs pointed out in 1999. 'It wasn't the other way around. Deluxe is quite a generic term in the film industry and is known worldwide. Rank is a very well-known name, too, but rather more in the UK, and the Rank Group is now mainly seen as a leisure and holiday business. I thought it was a good move and has certainly helped with our business.'

Jaggs' diplomatic explanation countered the widely held belief within the UK film industry that Andrew Teare was in fact grouping Rank's film divisions into a new entity to make a clean sale easier.

Though the City didn't appear terribly impressed with the CEO of Rank's plans thus far. In his first year at the helm, Teare declared that he expected to see a 15 per-cent return on capital for Rank's businesses. Yet Rank's shares had consistently under-performed by some 25 per-cent.

Andrew Hunter, leisure analyst at Hoare Govett, effectively placed a 'sell' rating on Rank shares from 1996 onward. The share price 'has fallen further than I had thought it would,' he warned.

Bad call

Mr. Hunter added that Butlins 'needed an awful lot more money spent on it to turn it around' and considered this one of the main problems the group faced. He said he thought Mr. Teare had realized it will take him a lot longer to turn the business around than he had hoped.

Teare next promised a review of US holiday activities and suggested Rank might quit the US holiday market altogether, though their experience there illuminated an opportunity in an area which, to date, had been under-developed in Britain – gaming.

Just over two years from him taking the helm, the financial press reported Mr Teare had spent more than £400 million on acquisitions:

- Duplico (a European video duplicator) for £29 million.
- Tom Cobleigh for £123 million.
- Hard Rock Cafes, where they did not already own the brand rights, namely in the Caribbean and Argentina; and,
- a logistical distribution business for video duplication in North America for a total consideration of £43 million.
- in March 1998, Rank bought Parkdean Holidays, a UK holiday park operator for £38 million.
- Teare then instigated spending £150 million on a major overhaul of Butlins.
- ordered more multiplex cinemas and renovation of some of its existing 76 Odeon cinemas.
- and pledged an additional annual £40 million a year in Tom Cobleigh since acquiring it.

Teare also disposed of freehold property for £161 million to a joint venture with The British Land Company PLC under a sale and leaseback arrangement and in July 1999 invested £10 million in Campotel, a campsite business in France.

Despite all his spending power, Teare found Rank's return on capital remained 'well below target'. Third quarter profits slumped 20per-cent to £11 million.

Gloom

As Rank issued its gloomy trading update it showed that the crucial summer months were even worse than expected. The figures included a disastrous period at Deluxe with Rank's video duplication business profits falling 17 per- cent to £24 million as it struggled to handle demand for copies of the video of *Titanic*. Rank said manufacturing problems and a short deadline had led it to subcontract a substantial part of the contract, which reduced profit.

The results shattered any remaining confidence Rank's board had in Mr Teare.

Management consultant Bain & Co were drafted in for a strategic review. The writing was on the wall for Teare.

On October 29, 1999 Andrew Teare accepted responsibility for the group's dire performance and resigned. Company chairman Sir Denys Henderson, who was responsible for hiring Mr Teare and supporting his strategy, said, 'The Board believes an even more determined approach to drive the business forward is required and that this is the time for new leadership.'

City analysts said Mr Teare's departure was likely to signal a change of strategy at Rank. 'The company won't exist in its current form for too long,' one expert predicted. Rank shares jumped 13p to 239p as analysts calculated that the group's break-up value was at least 320p a share. Under Mr Teare's short tenure, Rank's share price had more than halved.

Although compensation had not been initially agreed Mr Teare, who was on a two-year rolling contract and was paid £512,000 in his final year, was rumoured to receive more than £1 million in his goodbye handshake.

Douglas Yates, Rank's commercial director, took over as acting chief executive and put himself forward for the job. However, outside head-hunters were appointed.

⭒ 7 ⭒

The Mike Smith Years
(CEO, 1999–2006)

B y 1999 it was apparent that Rank was suffering under a major debt load. Its acquisition activity over the past several years had failed to produce positive financial results. As such, Rank approached betting and gaming industry executive Mike Smith as new CEO, to oversee the company's turnaround, in April 1999.

Bingo and gambling

Smith believed the company's future mainly lay in gaming and the Hard Rock Café brand. The former CEO of Ladbrokes immediately began a major streamlining effort designed to restore profits and reshape the company.

In August 1999 Rank, announced it was cutting 465 jobs (to include management) as part of a wide-ranging attempt to boost its earnings, and pledged it would also reduce spending and cut shareholder dividends.

News of the cost-cutting strategy came as Rank announced its results for the half-year. Profits were £80 million, slightly down on the previous year's figure, and turnover remained flat at £916 million.

'Results that only match those of last year need to be improved,' said Smith.

'I recognise that this performance is still not at the required level for the longer term and therefore we are taking firm action now to improve our future profits and cash position.'

Rank's spending on investment projects was immediately halved to £250 million and borrowing increased to a massive £1.3bn.

It was clear The Rank Group needed to generate more cash to repay its debts.

'We are reviewing our portfolio to establish how we can unlock value to shareholders by reshaping our business interests,' concluded Smith.

The Tom Cobleigh pub chain, which had failed miserably, had already been placed up for sale, and speculation was rife that its nightclub and amusement machines businesses would also be sold off.

But the problem with selling the smaller businesses was that they simply would not bring in enough cash to solve Rank's problems – and so attention turned to its bigger divisions such as Odeon and Hard Rock.

Mr Smith was more optimistic about the second half of 1999, and particularly singled out the cinema chain Odeon. He said poor film releases early in the year should be balanced by the successful performances of films such as *Notting Hill* and the new *Star Wars* movie. Salesman talk if ever there was…

The market gave Smith's strategy a lukewarm reception, and the company's shares fell 2per-cent to 269p.

So, Smith decided to divest holdings that were considered unrelated to its core businesses.

Holiday offers

In September 2000, half yearly losses at Butlin's had almost doubled to £10 million, and that news had the potential to scupper Mike Smith's plans to sell the whole holiday division. However family owned Bourne Leisure, a holiday and caravan site company founded in 1964, had recently been identified as the most likely buyer of the Rank holiday division, which also included Haven, Warner and Oasis for a suggested £650 million price tag.

Admittedly, of Rank's four remaining businesses, holidays showed the best operating profit growth of 27per-cent, mainly due to Resorts USA, though rumours in the City suggested the sale price was reducing.

In its other divisions, the half year to June 30, saw operating profits fall by 11per-cent at Deluxe, though gaming grew by 27 per-cent to £39.5 million, and the Hard Rock Cafe chain grew by 20 per-cent at £21.9 million.

Smith managed to bring debt down to £775 million, though reported £184.6 million of 'exceptionals' including losses on the sale of Tom Cobleigh and Rank's share in Universal Studios, which sent overall group losses for the year up to £142.5 million.

In November 1999, the Nightscene (nightclub) business was disposed of for £150 million to help shore up those losses.

The film division

All eyes shifted to Odeon cinemas and Rank's historic film home, Pinewood Studios.

TV boss and entrepreneur Michael Grade had approached Rank in 1993 about buying all its film interests, and led a consortium, pitching in at £400 million. But Rank said that it was not considering selling the business and instead set out its plans for a shake-up of the business, which many in the industry – including Grade – felt has lost its way.

Former CEO Michael Gifford said he had been aware of the interest for around four months, but 'at no time had Rank been approached'.

'We will not have conversations even if we are approached,' he concluded, 'as the division is not for sale.'

In late 1999 when Grade publicly expressed intertest in buying Pinewood again, Mike Smith told him they were only willing to sell Deluxe as a whole. Grade in turn told them he was only interested in the studio. The year prior, Pinewood made a profit of £4.4 million on turnover of £13.2 million.

On February 21, 2000 Rank announced a deal had been agreed to sell its Odeon cinema chain to venture capital group Cinven for £280 million. Rank said the cash raised would be used to reduce its debts. The business was to be merged with ABC Cinemas, already owned by Cinven.

The very next day Pinewood Studios was sold for £62 million to Michael Grade's group.

The spin-off of Pinewood wasn't unexpected, as the Rank Group proved unable to attract a buyer for the whole of its Deluxe division.

On the same day as announcing the Pinewood sale, Rank also revealed that it was buying a DVD facility in Los Angeles. It sent mixed if not

3.27 Lord Michael Grade was always keen on acquiring parts of Rank's film division.

confused messages to the City – the company which did not consider film a core part of its portfolio, was divesting itself of one major part only to buy a fresh interest in another. Rank shares fell 13.5p to 147p. They had been on a steady downward trend since they peaked at 550p in 1996.

Smith confirmed that the 'clear-out' was likely to continue, with several buyers interested in the group's holiday arm.

'At some stage we will have to consider whether Rank is an appropriate name. When Rank was in films it was obviously very relevant but since then we've moved off in other directions and you wonder whether the Rank name has any goodwill left in it,' he stated, as he contemplated a name change for the Group.

Write-downs on the sale of poorly performing businesses resulted in a £142 million pre-tax loss for the six months to June 2000. But operating profits on ongoing businesses rose 24 per-cent.

On September 28, 2000 it was announced Rank had agreed to sell its holiday businesses for slightly higher than anticipated, at £700 million, to Bourne Leisure. The sale marked the end of a three-year failed effort to revive Butlins. Under Andrew Teare, Rank had invested heavily in the relaunch which included enclosing large areas in all-weather Skyline

Pavilions, calling in the designer Jeff Banks to spruce up the Redcoats' uniforms and renaming camps 'family entertainment resorts'. But the seemingly old-fashioned holiday camps could not compete with cheaper foreign holidays once the budget airlines such as Easyjet came along.

Though matters weren't helped when Teare organised a big press launch for the Butlins overhaul in 1997, drafting in children's favourite, Noddy.

'If you ask me why this wasn't done years ago, the answer is I don't know,' Teare told the bemused press.

'People on social security are finding they can stay cheaper at home,' suggested financial director Nigel Turnbull to the same press when asked why he thought Butlins had lost some of its popularity in recent years.

'We don't want anyone to think we are trying to turn Butlin's into an upmarket product,' chipped in Head of Rank Holidays, Jerry Fowden.

With PR like that, who needs enemies?

Rumours

Suggestions followed that the next business on the block could be Deluxe – scaled down and with a cheaper price tag.

Smith had by now raised £1.4bn through disposals, and Deluxe stuck out like a sore thumb amongst Rank's remaining businesses — Mecca bingo halls, Grosvenor casinos and Hard Rock Cafes.

Smith believed that imminent deregulation of betting and opportunities to create online gaming ventures made gambling a more promising area and said he intended to use the Hard Rock brand to open a chain of casinos.

Whilst trying to offload Deluxe, Smith approved an odd move to pay £12 million for a DVD manufacturing facility in California – Pioneer Video Manufacturing Inc. – in 2001.

At the same time he acquired the Park Tower Casino in London for £14 million to bolster Rank's gaming ambitions.

In June 2001, Deluxe Video completed the sale and leaseback of the plant and machinery at the video duplication facility in Arkansas for £27 million. In December 2001, Deluxe Video also completed the sale and leaseback of the real estate in Arkansas for £22 million. The two transactions taken together realized a profit on disposal of £12 million.

The Group's internet gaming site, Rank.com, was launched in November 2001, followed by the launch of hardrockcasino.com in July 2002, yet curiously again they were still expanding Deluxe – perhaps in the belief it would attract a sale? – and entered into a venture with Ritek Corporation of Taiwan to combine the DVD assets of Deluxe and Ritek in North America and Europe. Deluxe paid a total of £34 million to Ritek, spread over three years for its 80 per-cent interest in the venture.

Then in November 2002, Deluxe acquired Capital FX – a leading player in the UK laser, sub-titling and digital effects market – for £9 million.

Switching focus, in January 2003 the Rank Group acquired Blue Square Limited, one of the UK's leading internet and telephone betting businesses for a consideration of £65 million. (Ten years later they sold the failed division for just £5 million).

Six months later, Deluxe was centre to Rank activities again when the Group acquired Disctronics, one of the largest independent DVD and CD replicators in Europe for £34.3 million.

Had Rank again lost focus? What in fact was its core activity to be? Was Deluxe to be part of it still?

In 2004 the answer was forthcoming as a succession of disposals began:

- The sale of Rank Leisure Machine Services netted £30 million.
- In 2005 Deluxe film processing was sold to MacAndrews & Forbes and netted £437 million.
- The exclusive West End casino the Clermont Club was sold to Quek Leng Chan's BIL International for £31 million.
- Next came the sale of the Hard Rock Cafe business for £490 million to the Seminole native American tribe in Florida – the business had made a pre-tax profit of £35 million in 2005 and had 132 outlets worldwide.
- Finally, the remaining UK operations (DVD duplication) of Deluxe Media were sold to Sony for £5.9 million in 2006.

This latter sale – which had supposedly been on the table for over a year – signalled the end of Rank's long association with the film industry.

Mike Smith had overseen the biggest shake up in Rank's history and its departure from all areas of the UK film industry with which it was so synonymous for 60 years.

Time to leave

Having raised a significant sum from disposals and balanced the books better, Smith announced he was to leave, after seven years, and stepped down ahead of his 60th birthday at the annual shareholders meeting in March 2006.

Investors were said to be 'disappointed' by the net proceeds of the Deluxe sale – of about £300 million – but Rank's Chairman Alun Cathcart denied Mr Smith's departure was related to investor feeling and pointed out that they'd started looking for a successor in the previous October to ensure an 'orderly handover'.

Alun Cathcart concluded, 'Since Mike joined Rank in 1999, he has brought about a major transformation of the company, creating a focused business that is well positioned to exploit growth opportunities in the gaming and leisure markets. Under his leadership, Rank has generated significant value for its shareholders through a programme of restructuring and development. On behalf of the Board I would like to express our deep appreciation for all Mike's hard work and dedication over the last seven years.

'We have been fortunate to identify Ian [Burke] so early in the process [to take over as new CEO]. With his track record in leisure and hospitality and his experience of brand development and franchising, he is well-equipped to lead Rank's continued development.'

There, the story of the Rank Organisation / Group and the film industry really ends. From the 1930s to the turn of the century, Rank and its famous Gong man logo had been synonymous with filmmaking and cinema.

Even though its 1996 move back into full-financing via Rank Film Distributors had been incredibly short-lived, it demonstrated the ambition and potential of the company – a company that had tried to support British films each and every year, albeit on a modest basis compared to Hollywood standards.

There is no denying RFD's strategic partnerships around the world were enviable and its repositioning itself as a 100 per-cent financier was the breath of fresh air the UK industry was looking for.

If only …

Part 4

Today

1

The Rank Group

Under Mike Smith's successor, Ian Burke (CEO and Chairman between 2006–2014), shares tumbled 24 per-cent in his first year at the helm in part due to the smoking ban – the biggest piece of legislation to hit the gaming industry in 40 years – as well as the shock of higher taxes when Gordon Brown, in his last budget as Chancellor, surprised the industry by hiking casino taxes thus blowing an £8 million hole in Rank's profits.

'Short-term challenges' was how Burke described it.

'We were disappointed. It took the wind out of our sails. We were just getting our investors to the point where they thought they understood all the issues that were facing our business and that came completely out of the blue.

'This is not a business that makes super profits, and therefore it is not a business that should suffer super taxes.'

Rank's profits certainly were not vast – they were just £44.4 million in 2006, and the business was unrecognisable as the leisure conglomerate it once was.

Focus

It was estimated 50 per-cent of Mecca's customers smoked and the impact on bingo halls north of the border (where the ban was first introduced) was enormous, sending underlying sales down 17 per-cent in the first year after the embargo.

Ahead of English and Welsh club smoking bans Burke said, 'We felt we did learn a number of lessons in Scotland in the first 12 months and we have had more time to execute additional actions – mainly around making sure customers are still going to enjoy bingo.'

Shelters sprung up outside Meccas so that customers could still puff away between cards, while the chain got rid of older sites that it could not modernise.

But Burke still had a lot of work in front of him. As well as the casino and bingo tax issues and the smoking ban, he had to prepare the company for the new gambling laws coming into force. The legislation allowed Rank to introduce new games – in bingo it could roll over stakes into big jack pot prizes and at its Grosvenor sites punters could now play Texas Hold'em, a hugely popular online game previously banned in casinos. It also meant Rank could, for the first time, advertise its casinos.

Burke took steps to modernise the business 'to broaden the appeal to a wide range of leisure customers', as he put it, with glitzier operations that had a wider choice of restaurants and bars to woo a bigger audience.

Moving on

In 2007 Rank moved from their plush Mayfair offices at 6 Connaught Place, Marble Arch, to Maidenhead in Berkshire and to the building they previously ran their Leisure Machine Services from. Less than a decade later, numbers 5 & 6 Connaught Place became a £100 million apartment complex consisting of seven 'ultra-prime' apartments – costing between £12 million and £20 million each.

The complex was deemed so posh, developers opted against a Waitrose on the ground floor – instead letting Harrods help residents with their shopping with a 24/7 concierge from the Knightsbridge store, 365 days-a-year, situated in the foyer.

In March 2008, the Rank Group hit the headlines again with the announcement it was off-loading its £700 million pension scheme. The move, which was believed to affect 20,000 past and present employees, was a sign that the struggling company was considering putting itself up for sale.

4.1 Ian Burke took over from Mike Smith in 2006

4.2 Rank's most recent CEO John O'Reilly was appointed in 2018

Rank finance director Peter Gill said, 'Our job is to put the company on the best financial footing. If that means it is attractive for someone to buy – so be it.'

4.3 One of the newer Mecca Bingo Halls in Wrexham

The Group looked vulnerable as its share price had more than halved in the year prior as the effects of the smoking ban were felt.

Profit at Rank's 100 bingo halls fell more than 30 per-cent to just under £44 million and the Group's 34 casinos reported profits down 18 per-cent to £30 million. A dividend pay-out to shareholders was scrapped.

The pension fund was to be handled by a subsidiary of American investment bank Goldman Sachs, Rothesay Life, which paid Rank £50 million. It said it expected to earn enough from the fund's investments to honour pension commitments and make a profit. Though a GMB union spokesman warned, "The pension funds regulator needs to step in to ensure the assets aren't stripped by Wall Street banks".

The Group survived however and in 2012 consolidated its position in the gambling arena when it bought Gala casinos for £205 million.

Two years later the Group reported an operating profit of £72.4 million on a turnover of £707.7 million from its three divisions: Mecca Bingo, Grosvenor Casino and Enracha (Spain) Bingo. With the company looking healthier now than when he inherited it, Burke decided it was time to leave.

New CEOs

In 2014 Henry Birch was ushered in as new CEO.

With 20 years of experience in the betting and gaming sector and in online and broadcast media he had been, most recently, the chief executive officer of betting company William Hill Online. He remained with the Group, and steered a steady ship, until 2018 when he chose to resign and take over as chief executive of online retailer Shop Direct.

In April 2018 Rank announced, 'betting industry veteran' and former Ladbrokes and Gala Coral executive John O'Reilly would take over as chief executive. He had led Ladbrokes' digital operations up until 2010 and joined Gala Coral the year after (before its merger with Ladbrokes) to relaunch the Coral brand online.

O'Reilly started his new job just one month from when Rank issued a profit warning after bad weather reduced visits to its Mecca bingo halls and high rollers contributed less at its Grosvenor Casinos. The company reported full-year operating profit would be in the range of £76 million – £78 million, below the £83.5 million it achieved the year prior.

The Group, along with many other companies, was hit hard in 2020 when the coronavirus pandemic hit. All sites were shuttered for months, seven-thousand employees were furloughed. After a phased reopening, by September 2020 Rank confirmed that it will not be paying a final dividend after annual profits plunged by 66 per-cent to £9.4 million

Chief executive John O'Reilly said, 'With positive momentum from the transformation programme, Rank performed very strongly during the first part of the year and into the second half.

'Despite continued good growth in our digital brands, with our venues closed from mid-March, the impact of the COVID-19 pandemic on the group has been significant.

'However, with the huge commitment and dedication of our colleagues, very tight cost control across the business and the support we have received from government, we have carefully navigated the past few months and are now beginning to successfully emerge. We know the recovery will take time, but the underlying strength of our business provides us with confidence that we are well equipped to return to full strength.'

Time will, of course, tell.

Looking back across the Group's 80-odd year history, one can't help but think what devout Methodist J Arthur Rank would make of his once great film empire having been carved up and sold off, leaving it standing today only as a gambling business?

2

Pinewood Studios

The 2000 management buy-out of Pinewood led by Michael Grade, Ivan Dunleavy, and studio MD Steve Jaggs, was financed by some personal investment and further backed by venture capitalist firm 3i.

3i were well known in the city for backing acquisitions, on a fairly short-term basis before wanting to cash out.

In February 2001, Grade & Co led an approach to rival studio Shepperton in a £35 million bid to purchase it; a deal was cemented, and the two operations merged.

Just over three years later, mindful 3i wanted 'out', in May 2004, Grade floated the combined company on the UK stock exchange and reportedly scooped a £250,000 when shares started trading.

The company issued new shares and raised £46 million through its flotation on the stock exchange and Grade reduced his stake in the studios from 4.2per-cent to 1.35per-cent.

However, in retaining 620,486 shares, worth around £1.2 million, Mr Grade had made a pretty good return on his investment.

Grade and Dunleavy continued to run the studios whilst expanding opportunities for the 'Pinewood brand' by establishing outposts (mainly by licensing their name and marketing expertise) at Pinewood Toronto Studios, Pinewood Indomina Studios, Pinewood Studio Berlin, Pinewood Iskandar Malaysia Studios, and a joint venture in the US with Pinewood Atlanta Studios. They also took over the last 9 years of the lease at Teddington Studios for £2.7 million when parent company The Studio Broadcasting Company Limited (SBC) went into administration.

4.4 Ivan Dunleavy lead the management buy-out with Michael Grade and became CEO of Pinewood in 2000

Teddington, which is based in south west London, had a long history of film production stretching back to the silent era. It was Warner Bros' UK base in the 1930s when stars such as Rex Harrison and Errol Flynn made movies. In the late 1950s, Teddington was re-customised as a TV studios and went on to house some of the UK's top comedy shows, from *Benny Hill* to *George and Mildred* and – in later years – *The Office, My Hero* and *Harry Hill* among them.

The acquisition came at a time when British studios were beginning to feel the pinch as a result of the widespread uncertainty surrounding the future of UK producer tax breaks due to a government review. In late March 2005, shares in Pinewood Shepperton fell by 13 per-cent, after the company admitted it was facing stiff competition from cheaper locations and studios in Eastern Europe, and the exchange rate against the dollar created a difficult business environment.

Pinewood saw its latest acquisition of Teddington as a way to diversify and strengthen its presence in the television and sound services business. In a statement, Ivan Dunleavy, Chief Executive of Pinewood Shepperton plc commented, 'This is an exciting opportunity for Pinewood Shepperton and is in line with our long term strategy to diversify our revenue streams in our integrated media businesses. Teddington Studios and SBC, combined with our existing business in television and sound services, significantly enhances our presence in the marketplace. We will be working closely with the management of Teddington Studios and SBC to maximise the benefit of our enlarged television and sound services activities.'

A couple of months later shares in Pinewood Shepperton dropped another 20 per-cent after the studio issued a profit warning.

Paramount's $120 million superhero thriller *Watchmen* had recently abandoned plans to shoot at Pinewood and the latest Bond, *Casino Royale*, shifted to Prague's Barrandov Studios having previously stuck loyally with the UK, and most often Pinewood.

The company said it expected interim operating profits to be a little below market estimates at £2 million.

The studio pointed out that the results reflected a broader picture of reduced film production investment in the UK in the first half of 2005. It said that overall UK production spend halved to £335 million compared to £668 million in the same period of 2004.

Pinewood said that 'only two significant Hollywood productions' shot in the UK in the first half, both of which are being serviced at Pinewood Shepperton: *The Da Vinci Code* and *Basic Instinct II*. It added 36 films overall began shooting in the UK during that period. Chairman Michael Grade commented, 'We welcome the Government's commitment to continuing fiscal incentives for the UK film sector, and the fact that the issue is now on its way to a positive resolution. Inevitably, some uncertainty will remain while the details are finalised, expected by the Spring of 2006.'

The producer tax incentive was renewed, and production (both film and television) did pick up, and even James Bond returned for his 2008 outing *Quantum Of Solace*.

BAFTA

At the 2009 annual British Academy Film Awards, the BAFTA for Outstanding British Contribution to Cinema was presented to Pinewood and Shepperton Studios.

Finola Dwyer, Chair of BAFTA's Film Committee said, 'Pinewood and Shepperton Studios have been at the creative heart of British filmmaking for over 70 years. This award recognises the role they have played in bringing to life some of the most memorable and iconic images in cinema history.'

Actor Jason Isaacs presented the award itself on the evening to (then) CEO Ivan Dunleavy. It remains on display in Pinewood's main admin building foyer.

Unrest

By June 2010 Grade was coming under pressure from Crystal Amber, the activist investment fund, who called for his resignation at the annual general meeting.

The fund, owned 18per-cent of Pinewood, and believed that board renewal was 'now essential to improve the performance of the group, which has seen profits and return on capital fall by more than half in the six years since the business was floated in May 2004'. Richard Bernstein, investment adviser to Crystal Amber, commented, 'We began investing in Pinewood 18 months ago because we believed there was underlying value in the business that was not fully appreciated by the market.

'We then sought to engage with the board and management in a constructive manner, offering proposals to enhance perceptions of the value in the business. Those proposals centred on creating greater transparency of the costs and profitability of the operating divisions and the value of Pinewood's property assets.

'Although these proposals were initially received well by management, we have seen no action and subsequent meetings with Mr Grade have been unproductive.'

Grade resisted their call to resign, though it's true to say Crystal Amber became a thorn in his side thereafter and in April 2011 it was no real surprise the studio board gave its backing to a takeover offer from John Whittaker's Peel Holdings following rival interest from former Harrods owner Mohamed Al Fayed.

Expansion

Peel, the Manchester-based commercial property group which leased part of Salford's MediaCityUK site to the BBC, upped its original bid by around

4.5/4.6/4.7 An artists impression of Project Pinewood

£8 million, valuing the business at £96.1 million. It already owned 29.8per-cent of Pinewood.

The board of Pinewood said Peel had been a supportive shareholder and the takeover proposal provided the business with the 'long-term stability it needs to build on the success of the past few years'.

Pinewood announced an ambitious £200 million expansion plan, Project Pinewood, on Green Belt land which it owned opposite the existing studio site.

The audacious 'Project Pinewood' was for a 100-acre development that provided permanent 'living and working' sets comprising streets and squares designed architecturally in the generic styles of popular filming locations. These included a Parisian square, a New York street, Brooklyn Brownstones, an Amsterdam canal front and even a Venetian canal, intended to offer producers a wide array of location choices to film next to the stages.

Though not only would the sets be permanent, they would self-gener-ate the financing required by incorporating living accommodation in the set buildings. 1,500 new homes were promised as an integral part of the expansion.

4.5/4.6/4.7 An artists impression of Project Pinewood

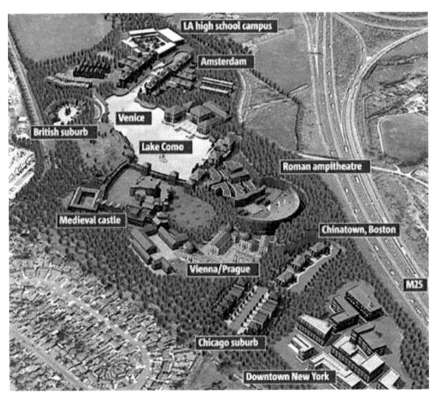

4.5/4.6/4.7 An artists impression of Project Pinewood

Predictably, local residents were shocked by the plans and the impact on the area, and immediately set up an opposition group, 'Stop Project Pinewood' (SPP). The immodest 'Project Pinewood' had seemingly already lost the goodwill of the local community who had so admired and supported Pinewood – in fact it fuelled considerable anger amongst the deep-pocketed residents.

In October 2009, the plan was rejected by the South Bucks District Council Planning Committee, who concluded it would harm the quality of life for local residents and cause 'significant degradation' of the local environment.

Six months later, after lengthy consideration and consultation, Pinewood appealed. In April 2011, a public enquiry was launched and a month later the hearings were concluded, and a report written.

'Project Pinewood' was again rejected as not meeting the 'Very Special Circumstances' required to justify planning permission for development in the Green Belt.

Isle Of Man

Brokered through its links with Peel Holdings, in February 2012 it was announced, the Isle of Man government planned to merge its film arm, CinemaNX, into the Pinewood Group, and hand over running the island's £25 million Media Development Fund to the studio management. Under the deal, the Isle of Man took a stake of up to 19.9per-cent in the Group and CinemaNX executives, including founder-chairman Steve Christian, joined the studio's board.

Pinewood next announced an initiative to support low-budget British films. It traded studio space for equity participation at first and then grew the division, under Steve Christian, to invest Isle of Man and Welsh Government film finance funds, in exchange for an equity position and distribution rights. The first was A Fantastic Fear of Everything (2012) starring Simon Pegg, others included The Christmas Candle (2013), Belle (2013), Dom Hemingway (2013), Powder Room (2013), The Riot Club (2014), and Spooks: The Greater Good (2015). Overall, the films received mixed reviews

4.8 The protestors were vocal and visual – this sign was opposite the studio entrance

and box-office returns, and Steve Christian admitted their investment was driven mainly by the deal, rather than the script.

Planning

In February 2012 Pinewood submitted a new planning application to South Bucks District Council, 'The Pinewood Studios Development Framework' (PSDF). It was a far more conservative plan this time around comprising purely new production facilities: stages, offices, workshops and 1,000 car parking spaces.

The building design was more sympathetic to the local environment and significantly did not propose the intensity of development and residential units that were part of 'Project Pinewood' and so opposed by the locals. Furthermore, the stages would have grass roofs to compensate for loss of grassland habitat, while set out on the development site so as to soften the horizon and sightlines from the village.

PSDF was deemed a more appropriate development and one taking a more sensitive approach to the local area.

Just over a year later, in May 2013, and with the PSDF planning application still under review, the Pinewood PR machine slipped into gear and former Chancellor George Osborne announced that *Star Wars Episode 7* would be made in the UK – at Pinewood. It planned to utilise a vast number of stages and backlot and proved the demand for greater capacity.

On May 15 at 4pm, a planning application hearing took place at South Bucks District Council where a committee of ten listened to petitions from Ivan Dunleavy, Lord Grade, The Earl of Stockton, local residents as well as district and county councillors. Pinewood produced letters of support from Disney and Universal Studios. Vince Cable, the then Business Secretary, also sent a letter of support. The expansion was described as of 'national importance' and its positive economic impact would have surely weighed favourably among the Very Special Circumstances required to develop the site.

The vote was 6-4 against. Chairman of the Planning Committee Mr Ralph Bagge explained, 'The Pinewood proposal is one of the most contentious and difficult planning applications that the Council has had to deal with…

'Having carefully considered all the arguments for and against the proposals, the Committee was on balance of the view that to have allowed this development of over 110 acres in the Green Belt and Colne Valley Park, would not only have caused significant degradation to the local environment but also harmed the quality of life for local residents.

'It is of course open to Pinewood to appeal the Council's refusal decision and if they do so then a Government Inspector will hold an Inquiry and decide whether to support the Council's refusal or to grant permission against the local decision.'

Appeal

On May 31, 2013 Pinewood applied to appeal the decision to the Planning Inspectorate, who undertook a hearing and produced a report with a recommendation to Eric Pickles MP, Secretary of State for Communities and

Local Government. The hearing was set for six-months later, in November, and lasted 16 days.

Meanwhile on February 17, 2014, Pinewood announced an agreement with the Welsh Government to act as advisors on their £30 million fund for a new studio facility near Cardiff. It was known as 'Pinewood Studio Wales'.

On June 19, 2014, the UK Government allowed the appeal granted the planning application for the PSDF, with Eric Pickles in broad support of the independent planning inspectorate which had recommended approval.

Initially five new stages were constructed with associated office space and workshops which opened in June 2016. The second phase, building another five stages, broke ground in 2018.

Meanwhile, in February 2016 board room politics came to a head and the company announced it had hired Rothschild to carry out what it called a 'strategic review' of the company's structure and ownership.

Pinewood's management had become frustrated with the company's three large investors, who held 79 per-cent of the stock between them, which in turn barred the studio from listing on the London Stock Exchange – something that would have given it access to greater fundraising ability as it expanded capacity in phase two and a planned third stage of development in the coming years.

A changing of the guard

Ivan Dunleavy, chief executive, said the shareholder arrangement was 'stifling' the company's efforts.

The unusual investor structure came about in 2011, when Peel Holdings, the Manchester-based conglomerate, used its shareholding to launch a bid for the whole company.

Its overtures were rendered unsuccessful after Warren James, the UK jeweller, took a significant stake in the business and blocked the deal. The pair remained the two largest investors, with 39 per-cent and 26.1 per-cent of the stock, respectively. Aviva Investors was the third largest with 13.1 per-cent.

So, the Pinewood board decided to look at 'all options for the business', including a partner investor or even a full sale.

Later that year, it was announced Pinewood was to revert to private ownership in a £323 million deal with Aermont Capital, a London-based asset management business, which valued each Pinewood share at 560p.

Lord Grade, chairman of Pinewood, said the takeover was an attractive offer for investors that would give Pinewood 'the platform required for future growth'.

Pinewood's directors stood to make a combined £1.82 million if they sold their entire holdings, including a £1 million windfall for the chief executive, Ivan Dunleavy.

In the takeover, Paul Golding was appointed Chairman and Lord Grade stood down. CEO Ivan Dunleavy stayed on, but after overseeing what was essentially a six-month handover period after serving 17-years at the helm, he stood down and Golding took over as interim chief executive – a position he still holds at the time of writing.

In an announcement to staff Paul Golding told them, 'Ivan has played a huge role in the success of Pinewood. When we became owners six months ago, we were delighted that he stayed on. Now, having overseen a smooth transition from public company to private ownership and with the business in such great shape, he has suggested the time is right to move on'.

In the following months, Pinewood's various initiatives were, one by one, closed down – including their Pinewood Pictures investment and production programme. Aermont was a property company and saw the value of the studio being in property and not in financing.

Ambition

The development plan to expand the studio continued apace and in a somewhat surprising move, in September 2019, The Walt Disney Studios announced a 10-year exclusive lease of Pinewood, to start in 2020. They were effectively taking over the whole studio, aside from the three TV and the underwater stages. They had first call on all facilities, offices and backlot space but agreed a deal – if the space was not being used – for Pinewood to sublet it to other productions.

At the same time, a further five stages (in place of existing buildings on the main site) received the go-ahead.

4.9 J Arthur Rank's presence is still felt at Pinewood today, not least with the main board room being named after him.

Though perhaps the most ambitious of all Pinewood Studios plans came in the summer of 2020 when a huge £450 million expansion – which will include a tourist attraction and new film production facilities – was announced.

Screen Hub UK will feature the 'Pinewood Studio Experience', a 350,000 square foot international visitor attraction and a training and skills hub and will be based on a 77-acre site to the south and immediately adjacent to their existing site.

Pinewood said the new hub will create around 3,500 new jobs, add £230 million a year into the economy and £125 million a year into the tourism industry.

A planning application was being prepared and consultations with the community started within weeks of the announcement.

Pinewood Studios has grown, diversified, developed, and become ever more synonymous with big budget Hollywood movies, as well as continuing to be the home of 007 – so we're assured by Disney and management.

Odeon

After purchasing the chain from Rank, Cinven then merged Odeon with ABC Cinemas (which it already owned) and rebranded the combined company as 'Odeon'. It became the UK's largest cinema chain.

By 2003, as a result of a £75 million modernisation, refurbishment and new-build programme, Odeon operated from 97 multiplex and city centre sites, consisting of 608 screens.

In March that year, Cinven announced it had agreed a deal to sell Odeon Cinemas to a syndicate of investors led by WestLB AG and the Entertainment Group for £430 million.

Commenting on the sale Richard Munton, a director of Cinven said, 'When we invested in Odeon, we backed a plan to drive the business forward through investment in both new multiplexes and the existing cinema portfolio. This was in line with Cinven's strategy of finding growth opportunities in market leading companies.

'We are clearly delighted that the management team has delivered on this business plan with consequent positive effects on the financial performance of the business. Odeon has been a very successful investment for us, and we wish the company well for the future.'

Sold again

A year later, in 2004, the chain was purchased by Guy Hands' Terra Firma for £570 million and merged with United Cinemas International to produce the largest cinema chain in Europe! As a condition of the merger (imposed by the Office of Fair Trading), Odeon had to dispose of six sites and a deal was agreed with Empire Cinemas.

In March 2012, the Odeon, and UCI Cinemas Group under Terra Firma's control, reported a £70 million loss for the previous year. Terra Firma announced in February 2015 that it planned to sell Odeon and UCI Cinemas for around £1 billion and in April that year the company agreed to sell its cinemas in Gerrards Cross, Esher, Muswell Hill and Barnet to its smaller rival Everyman Cinemas for £7.1 million.

Revenue increased at the cinema chain to £707 million in 2013, due to some high profile Hollywood blockbusters such as *Iron Man 3, The Hunger Games: Catching Fire, Man Of Steel, Frozen, Fast And Furious 6, Star Trek: Into Darkness, The Hobbit: The Desolation of Smaug,* but fell slightly to £657 million in 2014.

At the tail end of 2013 Odeon had made use of a financial tool to free up capital – sale and leaseback. It sold 10 of its cinemas to LondonMetric Property for £80.6 million and agreed to rent them back (with a tax incentive as a result) for £5.9 million per annum. The proceeds from the sale were used to repay its property group's debt.

AMC

Eventually, in July 2016, the company was bought for $921 million by the American company AMC Theatres, owned by Chinese conglomerate Wanda Group.

Odeon Cinemas Group was created and became a wholly owned subsidiary of AMC Theatres. AMC thus became the largest movie exhibition company in the world.'

On March 17, 2020, all Odeon cinemas in the UK temporarily closed due to the coronavirus pandemic. AMC had already seen a drop in its stock market price and rumours began circling that it was ripe for a takeover, and that Amazon was circling. Whether discussions took place or not was never confirmed but at the time of writing AMC is still the owner of Odeon.

~ 4 ~

Rank Film (Deluxe) Laboratories

In March 2014, the (former) Rank film processing laboratory closed its doors after 78 years. The last surviving building of the former Denham Studios, on the North Orbital Road, had seen a steady reduction in work since the popularity of digital photography overtook shooting movies on 35mm film.

The firm's operations and engineering manager, Colin Flight explained, 'This site is fundamentally here for processing reels of film. Really, since [James Cameron's science fiction blockbuster] *Avatar* came out in 2009 there has been a very fast transition to digital filming, especially for the use of 3D. It's not unexpected, and it has been a steady process getting to this stage.'

The site employed 70 people, and while many of them were going to retire, Deluxe tried to minimise the impact of the closure.

Over the years Rank Labs/Deluxe had enjoyed a close relationship with Pinewood Studios up the road at Iver Heath. Stanley Kubrick was known to be a fan, and would always insist his films were processed there, while more recently to the closure date, Steven Spielberg used Deluxe for the processing of his Oscar nominated film *War Horse*. Amongst the hundreds of films edited and processed at Denham were *Brief Encounter, The Great Escape, Alien* and *Aliens, ET, Superman 1, 2* and *3* and many of the *Star Wars* and Bond movies.

The future of Deluxe's art deco Grade II listed building seemed unsure, but a covenant in the original deeds required part of the site to remain in use for 'film purposes'.

Within two years of closure, in 2016, Weston Homes announced the main building (renamed Korda House) would be converted into 49 elegant apartments, bordered by three new four storey apartment buildings providing 105 new homes.

'Around the eastern side of the site there will be avenues of new three and four storey terraced housing, and to the northern section two and three storey detached townhouses' their publicity stated.

To satisfy the covenant, Weston Homes refurnished and upgraded the labs' art deco viewing theatre on site.

❦ 5 ❦

Other Interests

The Rank name also continued, and indeed still continues, in other areas of business and charitable causes started by Joseph Rank and J Arthur Rank (outside his conglomerate). They are:

(i) Rank Milling / Joseph Rank Ltd / Rank Hovis McDougal

In 1943 James Rank became Chairman following his father's death, and two-years later – assisted by Cecil Loombe, who had become a director – he set about rebuilding the mills that had been destroyed by bombing. Despite Hitler's best efforts to starve Britain, Joe, and James Rank after him, kept the mills turning and employed some 3,000 workers, many of them women.

In 1952, James Rank was succeeded by his brother J. Arthur Rank as Chairman. Arthur explored ways of improving quality control in food production founding RHM Technology and its research centre at High Wycombe.

The company acquired the Hovis-McDougall Company, which had been formed in 1957 with the merger of bakers Hovis Bread Flour Company and McDougall Brothers. It became Ranks Hovis McDougall Limited (RHM).

RHM expanded in 1968 when it bought the Cerebos food group, which had interests in Australia, Argentina, Canada, France, New Zealand, the United States and South Africa. In 1969 Arthur's nephew, Joseph Rank, took over the Chairmanship of the Company.

During the 1970s Joseph Rank encouraged research work in crustacea farming, cereal and seed production, and wheat hybrids. He also pioneered protein production from starch.

By the late 1970s, RHM and its competitor, Associated British Foods PLC, monopolized their industry. In 1981 Sir Peter Reynolds took over as Chairman from Joseph Rank and oversaw a number of important acquisitions during the decade in the United Kingdom, the United States, and the Far East.

By 1984 research had advanced to the point that the company was ready to undertake a joint venture with ICI, Britain's largest industrial company, to form Marlow Foods, a company dedicated to producing and promoting mycoprotein food, and created the meat substitute product Quorn.

The late 1980s was marked by a series of takeover battles and in 1988 there was a hostile takeover attempt by Australia-based food concern Goodman Fielder Wattie Limited, which owned 29.9 percent of RHM's shares. After that bid was thwarted by British regulators, the Australian firm began negotiating with third parties to sell its RHM stake and in May 1989 RHM sold its 29.9 per-cent stake in RHM to Anglo-French financier James Goldsmith, but in early 1991 he sold his entire RHM stake, leaving the largest single stake in the company under five percent.

Meanwhile, RHM paid £80 million to purchase the UK ready-to-eat cereal business of RJR Nabisco in 1988 and brands included Shredded Wheat and Shreddies, but after facing a tough battle with US cereal company and market dominator Kellogg, RHM decided to exit from the cereal business, selling the business to a joint venture of Nestlé S.A. and General Mills Inc. for £93 million in mid-1990.

RHM's profits and stock price were battered in the early 1990s by a recession and bread consumption declined. Another hostile takeover bid emerged, this time a £780 million offer from Hanson PLC; the bid was rejected by the RHM board, who then announced a three-way demerger as a defence – splitting company into three separate units: a milling and baking group, a grocery products company, and a cake business.

In late October 1992, an Anglo-U.S. conglomerate Tomkins PLC, bid £935 million for RHM, which the board accepted.

Ranks Hovis McDougall Limited became the food division of Tomkins which, in 1995, acquired Lyons Cakes, which two years later was integrated into Manor Bakeries Limited.

Also, in 1997, RHM merged two of its subsidiaries -Tiffany Sharwood's Frozen Foods and Abercroft Cakes – to form RHM Frozen Foods Limited, which gained strong market positions in meat and pastry pies, ethnic ready-to-eat meals, individual cakes, and other desserts.

Beginning in September 1996, Tomkins's began a disposal program to sell off non-strategic businesses.

In March 1998 Tomkins acquired six flour mills in the United Kingdom from Kerry Group, but UK regulators ruled that the purchase would give Tomkins too large a share of the domestic flour market and ordered the company to sell four of the six mills, allowing it to keep mills at Birkenhead and Cambridge.

In May 1998 Tomkins paid £35.6 million for Le Pain Croustillant Limited, a maker of specialty breads sold to major supermarket chains and made it a subsidiary of RHM.

In July 2005 RHM was relisted on the London Stock Exchange, and two-years later, in March 2007, was acquired by Premier Foods for £1.2bn.

In January 2014, Los Angeles private equity Gores Group acquired a 51per-cent stake in RHM for £30 million. They announced the brand, alongside other bakery brands such as Mothers Pride, was to be housed in a joint venture called Hovis Limited, and by October 2018 it emerged the 'Rank Hovis' brand would no longer be used.

Quietly, and without fuss, the name of Rank disappeared from the world of flour and bread.

(ii) The Rank Foundation

The Rank Foundation was the major charitable legacy of Joseph Arthur Rank, initially being established as The J Arthur Rank Group Charity in 1953.

Its work continues under the Chairmanship of Arthur's grandson, Joey Newton.

The wealth from J Arthur Rank's film companies provided the basis for the endowment which has enabled the Foundation to make charitable grants for over sixty years.

J Arthur Rank's strong simple faith echoed that of his father, who was a committed Methodist, and that faith lay behind his concern to help others, especially young people, whom he regarded as 'the seed corn of the future and the leaders of tomorrow'.

The foundation's aim is to improve the lives of people and their communities across the UK, by encouraging and developing leadership and promoting enterprise and innovation.

(iii) The Joseph Rank Trust

The trust established in June 2002, as an amalgamation of a number of charities established by Joseph Rank and members of his family.

An independent Christian grant-maker, the trust works with all Christian denominations in the United Kingdom 'to advance the Christian Faith'.

Its two main areas of interest are in

- Projects that demonstrate a Christian approach to the practical, educational, and spiritual needs of people of all ages.
- The adaptation of Church properties with a view to providing improved facilities for use by the church and its work in the community in which it is based.

(iv) CTVC

CTVC is a multi-BAFTA-winning and Grierson nominated independent production company producing content that raises important ethical and moral issues, with the aim of getting people thinking and talking.

Established in 1978 in memory of Lord and Lady Rank, CTVC is a registered charity which receives a grant from the Rank Foundation.

The Centre for Television and Communication, as it became known, saw the thriving operation move to newly built studios in a converted country house named 'Hillside'.

Based in Bushey, North London, an early production, *Will the Real Jesus Christ Please Stand Up?* featured a fresh faced, young Hugh Grant.

With rainbow-like brilliance colours spray from a bunch of tiny 'light-pipes'. Called Fibre Optics, this new technology—which is also featured on the front cover—has important applications in many fields, ranging from medicine to aviation. The Taylor Hobson Division of The Rank Organisation is among the world leaders in the development of fibre optics, and last year became the first Company in Britain to put the fibres into mass production.

4.10 *The Rank Prize Fund bestows bi-annual awards, one being in the field of Optoelectronics which, as this ad from 1966 shows, the Rank Organisation was at the forefront of research back then.*

4.11 Lord and Lady Rank

In 2005 the name was changed to CTVC Ltd and the principles laid out by Lord Rank's vision are still at the heart of everything they do, and as such they are passionate believers in the power and importance of media to educate, challenge and inspire – as indeed was he.

(v) The Rank Prize Funds

The Rank Prize Funds is a charitable organisation which seeks to recognise excellence in specific fields of research and reward innovators for their dedication and outstanding contribution.

4.12 A plaque on the former Rank Organisation HQ in South Street, central London

The Funds have as their objectives the advancement and promotion for the public benefit of knowledge, education and learning in all or any of the following sciences:

- NUTRITION FUND (Human and Animal Nutrition and Crop Husbandry)
  Crop husbandry
  Human nutrition
  Animal nutrition (as distinct from animal husbandry)
- OPTOELECTRONICS FUND
  The inter-face between optics and electronics and closely related phenomena.

The Funds were established by the late Lord Rank on February 16, 1972, shortly before his death in March of that year. The Rank Prize is awarded every two years and acknowledges those individuals who have made a significant contribution to the two fields.

Stuart Cowen, Chairman of the Rank Prize Funds, introduced the January 2020 bi-annual awards and said, 'It's both humbling and wonderful to see how the legacy of my grandfather, Lord Rank, has developed. He set up the prizes to support research into two areas of science that had supported his businesses' and recognised that without research, his businesses would not have thrived. He lives through an age where movie films had been created, transitioned to sound and then on to colour. I think he'd be amazed at the advances that have occurred since 1972, and I'm only sad he can't be here now to see how applicable his vision was, and how his legacy has continued.'

Appendix 1:

Brief History of 'Rank' – Charting the Rank Company History

1875   Joseph Rank Ltd was incorporated

1890   Gaumont Company founded in UK

1922   Ostrer brothers take control of Gaumont-British production, distribution, and exhibition group

1927   Billy Butlin opens first amusement park

1927   Piccadilly/Gainsborough absorbed by Gaumont-British

1928   Gaumont-British expands exhibition interests, becomes Gaumont-British Picture Corporation

1932   J Arthur Rank forms British National Films Company

1934   Pinewood Studios formed by Henry Boot & J Arthur Rank, and opens for business in 1936

1936   J Arthur Rank and C M Woolf form General Cinema Finance Corporation (GCFC)

1936   GCFC buys General Film Distributors (UK distributors for Universal Pictures)

1937   Odeon Theatres becomes public company headed by Oscar Deutsch

1937   J Arthur Rank forms The Rank Organisation as vehicle for interests in Pinewood Studios and Denham Studios

1938   The Rank Organisation buys Odeon cinema chain

1938   Rank Screen Advertising founded as subsidiary of Odeon Theatres

1938	The Rank Organisation buys Amalgamated Studios in Elstree
1941	The Ostrers sell Gaumont-British Picture Corporation stake to J Arthur Rank
1945	The Rank Organisation buys 50per-cent of Australian Greater Union Theatres
1949	The Rank Organisation sells studio in Islington
1949	The Rank Organisation sells Shepherd's Bush studio to BBC
1949	The Rank Organisation buys radio manufacturer Bush (Bush Radio)
1952	Denham Studios closed down
1955	The Rank Organisation merges its Odeon and UK Gaumont cinema chains
1956	A partnership agreed with Haloid Corporation as Rank Haloid (later Rank Xerox)
1960	The Rank Organisation sells its Top Rank Records to EMI
1962	The Rank Organisation acquires radio manufacturer Murphy, forms Rank Bush Murphy Group
1969	A restructuring of the Xerox partnership, establishes Rank Xerox as joint-venture company
1971	First Hard Rock café opened in London by Isaac Tigrett and Peter Morton
1977	The Rank Organisation appointed Tony Williams head of production and over two years Rank made eight films worth £10 million
1978	Rank Bush Murphy Group is sold to Great Universal Stores
1980	At the Cannes Film Festival in 1980 Ed Chilton of Rank announced a £12 million slate of projects. The plan was not seen through.
1984	Australasian company, Amalgamated Holdings Limited (AHL), buys Rank's stake in Greater Union Theatres
1988	Mecca Leisure buys Hard Rock chain
1988	The Rank Organisation forms a partnership with MCA to develop Universal Studios Escape in Florida
1990	The Rank Organisation buys Mecca Leisure for £895 million
1995	The Rank Organisation sells part of stake in Rank Xerox for £620million; disposes of Rank Motorway Services

1996	Carlton buys Cinema Media (former Rank Screen Advertising) for £58.8m, subsequently renamed Carlton Screen Advertising
1996	The Rank Organisation buys Duplico video duplicator
1996	The Rank Organisation buys Tom Cobleigh chain of pubs and restaurants.
1996	The Rank Organisation acquires Hard Rock Café Canada
1996	The Rank Group replaces The Rank Organisation
1997	The Rank Group acquires Hard Rock Cafes and brand rights for Caribbean and Argentina
1997	The Rank Group sells more of remaining interest in Rank Xerox
1997	The Rank Group buys Parkdean Holidays
1997	Carlton buys Rank Film Distributors and film library for £65 million
1999	The Rank Group sells Nightscene nightclubs to Northern Leisure for £150 million
1999	The Rank group sells five Butlin's hotels – in Brighton, Margate, Llandudno, Scarborough and Blackpool – to entrepreneur Kevin Leech for £20 million
2000	Butlins, Warner Hotels, Haven Catered Parks and Oasis sold to Bourne Leisure for £700 million
2000	Pinewood Studios was sold for £62m to consortium led by Michael Grade
2000	Odeon chain sold to Cinven for £280m
2000	The Rank Group divested its Holidays Division for £700 million to Bourne Leisure
2000	The Rank Group buys Pioneer Video Manufacturing Inc.
2000	The Rank Group buys Park Tower Casino
2000	The Rank Group sells Tom Cobleigh pub restaurants business for £90 million
2000	The Rank Group sells 50per-cent stake in Universal Studios Escape (Florida) for £182 million
2003	The Rank Group buys Blue Square Limited for £65 million
2004	The Rank Group sells Rank Leisure Machine Services for £30 million
2005	The Rank Group sells Deluxe film processing arm to MacAndrews & Forbes for £437 million

2006   The Rank Group sells the UK operations of Deluxe Media to Sony for £5.9m

2006   The Rank Group sells exclusive West End casino the Clermont Club to Quek Leng Chan's BIL International for £31m; disposed of the Hard Rock Cafe business for £490 million.

2012   The Rank Group buys Gala casinos for £205 million

2020   The Rank Group now comprises: Grosvenor Casinos, Mecca and Enracha with the ambition of becoming a £1 billion revenue international gaming company by 2023

Appendix 2:

Rank Management over the Decades

J Arthur Rank (1888–1972)
Managing director/Chief Executive from formation of company until 1952
Appointed Chairman in 1952, a position held until 1962 when he became Life President until his death in 1972

John Davis (1906–1993)
Appointed Managing Director in 1948
Appointed Chairman & Chief Executive in 1962
Stepped down as Chief Executive in 1974, but remained Chairman
Appointed President in 1977, until 1983

1974 Graham Dowson promoted from assistant Chief Executive to Chief Executive
1975 Dowson forced to resign as Chief Executive after 8 months in the role Russell W Evans appointed Chief Executive
1976 Harry Smith appointed Deputy Chairman
1977 Harry Smith succeeds John Davis as Chairman
1982 Russell W Evans appointed Chairman
J B Smith appointed Chief Executive
1983 Sir Patrick Meaney appointed Chairman
Michael B Gifford appointed Chief Executive

1992	Sir Leslie Fletcher appointed Chairman
1995	Sir Denys Henderson appointed Chairman
1996	Andrew Teare appointed Chief Executive
1999	Mike Smith appointed Chief Executive
2001	Alun Cathcart appointed Chairman
2006	Peter Johnson appointed Chairman
	Ian Burke appointed Chief Executive
2011	Ian Burke appointed Chairman and Chief Executive
2014	Henry Birch appointed Chief Executive
2018	John O'Reilly appointed Chief Executive
2019	Alex Thursby appointed Chairman

Appendix 3:

Rank Films

FILMS EITHER PRODUCED BY RANK, OR DISTRIBUTED BY GENERAL FILM DISTRIBUTORS/ RANK FILM DISTRIBUTORS

NB: General Film Distributors kept its own name within the Rank Organisation until 1955, when it was renamed J. Arthur Rank Film Distributors, which in turn was renamed Rank Film Distributors Ltd. in 1957.

YEAR / TITLE

1935

    Turn of the Tide
    No Monkey Business
    Moscow Nights
    The Iron Duke
    Heat Wave
    Bulldog Jack
    The 39 Steps
    The Clairvoyant
    Stormy Weather
    Boys Will Be Boys
    Car of Dreams
    The Guv'nor
    Foreign Affaires

1936

Limelight
The Improper Duchess
King of the Castle
When Knights Were Bold
Public Nuisance Number 1
Rhodes of Africa
Fame
Debt of Honour
Pot Luck
Tudor Rose
The Secret Agent
Love in Exile
The Marriage of Corbal
Where There's a Will
Seven Sinners
Everything is Thunder
East Meets West
Dishonour Bright
Millions
Southern Roses
Tropical Trouble
The Secret of Stamboul
Land without Music
This'll Make You Whistle
You Must Get Married
Sabotage
Windbag the Sailor

1937

Splinters in the Air
London Melody
Head Over Heels
The Great Barrier
For Valour
The Frog

The Gang Show
Our Fighting Navy
Okay for Sound
Take My Tip
Sunset in Vienna
King Solomon's Mines
Said O'Reilly to McNab
Gangway
Dr Syn
Command Performance
School for Husbands
Non-Stop New York
Smash and Grab
Oh, Mr Porter!
The Sky's the Limit
Young and Innocent
OHMS
Good Morning, Boys

1938

The Lady Vanishes
Sweet Devil
Owd Bob
Bank Holiday
Second Best Bed
Sailing Along
Kate Plus Ten
Strange Boarders
Convict 99
Kicking the Moon Around
Break the News
Alf's Button Afloat
Follow Your Star
A Spot of Bother
Hey! Hey! USA
Crackerjack

Lightning Conductor
Pygmalion
Old Bones of the River

1939

The Mikado
A Girl Must Live
A Window in London
The Arsenal Stadium Mystery
On the Night of the Fire
The Frozen Limits

1940

Band Waggon
For Freedom
Charley's (Big-Hearted) Aunt
Old Bill and Son
Gasbags
Neutral Port

1941

The Ghost Train
Major Barbara
Cottage to Let
He Found a Star
Jeannie
I Thank You
a49th Parallel
Hi Gang!
Freedom Radio

1942

Hard Steel
Back Room Boy
The Day Will Dawn
Uncensored

The First of the Few
Secret Mission
The Great Mr Handel
In Which We Serve
King Arthur Was a Gentleman
Unpublished Story

1943

The Silver Fleet
It's That Man Again
We Dive at Dawn
The Gentle Sex
The Life and Death of Colonel Blimp
The Man in Grey
They Met in the Dark
Dear Octopus
The Flemish Farm
Millions Like Us
The Lamp Still Burns
The Demi-Paradise

1944

Bees in Paradise
On Approval
Tawny Pipit
This Happy Breed
Fanny By Gaslight
A Canterbury Tale
The Way Ahead
Give Us the Moon
2,000 Women
Mr Emmanuel
Love Story
Don't Take It To Heart
Madonna of the Seven Moons
English Without Tears

1945

Waterloo Road
Henry V
A Place of One's Own
Blithe Spirit
They Were Sisters
The Way to the Stars
I'll Be Your Sweetheart
Johnny Frenchman
They Knew Mr. Knight
Dead of Night
The Seventh Veil
Brief Encounter
I Know Where I'm Going!
The Wicked Lady
Pink String and Sealing Wax
The Rake's Progress
Here Comes the Sun

1946

Caesar and Cleopatra
The Captive Heart
Bedelia
Caravan
The Years Between
Beware of Pity
I See a Dark Stranger
Men of Two Worlds
London Town
The Magic Bow
The Overlanders
Carnival
A Matter of Life and Death
School for Secrets
Great Expectations

Green for Danger
Daybreak

1947

Hungry Hill
Odd Man Out
The Root of All Evil
Hue and Cry
Nicholas Nickleby
The Man Within
Black Narcissus
Take My Life
The Brothers
Bush Christmas
Dear Murderer
The Loves of Joanna Godden
Frieda
The Upturned Glass
Holiday Camp
Jassy
Master of Bankdam
Captain Boycott
The October Man
Fame is the Spur
Uncle Silas
The White Unicorn
The End of the River
The Woman in the Hall
It Always Rains on Sunday
When the Bough Breaks

1948

The Mark of Cain
Vice Versa
Easy Money

Against the Wind
Blanche Fury
Miranda
Broken Journey
One Night with You
Good Time Girl
Corridor of Mirrors
The Calendar
Hamlet
My Sister and I
Oliver Twist
My Brother's Keeper
London Belongs to Me
The Red Shoes
Mr Perrin and Mr Traill
Saraband for Dead Lovers
The Weaker Sex
The Blind Goddess
Esther Waters
Sleeping Car to Trieste
Woman Hater
Quartet
Here Come the Huggetts
It's Hard to Be Good
Another Shore
Scott of the Antarctic
The Fool and the Princess
Look Before You Love
Once a Jolly Swagman

1949

Portrait from Life
Warning to Wantons
Third Time Lucky
Eureka Stockade

Once Upon a Dream
The Passionate Friends
Vote for Huggett
The History of Mr. Polly
All Over the Town
The Blue Lagoon
Fools Rush In
Bad Lord Byron
Floodtide
It's Not Cricket
A Boy, a Girl and a Bike
Passport to Pimlico
The Huggetts Abroad
Adam and Evelyne
The Perfect Woman
Stop Press Girl
Marry Me
Christopher Columbus
Whisky Galore
Kind Hearts and Coronets
Poets Pub
Helter Skelter
Don't Ever Leave Me
Madness of the Heart
Trottie True
Train of Events
The Lost People
Dear Mr Prohack
The Chiltern Hundreds
Diamond City
Give Us This Day
The Spider and the Fly
A Run for Your Money
The Romantic Age
Boys in Brown

The Rocking Horse Winner
Traveller's Joy
The Cardboard Cavalier

1950

The Blue Lamp
Golden Salamander
Madeleine
Morning Departure
The Astonished Heart
They Were Not Divided
The Reluctant Widow
Prelude to Fame
So Long at the Fair
Dance Hall
Tony Draws a Horse
Waterfront
Bitter Springs
Trio
Cage of Gold
The Woman in Question
The Magnet
The Clouded Yellow
Highly Dangerous

1951

The Adventurers
Scrooge
Blackmailed
The Dark Man
Pool of London
The Browning Version
White Corridors
The Lavender Hill Mob
Hotel Sahara
The Man in the White Suit

Valley of the Eagles
Appointment with Venus
High Treason
Where No Vultures Fly
Encore

1952

His Excellency
Secret People
Hunted
The Card
I Believe in You
Curtain Up
The Importance of Being Earnest
Something Money Can't Buy
Penny Princess
Mandy
Meet Me Tonight
The Planter's Wife
Venetian Bird
The Gentle Gunman
It Started in Paradise
Made in Heaven

1953

The Long Memory
The Net
Top of the Form
The Titfield Thunderbolt
Street Corner
Desperate Moment
The Final Test
The Cruel Sea
Turn the Key Softly
Genevieve
Malta Story

The Square Ring
Wheel of Fate
Always a Bride
A Day to Remember
Personal Affair
Small Town Story
Meet Mr. Lucifer
Trouble in Store
The Kidnappers

1954

The Million Pound Note
The Love Lottery
The Maggie
You Know What Sailors Are
Fast and Loose
Star of My Night
Doctor in the House
West of Zanzibar
Forbidden Cargo
The Rainbow Jacket
The Seekers
Up to His Neck
The Beachcomber
The Young Lovers
Romeo and Juliet
The Purple Plain
Lease of Life
Mad About Men
The Divided Heart
One Good Turn

1955

To Paris with Love
Simba
Out of the Clouds

As Long as They're Happy
The Night My Number Came Up
Above Us the Waves
Passage Home
The Ship that Died of Shame
Doctor at Sea
Value for Money
The Woman for Joe
Man of the Moment
Touch and Go
Simon and Laura
An Alligator Named Daisy
The Ladykillers
All for Mary

1956

Lost
Jumping for Joy
A Town Like Alice
Who Done It?
The Black Tent
The Feminine Touch
The Long Arm
Reach for the Sky
Jacqueline
Eyewitness
House of Secrets
Checkpoint
The Battle of the River Plate
The Spanish Gardener
Tiger in the Smoke
Up in the World
The Big Money

1957

Ill Met by Moonlight

The Secret Place
True as a Turtle
Doctor at Large
High Tide at Noon
The Crooked Sky
Miracle in Soho
Hell Drivers
Manuela
Across the Bridge
Seven Thunders
Robbery Under Arms
Campbell's Kingdom
The One That Got Away
Just My Luck
Dangerous Exile
The Naked Truth
Windom's Way
Slim Carter
The Monolith Monsters
The Mark Of The Hawk
Love Slaves of the Amazons
La Parisienne
Summer Love
The Sea Wall

1958

Violent Playground
The Gypsy and the Gentleman
A Tale of Two Cities
Carve Her Name with Pride
Rooney
Innocent Sinners
Heart of a Child
A Night to Remember
Nor the Moon by Night
Sea Fury

The Wind Cannot Read
Rockets Galore
Passionate Summer
Sea of Sand
Floods of Fear
The Square Peg
Bachelor of Hearts
The Wonderful Years
Monster on the Campus
Strictly for Pleasure
From the Earth to the Moon
Ride a Crooked Trail
Joy Ride
Money, Women and Guns
The Saga of Hemp Brown
Step Down to Terror
Once Upon a Horse…
Kathy O'
Voice in the Mirror
The Naked and the Dead
Raw Wind in Eden
The Last of the Fast Guns
Twilight for the Gods
Wild Heritage
The Thing That Couldn't Die
This Happy Feeling
Dracula
A Time to Love and a Time to Die
Live Fast, Die Young
Girls On The Loose
Touch Of Evil
Salmon Yeggs (Animation)
The Diplomatic Corps
Damn Citizen
Watch The Birdie (Animation)
The Big Beat

The Lady Takes A Flyer
Day of the Badman
Maigret Sets a Trap
The Female Animal
Above All Things

1959

The Captain's Table
Operation Amsterdam
Hidden Homicide
Too Many Crooks
The 39 Steps
Whirlpool
Sapphire
The Heart of a Man
Ferry to Hong Kong
Upstairs and Downstairs
Blind Date
The Night We Dropped a Clanger
North West Frontier
SOS Pacific
Desert Mice
Follow a Star
Tiger Bay
Witness in the Dark
Devil's Bait
Desert Mice
Operation Petticoat
Pillow Talk
We Are The Lambeth Boys
The Mummy
The Sinner
This Earth Is Mine
Curse Of The Undead
The Wild and the Innocent
Antarctic Crossing

The Boatmen
Imitation Of Life
Verboten!
No Name On The Bullet
Never Steal Anything Small
A Stranger In My Arms
Hidden Homicide

1960

Too Young to Love
The Shakedown
The Royal Ballet
Conspiracy of Hearts
Faces in the Dark
Your Money or Your Wife
The League of Gentlemen
Beyond the Curtain
The Challenge
Never Let Go
Make Mine Mink
Snowball
Doctor in Love
Piccadilly Third Stop
Man in the Moon
The Bulldog Breed
The Pharaohs' Woman
Chartroose Caboose
The Great Imposter
Fowled Up Falcon (Animation)
Faces In The Dark
Midnight Lace
Spartacus
College Confidential
Seven Ways from Sundown
The Brides Of Dracula
Dinosaurs!

Portrait In Black
Macario
The Leech Woman
Pistol Packin' Woodpecker (Animation)
The Savage Innocents
Teenage Lovers
The Cossacks
Hell Bent For Leather
Carthage in Flames
The Private Lives of Adam and Eve

1961

The Singer Not the Song
No Love for Johnnie
Very Important Person
Flame in the Streets
Whistle Down the Wind
Information Received
No, My Darling Daughter
Victim
In the Doghouse
The Outsider
Lover Come Back
Doc's Last Stand
Over the Odds
The Choppers
El Cid
Flower Drum Song
Case of the Red-Eyed Ruby
Back Street
The Sergeant Was a Lady
Tammy Tell Me True
Come September
The Last Sunset
Romanoff and Juliet
The Gambler Wore a Gun

The Shadow of The Cat
Gun Fight
The Curse of The Werewolf
The Secret Ways
Tomboy and the Champ
Blast Of Silence
The Bird Who Came to Dinner (Animation)
Wings of Chance
Posse from Hell
Frontier Uprising
The Grass Is Greener

1962

All Night Long
A Pair of Briefs
The Traitors
Tiara Tahiti
Life for Ruth
The Day of the Triffids
Der Rosenkavalier
Band of Thieves
Billy Budd
The Wild and the Willing
Stranglehold
The Fur Collar
The Fast Lady
On the Beat
Waltz of the Toreadors
40 Pounds of Trouble
Mediterranean Holiday
Freud
The Legion's Last Patrol
King Kong vs Godzilla
If A Man Answers
Sodom and Gomorrah
Island Escape

Stagecoach to Dancers' Rock
The Spiral Road
The Phantom of The Opera
Captain Clegg
The Traitors
A Touch of Mink
Lonely Are the Brave
Cape Fear
Hair of The Dog
Six Black Horses

1963

This Sporting Life
Bitter Harvest
The Bay of St Michel
Call Me Bwana
80,000 Suspects
Doctor in Distress
The Eyes of Annie Jones
Live It Up
Farewell Performance
The Informers
A Stitch in Time
Father Came Too
Hot Enough for June
The Raiders
Charade
Captain Newman MD
Live It Up
Bomb In The High Street
The Kiss Of The Vampire
For Love Or Money
The Thrill Of It All
A Gathering of Eagles
Tammy And The Doctor
Lancelot and Guinevere

The List Of Adrian Messenger
Showdown
Paranoiac
The Sadist
The Day Of The Triffids
Charlie's Mother In Law
The Ugly American
The Birds
Stranglehold

1964

Seance on a Wet Afternoon
The Beauty Jungle
The High Bright Sun
The Fall Of The Roman Empire
The Nightwalker
The Guns Of August
Taggart
Father Goose
The Hanged Man
Kitten with a Whip
Send Me No Flowers
The Lively Set
Bullet For A Badman
I'd Rather Be Rich
Marnie
The Killers
Island Of The Blue Dolphins
McHale's Navy
The Magnificent Showman
Bedtime Story
The Eyes of Annie Jones
Wild and Wonderful
The Evil of Frankenstein
The Chalk Garden
Deep Freeze Squeeze

Nightmare
He Rides Tall
The Brass Bottle
Man's Favourite Sport

1965

The Intelligence Men
Be My Guest
The Ipcress File
The Heroes of Telemark
Sky West and Crooked
The Early Bird
Dateline Diamonds
Doctor in Clover
I Was Happy Here
The War Lord
Strange Bedfellows
Guess Who? (Animation)
Andy
Mirage
The Truth About Spring
Bus Riley's Back in Town
Frosty
I Saw What You Did
The Sword of Ali Baba
Janie Get Your Gun (short)
The World of Abbott and Costello
The Secret of Blood Island
The Naked Brigade
The Wise Guys
Dateline Diamonds
That Funny Feeling
Love And Kisses
A Very Special Favour
McHale's Navy Joins the Air Force
Dark Intruder

Deadwood '76
Fluffy
The Art of Love
Shenandoah
Davy Cricket (short)

1966

That Riviera Touch
The Sandwich Man
They're a Weird Mob
The Trap
Romeo and Juliet
Press for Time
The Quiller Memorandum
Deadlier Than the Male
Don't Lose Your Head
Maroc 7
Gambit
The Doomsday Flight
Castle Of Evil
La Grande Vadrouille
Let's Kill Uncle
Dimension Four
Cyborg 2087
Texas Across the River
The Appaloosa
The Battle of Algiers
Beau Geste
They're a Weird Mob
The Plainsman
The Pad and How to Use It
Torn Curtain
Munster, Go Home!
Destination Inner Space
And Now Miguel
Arabesque

Out of Sight
Paddle to the Sea
L'homme de Marrakech
Spies Strike Silently
Blindfold
Gunpoint
A Man Could Get Killed
Incident At Phantom Hill
Madame X
The Rare Breed
Moment To Moment
The Ghost and Mr Chicken
Foot Brawl
Agent for HARM

1967

Tobruk
A Countess From Hong Kong
The Longest Hundred Miles
Gunfight in Abilene
The Magnificent Two
Stranger in the House
The Long Duel
The Trygon Factor
Follow That Camel
Winchester '73
Privilege
Carry On Doctor
Hell is Empty
Two Weeks in September
The Money Jungle
The Ballad of Josie
Arabella
Pretty Polly
Games
The King's Pirate

Rough Night in Jericho
Sullivan's Empire
Banning
King Kong Escapes
The Reluctant Astronaut
Palaces of a Queen
Two Weeks In September
Tammy and the Millionaire
The Jokers
The War Wagon
The Perils Of Pauline
The Young Warriors
The Ride To Hangman's Tree
Valley of Mystery
Degree Of Murder
The Champagne Murders
The Last Adventure
Thoroughly Modern Millie

1968

Carry On… Up the Khyber
Nobody Runs Forever
Subterfuge
Kill Them All And Come Back Alone
The Smugglers
Isadora
Emma Hamilton
House Of Cards
Hellfighters
Secret Ceremony
The Pink Jungle
Better a Widow
The Hell With Heroes
The High Commissioner
In Enemy Country
OSS 117 Murder for Sale

Did You Hear The One About The Travelling Saleslady?
The Shakiest Gun In The West
White Comanche
Work is a 4-Letter Word
Oedipus the King
Jigsaw
Three Guns For Texas
Kona Coast
The Counterfeit Killer
Boom
What's So Bad About Feeling Good?
Don't Just Stand There
Journey to Shiloh
A Lovely Way To Die
Counterpoint
A Man Called Gannon
Coogan's Bluff
Shadow Over Elveron
Madigan
Panic In The City
Charlie Bubbles
Prescription: Murder
Sergeant Ryker
The Secret War of Harry Frigg
New Face in Hell
The Destructors
Zita
Nobody's Perfect

1969

Some Girls Do
Carry On Camping
Ring of Bright Water
Carry On Again Doctor
Twinky aka Lola
Mister Jericho

Army Of Shadows
Topaz
Journey to the Far Side of the Sun
Secret World
The Love God?
This Savage Land
In Search Of Gregory
Change Of Habit
Dirty Mary
The Royal Hunt of the Sun
Tell Them Willie Boy Is Here
Anne of the Thousand Days
The Lost Man
Three Into Two Won't Go
Eye Of The Cat
Love of Life
Backtrack
Winning
Death Of A Gunfighter
Angel In My Pocket
Sweet Charity
The Night of the Following Day
Fear No Evil

1970

Carry On Up the Jungle
Doctor in Trouble
Carry On Loving
Toomorrow
Countess Dracula
The Firechasers
The World at Their Feet
I Love My Wife
Puzzle of a Downfall Child
Berlin Affair
The Intruders

Violent City
The Other Man
Company Of Killers
Lost Flight
Diary Of A Mad Housewife
Cockeyed Cowboys of Calico County
Colossus: The Forbin Project
A Clear and Present Danger
Two Mules For Sister Sarah
Skullduggery
Airport
Ritual Of Evil
The Challengers
Story Of A Woman
The Movie Murderer
The Gamblers

1971

Assault
Carry On at Your Convenience
Hands of the Ripper
Quest for Love
Carry On Henry
Countess Dracula
Revenge
Twins of Evil
Never Give An Inch
See The Man Run
The Devil And Miss Sarah
Duel
Stamping Ground
The Harness
Escape Of The Birdmen
Please Sir!
Catch Me A Spy
Play Misty For Me

The Hired Hand
Two Lane Black-Top
Shoot Out
They Might Be Giants
One More Train To Rob
The City
Johnny Got His Gun
Red Sky at Morning
Nickel Queen
The Andromeda Strain
How to Frame a Figg
Taking Off
The Neon Ceiling
The Beguiled

1972

All Coppers Are…
The Manhunter
The Screaming Woman
Carry On Abroad
Carry On Matron
Kidnapped
Rentadick
Frenzy
Black Jack
Slaughterhouse Five
Silent Running
Evil Roy Slade
The Hound Of The Baskervilles
Vampire Circus
A Quiet Revolution
The Couple Takes a Wife
The Victim
That Certain Summer
Death Line
Ulzana's Raid

Bless This House
Joe Kidd
The Groundstar Conspiracy
The Great Northfield Minnesota Raid

1973

The Belstone Fox
Carry On Girls
Father Dear Father
Nothing But the Night
Antony and Cleopatra
That's Your Funeral
Go for a Take
Double Indemnity
That Man Bolt
Showdown
Beg, Borrow ... or Steal
The Six Million Dollar Man
Barcelona Kill
You'll Never See Me Again

1974

Carry On Dick
Don't Just Lie There, Say Something
Soft Beds, Hard Battles
The Swordsman
When You Want One
The California Kid
The Apprenticeship of Duddy Kravitz
The Execution of Private Slovik
The Wrestler
Lacombe, Lucien
What next?

1975

I Don't Want to Be Born

Carry On Behind
Deadly Strangers
That Lucky Touch
The Ghoul
Sarah T. – Portrait of a Teenage Alcoholic

1976

Bugsy Malone
Carry On England
Voyage of the Damned

1977

Wombling Free
Holocaust 2000
The Devil's Advocate
Soldier Of Orange
Target of an Assassin

1978

To See Such Fun
Age of Innocence
The Uncanny
Power Play
The Shout
The Thirty Nine Steps
Tomorrow Never Comes
The Wild Geese
Carry On Emmannuelle
Circle Of Iron
Matilda
The Evil

1979

The Human Factor
That's Carry On
The Riddle of the Sands

Tarka the Otter
The Lady Vanishes
Eagle's Wing
A Man, a Woman and a Bank
Jaguar Lives!
City On Fire

1980

Bad Timing
Silver Dream Racer
The Sea Wolves
Terror Train
Loving Couples
The Fog

1981

Improper Channels
King Of The Mountain
Back Roads
Fort Apache, The Bronx

1982

The Boys in Blue
Nutcracker
Who Dares Wins
Six Weeks
Heidi's Song
Alone In The Dark
Class Reunion
Young Doctors In Love
The Soldier
Summer Lovers

1983

Educating Rita
The Honorary Consul

Heat and Dust
Gorky Park
Silkwood
Under Fire
Easy Money
Class
Breathless
Lone Wolf McQuade
BMX Bandits

1984

The Bostonians
The Chain
Secret Places
The Cotton Club
Heartbreakers
The Woman In Red
Finders Keepers
Grandview USA
Harry & Son
Lassiter
Broadway Danny Rose

1985

Defence of the Realm
The Girl in the Picture
Water
Turtle Diary
A Chorus Line
Target
Not Quite Jerusalem (aka Paradise)
Eleni
Flesh + Blood
Code Of Silence
Crimewave
Desperately Seeking Susan

The Mean Season
The Falcon and the Snowman
The Lightship
Star Quality: Mr & Mrs Edgehill
Star Quality: Bon Voyage
Me and the Girls
Mrs Cappers Birthday
What Mad Pursuit?

1986

Half Moon Street
Foreign Body
The Whistle Blower
Platoon
Three Amigos!
Best Shot
Something Wild
The Transformers: The Movie
Detective School Dropouts
Just Between Friends
Opposing Force
Power
The Longshot
Hannah and Her Sisters
Terry On The Fence

1987

The Fourth Protocol
Throw Mamma From The Train
The Big Town
No Man's Land
No Way Out
Bestseller
Malone
Robocop

The Believers
Radio Days

1988

Stealing Heaven
Switching Channels
Heart Of Midnight
Dirty Rotten Scoundrels
Without A Clue
Far North
Married To The Mob
The Blob
Monkey Shines
Bull Durham
Shakedown
A Time Of Destiny
Colors
Dominick and Eugene
Dead Ringers

1989

Scenes from the Class Struggle in Beverly Hills
Return From The River Kwai
Dealers
Wilt
All Dogs Go To Heaven
Crimes and Misdemeanours
Physical Evidence
Welcome Home
The Package
Millennium
Reunion
Miss Firecracker
Gleaming The Cube
Winter People

UHF
Great Balls of Fire
The Fabulous Baker Boys
Weekend At Bernies

1990

The Comfort Of Strangers
State Of Grace
Reversal of Fortune
Navy Seals
Robocop 2
King Of New York
Cadillac Man
Miami Blues
Blue Heat
Madhouse
Happily Ever After

1991

Rock-a-Doodle
Under Suspicion
Scorchers
Ambition
Off and Running
Pyrates
Missing Pieces
The Linguini Incident
The Magic Riddle
Til There Was You
Highway To Hell
Drop Dead Fred
Fried Green Tomatoes…
Barton Fink
The Silence of the Lambs
London Kills Me
Afraid Of The Dark

1992

Strictly Ballroom
Just Like A Woman
Bob Roberts
Paydirt
Ruby
Candyman
Glengarry Glenn Ross
Freddie as F.R.O.7.
Close To Eden
Only You
Reservoir Dogs
Over The Hill

1993

Sabu: The Elephant Boy
The Young Americans
Malice
Romeo Is Bleeding
Snake Eyes
Kalifornia
Only The Strong
Needful Things
The Ballad of Little Jo
Posse
Lake Consequence

1994

Andre
Four Weddings and a Funeral
Widow's Peak
S.F.W.
Wes Craven's New Nightmare
Shopping
The Woman with the Hundred Hairless Heads
Final Combination

Backbeat
The Shawshank Redemption
The Adventures of Priscilla, Queen of the Desert
The Hudsucker Proxy
The Pagemaster

1995

Dr Jekyll and Ms Hyde
To Die For
Circle Of Friends
Dolores Claiborne
The Run Of The Country
The Usual Suspects

1996

Getting Away With Murder
The Stupids
Heaven's Prisoners
Hamlet
Ghosts From The Past
SubUrbia
Extreme Measures
Lone Star
Michael
The Spitfire Grill
Some Mother's Son
Somebody Is Waiting

1997

Gold In The Streets
8 Heads in a Duffel Bag
Best Men
Lawn Dogs

THIS MODERN AGE series:

A monthly news cinemagazine, produced by the Rank Organisation. There were forty-one produced in all, from October 1946 to February 1951. Each issue was devoted to a single story, lasting around twenty minutes.

LOOK AT LIFE series:
Between 1959 and 1969 over 500 documentary shorts of approx. 8 mins were produced, replacing the old newsreel section of film shows.

ANIMATION DIVISION:
Musical Paintbox Series
(1948–1950)
Animation films: 10 x 8 mins

David Hand's Animaland Series
(1948–1949)
Animation films: 9 x 7 mins (approx.)

RANK'S CHILDREN'S ENTERTAINMENT FILMS:
1944

Tom's Ride (11 min)
Sports Day (24 min)

1946

Trouble at Townsend (23 min)
The Voyage of Peter Joe
Split into a six-part serial (146 min)

1947

Dusty Bates
Split into a five-part serial (115 min)
Bush Christmas (80 min)
Circus Boy (50 min)
The Little Ballerina (61 min)

1948

    The Secret Tunnel (49 min)

    Under the Frozen Falls (55 min)

1949

    A Journey for Jeremy (33 min)

    The Mysterious Poacher (59 min)

    Trapped by the Terror (56 min)

Acknowledgements

Ben Ohmart, for supporting this book from the moment I first mentioned it; Robin Harbour for his eagle eyes and also for allowing use of some of his photographs; Andrew Boyle for his computer skills; Richard Blanshard for allowing use of a couple of his photos; Al Samujh, for his shared interest in all things Rank; Steve Godwin, Will Hay Appreciation Society; Matt Boot, Trustee of Henry Boot Pension Trustees Ltd; Louise Etson for use of her grandfathers photos; Graham Higson, The Walmsley Society; David Wight; Damian Fox for his terrific cover artwork; Bernard Vandendriessche; John Scotney, Chairman, Hull Civic Society.

CPSIA information can be obtained
at www.ICGtesting.com
Printed in the USA
LVHW050206150222
711110LV00010B/83